Piers Plowman Studies VIII

IMAGINATIVE PROPHECY IN THE B-TEXT
OF *PIERS PLOWMAN*

The psychology underlying Passus 8–20 of *Piers Plowman* remains unexplored in its entirety, despite single articles on separate psychological personifications. Professor Kaulbach aims to remedy this huge gap in our understanding of Langland's poem, by adducing a psychology which not only illuminates previously mysterious relations between psychological actants, but also reveals that many apparently non-psychological figures (Piers Plowman, for example) are best explained by reference to psychological theory.

The body of psychological theory on which the author draws is that of Arabic, specifically Avicennan, theory of the prophetic mental act, the 'vis imaginativa', or 'ymaginatif' in Middle English. Professor Kaulbach argues that Ymaginatif, a power of the lower Anima, requires the first inner vision in order to teach Will the concrete words of 'kynde knowynge', and to motivate Will to the practice of patient poverty. Piers Plowman (the perfection of Ymaginatif and a power of the higher Anima) requires a second inner vision in order to inspire Free Will to preach and practise charity.

Beyond the original interpretative insights offered by this book, Professor Kaulbach also describes the intellectual and manuscript context in which Arabic psychology was made available to a late fourteenth-century English poet.

ERNEST N. KAULBACH is Associate Professor of English, Classics and (occasionally) Philosophy at the University of Texas at Austin.

Piers Plowman Studies

ISSN 0261-9849

Series Editor: James Simpson

I THE THEME OF GOVERNMENT IN PIERS PLOWMAN
Anna Baldwin

II THE FIGURE OF PIERS PLOWMAN
Margaret E. Goldsmith

III PERSONIFICATION IN PIERS PLOWMAN
Lavinia Griffiths

IV THE CLERKLY MAKER: LANGLAND'S POETIC ART
A. V. C. Schmidt

V PIERS PLOWMAN: A GLOSSARY OF LEGAL DICTION
John A. Alford

VI NATURE AND SALVATION IN PIERS PLOWMAN
Hugh White

VII A GAME OF HEUENE: WORD PLAY AND
THE MEANING OF *PIERS PLOWMAN* B
Mary Clemente Davlin, O.P.

Imaginative Prophecy in the B-Text of *Piers Plowman*

ERNEST N. KAULBACH

D. S. BREWER

First published 1993 by D. S. Brewer, Cambridge

D. S. Brewer is an imprint of Boydell & Brewer Ltd
PO Box 9, Woodbridge, Suffolk IP12 3DF, UK
and of Boydell & Brewer Inc.
PO Box 41026, Rochester, NY 14604, USA

ISBN 0 85991 357 0

British Library Cataloguing-in-Publication Data
Kaulbach, Ernest N.
　　Imaginative Prophecy in the B-Text of
　　"Piers Plowman". – (Piers Plowman
　　Studies, ISSN 0261-9849; Vol. 8)
　　I. Title II. Series
　　821.1
　　ISBN 0-85991-357-0

Library of Congress Cataloging-in-Publication Data applied for

The paper used in this publication meets the minimum requirements
of American National Standard for Information Sciences –
Permanence of Paper for Printed Library Materials, ANSI Z39.48-1984

Printed in Great Britain by
St Edmundsbury Press Ltd, Bury St Edmunds, Suffolk

Contents

Introduction   1

CHAPTER ONE
The Meaning and Function of Ymaginatif

Seven Functions of the "Vis Imaginativa Secundum Avicennam"   39
  1. Identified with Thou3t   40
  2. Produces "awe" and patient speech   48
  3. Appears in sleep and inner dreams   58
  4. Prophesies in inner dreams by converting images into
       speakers   61
  5. Produces shame   65
  6. Appears and disappears suddenly   66
  7. Teaches a poetic syllogistic   68

CHAPTER TWO
The "Vis Imaginativa secundum Avicennam" and
the Naturally Prophetic Powers
of Ymaginatif

The "Vis Imaginativa Secundum Avicennam" and the
    Mainstream of Medieval Psychology   77
An Introduction to "Augustinisme Avicennisant"   86
"Augustinisme Avicennisant" in England and in Worcester   104
An Introduction to Natural Prophecy   112
An Introduction to Prophetic Preaching   118
The Elevation of Ymaginatif's Sensory Prophecy   121
An Introduction to the Higher Psychology of
    "Augustinisme Avicennisant"   127
Certification by Inner and Outer Dreams and by "Makynges"   138
Conclusions and Suggestions   145

List of Primary Sources Quoted   149
Index of Lines   154

Introduction

The Depth Psychology Introduced by the First Vision of
the Vita in the B-Text

Even if students of the B-text of *Piers Plowman* bring some knowledge of modern depth psychology, say that of Sigmund Freud or Carl Jung, to the reading of the poem, they still may not perceive that the *PP*-poet takes sleep, dreams, images, the imagination and self-knowledge just as seriously as modern depth psychology takes them. The first part of his poem, commonly called the *Visio*, reads like the dream journal of a medieval client in the first stages of therapy. The "Prologue" records his vivid dream, followed by four more Passus of dream images (Passus 1–4), then by another dream of three Passus (Passus 5–7).[1] Like any intelligent client, the dreamer wants to know what his dream in the "Prologue" means. He asks an authority, holi chirche, to give him the "kynde knowyng" to interpret the dream (1, ll.138–9):

> 'Yet haue I no kynde knowyng', quod I, 'ye mote kenne me bettre
> By what craft in my cors it comseþ, and where.'

She dismisses him as a nitwit (1, l.140),

> 'Thow doted daffe!' quod she, 'dulle are þi wittes;'

and, after his repeated request, " 'Kenne me by som craft to knowe þe false' " (2, l.4), tells him only to " 'Loke' " (2, l.5). He looks all the way

---

[1] References to the B-text are taken from *Piers Plowman: the B Version*, ed. by George Kane and E. Talbot Donaldson (London: The Athlone Press, 1975). References to the A-text are taken from *Piers Plowman: the A Version*, ed. by George Kane (London: The Athlone Press, 1960). References to the C-text are taken from *Piers Plowman by William Langland: An Edition of the C-text*, ed. by Derek Pearsall (London: Edward Arnold, 1978). Occasional reference is made to Skeat's B-text and C-text (*The Vision of William concerning Piers the Plowman in Three Parallel Texts, together with Richard the Redeless by William Langland*, 2 vols. [London: Oxford Univ. Press, 1968]), to Skeat's notes (*Introduction, Notes and Glossary* in vol.2) and to A.V.C. Schmidt's text and notes (*William Langland, The Vision of Piers Plowman: A Critical Edition of the B-Text* (London: J.M. Dent & Sons, 1978).
English translations from the various Latin texts are mine, unless otherwise noted.

1

to the end of the *Visio* while his readers read; but neither he nor they find any explanation of the "kynde knowyng," "craft in my cors," or "wittes" to interpret the dream in the "Prologue." The *Visio* develops the dream journal more than the psychology of the dreamer.

The second part of the poem, commonly called the *Vita*, continues the dream journal, but develops the dreamer's psychology with a vengeance. In only the first vision of the *Vita* in the B-text (8,1.68–12,1.297), the dream journal is so interwoven with the dreamer's intent to find a kynde knowyng in the wits of his "cors" that readers of the B-text need training in an unusual medieval depth psychology, in order to understand how the nitwit becomes the interpreter of his own dreams by the end of the vision. For, awake at 13, 1.1, he claims to have learned a "konnynge" from Ymaginatif and from Kynde in an inner vision within the first vision (13, ll.5–15, referring to 11, ll.6–406). The *Vita* develops the dream journal as well as the dreamer's psychology.

In the first vision of the *Vita*, the expressions "kynde knowyng" and "craft in my cors" first refer to a series of mental acts in the dreamer's outer dream (8, 1.68, to 11, 1.5). Then, they refer to a clash of his mental acts in an inner dream (11, ll.6–406). At the height or depth of the inner dream, the same expressions refer to the mental act whereby Ymaginatif as "oon" brings images of Kynde's Reson and Wit into the dreamer's imagination (11, ll.321–68). By mental acts in an outer, inner, and again outer dream, the dreamer does arrive at a "konnynge" from a "kynde knowyng" by several "crafts in my cors," especially from Ymaginatif, whose effects are summarized in his waking at the end of the vision in 13, ll.5–15. The depth psychology we are to see accounts for Will's derivation of the "konnynge" from the several "crafts" and Ymaginatif, from an inner dream, inserted in the middle of the first vision (11, ll.60–406), and from a continuing outer dream which explains the inner dream (11,ll.407–12,1.297). It also accounts for a psychology of prophecy, represented in the rest of the visions in the *Vita*.

According to this depth psychology, the mental acts represented from 8, 1.70 (the introduction of Thouȝt in the dreamer's sleep), to 11, 1.319 (the confused thoughts of the dreamer in the inner dream), only lead up to and preface the mental acts from 11, ll.320–410 (the introduction of Ymaginatif as "oon" in the dreamer's inner sleep and awakening from inner sleep) and from 11,1.411–13,ll.14–9 (the "konnynge" learned from Ymaginatif and Kynde after the dreamer awakes from the first vision). The mental trek toward that "konnynge" begins at 8, ll.70 and 129, where the dreamer's mental acts of self-knowledge, comprised of hypostatized "þouȝt" and of himself as the hypostasis "wil," propose to find the kynde knowyng of Dowel, Dobet and Dobest, first from Wit in Passus 9 and then from Wit's wife, Dame Studie (10, ll.5–223). After

2

Dame Studie silences her husband (10, ll.140-4), she introduces Will (and the readers) into more learned mental acts of self-knowledge, represented by her cousin, Clergie (10, ll.238-335), and Clergie's wife, Scripture (10, ll.337-48). At the point where Will's thoughts learn enough from Wit, Dame Studie and Clergie to oppose Scripture's teaching (10,l.377-11,l.4), then Scripture, like holi chirche, also dismisses him: " '*Many know many things but nothing about themselves*' " (11, l.3). Dismissed as a formally educated nitwit, he is cast into an inner dream.

After 11, l.3, the psychology acquires a baffling depth, when, in the inner dream, Will is returned to a comparison between his wit and universal Wit (11, ll.6-406). At 11, l.7b, Fortune suddenly ravishes Will into the "Mirour þat hiȝte middelerþe" (11, l.9a), where Will sees and hears a motley procession of speakers (11, ll.7-319). Literally looking into the mirror, Will literally hears the sisters Concupiscence and Old Age and Holiness and Recklessness and Conscience and a friar and Lewte and Scripture (again) and Trajan and a speaker after Trajan. The speakers debate Will's confusion, some speaking his acts of innate knowledge, others speaking his acts of learned knowledge, others speaking his acts of naturally good desire, others speaking his acts of concupiscent desire. At 11, ll.44-5, Old Age and Holiness remind him of the forgotten depth psychology, i.e., his desire to learn from the wit in his "cors:"

'Allas, eiȝe!' quod Elde and holynesse boþe,
'That wit shal torne to wrecchednesse for wil to haue his likyng!'

Will is reminded of the mental act in 8, ll.128-9, where Thouȝt spoke his "purpos" to Wit:

'Wher dowel [and] dobet and dobest ben in londe
Her is wil wolde wite if wit koude [hym teche].'

Here at 11, l.48, Will's "likyng" makes him forget previous Thouȝt of Dowel (8, ll.78-110); but, previously in 8, ll.78-110, the same "likyng" contradicted Thouȝt's definition of Dowel, when Will called it "coueitise" (8, ll.112-3):

'Ac yet sauoreþ me noȝt þi seying, [so me god helpe!
More kynde knowynge] I coueite to lerne.'

By 11, ll.44-5, Will's covetousness overpowers the "entente," given him by Thouȝt and Wit (8, l.131), so that Will becomes and desires what Dame Studie predicted he would become and desire: "frenetike of wittes" and desirous of "lond and lordship on erþe" (10, ll.6b, 14). By 11, ll.40, 46-51, Will explicitly intends what the Sisters Concupiscence

3

intend: a "likyng" for "Concupiscencia carnis," "Coueitise of eiȝes" and "Pride of parfit lyuynge" (11, ll.13–5).

In other words, Will has confused one kynde knowyng by Thouȝt and Wit with another kynde knowyng, prompted by his own covetousness and by the Sisters Concupiscence. Confused senses of "kynde," confused intents of Wit, and confused stimuli from Will's "cors" transform Will into an hypostasis of confused desires by 11, l.319. Readers are baffled by the depth psychology, i.e., by the outer and inner dream, by the procession of speakers before and during the inner dream, and by the representation of Will's contradictory intents.

They understand that Will's sudden mental act at 11, l.320, reveals an essential component in his unusual depth psychology:

> And muche moore in metyng þus wiþ me gan oon dispute,
> And slepynge I seiȝ al þis.

For the "oon" who teaches Will to learn the depth psychology of "kynde knowyng" by a "craft" in his "cors" is later named with the unusual name "ymaginatif" (12, l.1):

> 'I am ymaginatif.'

But they are puzzled that Will credits to him the important "konnynge," after his awakening from the first vision in the *Vita* (13, ll.14–15b):

> And how þat Ymaginatif in dremels me tolde
> Of kynde and of his konnynge.

The inner dream, another component of the depth psychology, allows Will to think the confused thoughts spoken by the speakers, and thus allows Ymaginatif to answer Will's "likyng" by means of a twofold function: to return Will's sight to Wit (11, ll.320–406), and to teach Will the Clergie consequent upon the sight of Wit (11,l.415–12,l.297, and especially 12, ll.155–8). For, according to another component in the depth psychology, the continuing outer dream (11,l.407–12,l.297) would allow Ymaginatif to interpret the inner dream (11,ll.407–12,l.297) by answering Will's mental acts in the first part of the outer dream (8, l.74–11, l.5).

The *PP*-poet represents the dreamer's sleep, dreams, images, thoughts, speakers, imagination and self-knowledge with a depth psychology different from modern depth psychology. Outer dreams, inner dreams, and the acts of Thouȝt and Ymaginatif teach Will to find the "craft" in his body by which he learns a "konnynge." The self-taught "konnynge," in turn, helps him to differentiate the "likyng" in his wits and "cors" from the true intent in his wits and "cors." Without training in the parts of the depth psychology and the mental acts signified by the terms "wil," "craft," 'þouȝt," "wit," "cors," "kynde," "ymaginatif," and "entente," readers would find and have found all these acts of self-knowledge, represented in an outer dream (8,l.68–13,l.1) enveloping an inner dream (11, ll.6–406), so baffling as to be incoherent.

The depth psychology is supposed to be simple. Will develops it, in order to to learn how to discern the good from the evil in the minute mental acts which stem from Thouȝt and Ymaginatif, i.e., from powers of knowledge who interpret the intents Will receives from his Wit in his "cors." For Will is supposed to hypostatize desire, a desire who learns how to discern the true/good from the false/bad in the intents of the images, drawn from Wit and presented by Thouȝt and by Ymaginatif to his imagination. On the one hand, Will desires Thouȝt to teach him the good in his own Wit (Passus 9), such that Thouȝt and Wit stimulate him, as the *human* will, to recognize a false "likyng" or "coueitise" in the intent of his "cors." On the other, Will also desires Ymaginatif to teach him the Good in Kynde's Wit (11, ll.321b, 323b, 335–62), such that Ymaginatif and Kynde's Wit stimulate him, as the will in all *animals*, to recognize the Natural Good in the intent of his "cors." Minute mental acts are supposed to represent Will as the human will in the process of learning how to desire what the good is, i.e., how to will the true good innate to his wits and his "cors." Being both animal and man (for Will is by definition the "rational animal"), Will knows both his human and animal desires "kyndely" from the wits in his body. He, therefore, uses both Thouȝt and Ymaginatif, i.e., the hypostases of human sensory reasoning and animal sensory reasoning, to develop mental words for his desire from the wit in the "cors," i.e., from Inwit and his five sons, See-well, Say-well, Hear-well, Work-well-with-your-hand, and Go-well.

Will's development of a "kynde knowyng" by a "craft" in the "cors" is, then, somewhat comparable both to Freud's psychology of the non-Christian "id" and to Jung's psychology of the more Christian "Anima." If Will heeds the power of human Wit in his "cors," then his sensory kynde knowyng comes from Anima (" '*mens* þouȝte' " in 15, l.25, in the "R-group" of mss), is called Thouȝt (8, ll.70–4), and he is named human "wil" in the act of knowing his intent (8, ll.129, 131). His depth psychology resembles Jung's psychology of "anima." If Will heeds the power of Kynde's Wit in his "cors" (11, ll.322–3), then his sensory kynde knowyng comes from Kynde (11, l.322), is called Ymaginatif (12, l.1), and he is named "my name" (11, l.322), i.e., by the name "appetitus" in all animals who desire to do good and avoid evil (i.e., are attracted to pleasure and repulsed by pain). His depth psychology also resembles Freud's psychology of the "id." Whether the dreamer is named with the human name "wil" or with the name "appetitus" in all animals, i.e., " 'wheiþer he be man or [no man]' " (8, l.130), his dreams necessarily tell him about his intents. Like Freud's and Jung's, Will's depth psychology is founded upon dreams and the interpretation of dream images. Unlike Freud's or Jung's depth psychology, this psychology resorts to inner dreams. In this depth psychology, the minister of Will's Anima in the senses, the "vis cogitativa" (Thouȝt), would ordinarily overpower the minister of Kynde in Will's senses, the "vis imaginativa" (Ymaginatif), unless Will sleeps (8, l.68, to 13, l.1) and, in the deep sleep of an inner dream (11, ll.6–406), the "vis imaginativa" discerns the true/good intent in his images.

Three features of the unusual depth psychology help Will to prove the intent in his wits. First, he names the same sensory, reasoning and imagining power with two different names, Thouȝt and Ymaginatif. Second, Will knows that his "vis imaginativa" discerns his true intents and proves his wits, by overpowering the flawed, human rationality of his "vis cogitativa" in an inner dream. Third, Will logically reasons to a "konnynge" or infallible rationality within his "vis imaginativa," albeit that the rationality is instinctual.

Nevertheless, the depth psychology baffles readers. As a consequence, we do not perceive that the depth psychology is developed from Passus 13 to Passus 19. We do not understand that, after Will perfects patient poverty (Passus 13 and 14) and arrives at kynde knowyng (Passus 15, l.2), he comes to know the charity by which the human will is made free (15, l.150). This development allows Will, now named Free Will (" 'liberum arbitrium,' " in 16, l.16a), to perfect the power of Haukyn or Actif in himself (16, ll.1–2), to learn what charity means to free will in a second inner vision (16, ll.19–167), and to practise acts of free will in a continuing outer vision (16, l.167–17, l.356). All these developments, in turn, lead to the perfection of the depth psychology, i.e., to the mental acts by which Free Will's Conscience receives a grace from Grace to perfect his wits (19, ll.215–8):

> 'For I wole dele today and [dyuyde] grace
> To alle kynne creatures þat [k]an hi[se] fyue wittes,
> Tresour to lyue by to hir lyues ende,
> And wepne to fighte wiþ þat wole neuere faille.'

Readers do not understand that the psychology of free will is perfected, in order that his Conscience be tested from 19, l.335b ("pride it aspide"), to the last line of Passus 20. In the last two Passus, Free Will's Conscience practises the same discernment of good from evil in a more sophisticated moral situation, a situation first predicted by holi chirche in 2, l.51,

'And lat no conscience acombre þee for coueitise of Mede,'

and then predicted by Grace in 19, ll.219–20:

'For Antecrist and hise al þe world shul greue
And acombre þee, Conscience, but if crist þee helpe.'

According to the depth psychology, Will, having perfected his Ymaginatif by a series of dream visions, ought to awake to conditions where he wills and acts without necessity. The final Passus of the B-text begins with a contradiction to the maxim. Will awakens to Nede, to conditions of necessity and to the maxim, " 'nede haþ no lawe' " (20, l.10). Nede puts Free Will's Conscience in a quandary. If Conscience's freedom is removed by Free Will's necessity for food, clothing and shelter (20, ll.12–3), then Free Will may in this situation " 'come þerto by sleighte' " and " 'synneþ noȝt' " (20, ll.14b–15a). In case of need, Free Will is not free and, therefore, may beg, borrow or steal the necessities for life without committing sin, despite Ymaginatif's teaching to the contrary.

The Depth Theology in the First Vision of
the Vita in the B-Text

The B-text of *Piers Plowman* not only develops an unusual psychology from the conclusion of the A-text of *Piers Plowman*. It also develops a series of theological questions from the A-text, e.g., the question at B. 10, ll.104–36, which Ymaginatif is to answer (a question about the effects of original sin upon the "cors" of all mankind and upon Will's "cors"). In the B-text, Ymaginatif complements the Clergie which Will learns from his interactions with Thouȝt, Wit, Dame Studie, Clergie and Scripture in Passus 10 and 11 of the A-text. At B. 10, l.119, Dame Studie predicts Ymaginatif's theological prominence, when she correlates Ymaginatif's "answer" with Will's theological "purpos" (i.e., Will's development of theological questions)

'Ymaginatif herafterward shal answere to [youre] purpos.'

Ymaginatif is to " 'answere' " the " 'purpos" " of Will's theological inquiry, stated by Dame Studie in 10, l.119, and begun by Will in 8, l.125, where Will puts Thouȝt to a "purpos to preuen his wittes."

Up to the prediction, Will has developed an innate Clergie from his own Thouȝt, Wit and Dame Studie, i.e., from his innate acts of thought, innate acts of wit, and innate acts of the study of his wit. After her prediction, Will's wit is so silenced (10, ll.140–6) that Will develops an acquired Clergie from Dame Studie's cousin, Clergie, from Clergie's wife, Scripture, and from the motley speakers in the inner dream up to 11, 1.319, i.e., from mental acts of knowledge whose origins are not innate to Will. Innate Clergie and acquired Clergie clash at Will's mental act where Dame Studie describes the opposition between the theology of "heiʒe men" and the theology of " 'cler[gie]' " on the subject of the effects of the original sin upon Adam's " 'seed' " (10, ll.105–11).

The opposed Clergie's parallel Will's opposed intents. After 10, 1.119, Will hypostatizes two conflicting intents in his study of theological questions: one toward the good of human concupiscence (Will as a son of Adam) and toward a theology which justifies his concupiscence (ritual baptism and ritual salvation), and a second toward the good of natural desire (Will as "appetitus" or appetite) and a theology which justifies natural desire (baptism into patient poverty and salvation by Kynde). At 11, 1.319, the confusion in Will's mental acts of self-taught theology represents the promptings of opposed stimuli in Will's "cors:" one stimulus urging Will to take the ritually theological means to an easy salvation (11, ll.53–83, 115–39), another stimulus urging Will to take the naturally theological means to a surer salvation (11, ll.85–114, 140–53).

From 11, 1.320, to 12, 1.297, Ymaginatif answers to the intricate psychological and theological development of the Thouʒt in Will's "purpos," by showing and telling. First, he shows Will the Wit and Reson of Kynde acting instinctually in the bodies of all the animals of Kynde (11, ll.323b–68). Kynde's Reson and Wit allows them no concupiscence (11, ll.335–44) and thus preserves their species (11, ll.351–62). Will indeed sees a lack of Wit and Reson in the acts of human kynde (11, ll.331–4, 370–2) and well realizes that all animals are more rational than his species, but Will objects. Where Will ought now to recognize the concupiscence in all human wit and reason seen at 11, ll.344b, Will instead chooses to accuse Kynde's Wit and Reson of creating his and all human bodies for " 'mysfeet' " (11, ll.373–5):

> 'I haue wonder [in my wit], þat witty art holden,
> Why þow ne sewest man and his make þat no mysfeet hem folwe.'

Under Ymaginatif's showing, Kynde's Reson answers Will's "purpos:" the " 'matere' " in man's body is subject to the " 'fondynge of þe flessh and of þe fend boþe' " (11, ll.401–2), i.e., to the concupiscence Will's body inherits from Adam. The showing confirms what Old Age and Holiness have already said, " 'That wit shal torne to wrecchednesse for wil to haue his likyng!' " and proves that Will suffers the concupiscence because he inherited his "cors" ultimately from Adam. Shamed into

awakening from the inner dream (11, l.405b–406a), Will hears Ymagi-
natif tell. He tells Will about the true Clergie in that Wit and Reson of
Kynde (11,ll.415–12, l.297), i.e., about the Clergie in Will as ''appetitus''
(appetite) before he, like Adam, fell. Ymaginatif says that Will as
''appetitus'' would have kept the Clergie had Will not been urged by his
''cors'' to object to Kynde's Wit and Reson as Adam had objected (11,
ll.413–22). In short, the showing answers the concupiscence in the
matter of Will's body, and the telling corrects the concupiscence in
Will's Clergie (11, ll.413–6):

> 'Haddestow suffred', he seide, 'slepynge þo þow were,
> Thow sholdest haue knowen þat Clergie kan & [conceyued] moore
>   þoruȝ Res[on],
> For Reson wolde haue reherced þee riȝt as Clergie seide;
> Ac for þyn entremetyng here artow forsake.'

Will would have achieved the Clergie to know Dowel kyndely from a
''craft'' in his ''cors,'' had Will seen, thought and suffered in silence the
sight taught by Kynde's Reson: '' 'Suffraunce' '' (11, l.379a).

The ''konnynge,'' achieved at 13, l.15, comes from Ymaginatif's
Clergie or natural theology, a theology of seeing all and suffering evil.
By the end of the first vision, Will learns the natural theology of all the
animals in Kynde: to see all and to suffer the evil which cannot be
amended unless there is human amendment (11, ll.382–8). In the B-text,
such ''konnynge'' resolves Will's inner conflict between an innate
kynde knowyng of human wits and an acquired kynde knowyng of
human wits in the acts of naturally knowing an intended good, i.e.,
Dowel. Because of Ymaginatif's psychological and theological promi-
nence in the B-text, Will both falls like Adam (11, ll.417–420a) and rises
like Adam (11, l.440a). The acts of Ymaginatif's psychology and
theology teach Will the true intent of his wit and his ''cors'' by a ''craft''
unique to Ymaginatif.

Ymaginatif's ''answer,'' i.e., Ymaginatif's showing of Kynde's Wit at
11, l.323b, would make no sense to any reader, unless Will's ''purpos''
has been developed, i.e., Will's thought processes represented from
8, l.68, to the first part of the inner dream (11, ll.7–319). For the ''oon,''
enveloping the second part of the inner dream (11, ll.320, 410), has been
predicted to ''answer'' to Will's ''purpos.'' Only after Will's mental acts
represent his purpose from 8, l.68, to 11, l.319, can Ymaginatif answer
Will's purpose. While Ymaginatif shows Will the Wit and Reson in the
Kynde of all animals to Will's imagination (11, ll.323b–68), Will does
''study'' his human wit, as Ymaginatif says in 12, l.223b (''studiest'').

Will's study involves him in acts of an imaginative reason, i.e., a
reason which compares good images to good images and which divides

out evil images from good images. Ymaginatif brings images of
universal animality into Will's imagination, so that Will uses the images
to compare the intents in his human wit to the intents in the wit of all
other animals in Kynde (11, ll.369–72). In one group of images, Will
takes wit of the effects of the intents in the wit of man and his mate
(11, ll.331–4),

> Man and his make I myȝte [se] boþe.
> Pouerte and plentee, boþe pees and werre,
> Blisse and bale boþe I seiȝ at ones,
> And how men token Mede and Mercy refused.

In a second group of images, he sees that Kynde's Reson follows the
intents in the wits of every animal except man and his mate (11, l.335),

> Reson I seiȝ sooþly sewen alle beestes,

such that all animals act with a marvellous wit (11, ll.336–62). The
comparison of the effects of the opposed intents in the two types of wit
forces Will to a conclusion: ''mysfeet'' befalls man and his mate for lack
of wit, but does not befall any other animal (11, l.375).

Instead of suffering, Will's vehemence makes him fault Kynde's
Reson for making man and his mate unwitty (11, ll.370–4). Kynde's
Reson responds: although God (Kynde) could resolve the evil in human
wit in a minute (11, l.381), nevertheless Kynde and all creatures suffer
'' 'for som mannes goode' '' (11, l.382) while the human animal
grapples with the effects of the '' 'fondynge of þe flessh and of þe fend
boþe' '' in the human body (11, l.401), i.e., the effects of Adam's
original sin. Ymaginatif's showing forces Will to acknowledge that his
concupiscent ''purpos'' has infected his human intent, his human
thought, his human wit, his human study, his humanly acquired
knowledge, and his human intepretation of Scripture. Will is forced to
see that the ' ''matere' '' in his ''cors'' contains a concupiscence which
flaws his intents which, in turn, flaws his wit and thought, which, in
turn, flaws his speech (11, ll.387–402). Ymaginatif's ''answer'' would
make no sense unless the Sisters Concupiscence had turned Will's Wit
' ''to wrecchednesse for wil to haue his likyng,' '' and unless Dame
Studie had predicted this, i.e., Ymaginatif's answer to Will's ''purpos.''

As soon as the showing concludes at 11, l.406, Will looks up, at
11, l.410, and sees the same ''oon'' with whom he disputed at 11, l.320.
After Ymaginatif shows, he begins to tell. First, he tells by forcing Will to
define the Dowel intended in his human wit from 8, ll.128–31, up to
11, l.319 (11, l.412):

> 'To se muche and suffre moore, certes, is dowel.'

From Ymaginatif's showing of Kynde's Wit in all animals, Will concludes a Clergie that Thouʒt, Wit, Dame Studie, Clergie, Scripture and the rest ought to have shown and told him: that seeing much and suffering more is Dowel, that Dowel is the Clergie of Kynde's Wit, and, therefore, that Kynde's Wit is the foundation for any kynde knowyng from a "craft" in the "cors." Secondly, the "oon" tells by defining the Clergie in the next lines (11, ll.413–39): Clergie ought to originate in the Wit and Reson of Kynde, since such Clergie taught Adam to suffer in silence before Adam fell. Thirdly, the "oon" tells Will how important this Clergie will be when Free Will and Conscience are attacked by both shame and Nede in Passus 20, ll.4–51 (11, ll.432–4):

> 'Ac whan nede nymeþ hym vp for [nede] lest he sterue,
> And shame shrapeþ his cloþes and his shynes wassheþ,
> Thanne woot þe dronken [wye] wherfore he is to blame.'

Under the name "oon," Ymaginatif answers to Will's "purpos" by showing and telling from 11, l.320, to the end of the Passus. Under the name "ymaginatif" in 12, l.1, Ymaginatif answers to Will's "purpos" by only telling. Under both names, Ymaginatif prophesies what will happen in Passus 20.

By the end of the first vision, Will concludes the study of Wit with a "konnynge," i.e., the wit to know that his kynde is human and, therefore, fallen. Though nearly "witlees" by 13, l.1, he is not the natural nitwit he was at the beginning of the *Vita* nor the learned nitwit he was at the beginning of the inner dream in the first vision of the *Vita*. The "konnynge" he has learned from Kynde and Ymaginatif has taught him about the flaw in the " 'matere' " of his body and about the means to amend the flaw, i.e., the practical theology of repentance (13, ll.14–15b): "Ymaginatif in dremels me tolde of kynde and of his konnynge." "Konnynge" means that Will has learned an intricate "kynde know-yng" from a "craft in my cors." For Ymaginatif has forced Will to compare self-knowledge by his human "wittes" (developed from 8,l.128–11, l.319) to self-knowledge by Kynde's Wit (envisioned from 11, ll.324–68). "Self-knowledge" means that Will knows the false/bad in his intent toward kynde knowyng, because he has compared the desire in his human wit and reason to the Desire in Kynde's Wit and Reson. Will's "konnynge" is natural, since it comes from Kynde.

By the end of the first vision of the *Vita* in the B-text, Ymaginatif complements the psychology of kynde knowyng attempted at the end of the A-text, and responds to the theological "purpos" predicted by Dame Studie. According to this depth psychology, the laborious mental acts of Will, attempting to fathom his "entente" to know kyndely (8, l.131), achieve the intent in a flash of vision from 11, ll.320–406, although the minute mental acts are elongated and the realization is explained by both Will and Ymaginatif as something gradually achieved by Will only in his forty-fifth year (11, 1.47, 12, 1.3).

How Our Traditional Interpretation of Ymaginatif Leads to This Depth Psychology

In 1546, John Bale assessed *Piers Plowman* as a "learned work. . . somehow prophetic" ("Peers plowghman opus eruditum. . . quodammodo propheticum"). Explication of the depth psychology will support Bale's assessment, although, according to the first modern editor of the poem, the Rev. Walter W. Skeat, renaissance readers emphasized the theology of the poem more than the prophetic psychology.[2] In 1886, while separating the three texts of the poem into an A-text, a B-text and a C-text,[3] Skeat discovered the prominence of Ymaginatif in the B-text, and, in notes to B.X.,1.115 ("See. . .xi. 399–402") and C.XV.,1.1, pointed out that Ymaginatif is the "oon" who does answer to Will's "purpos," as predicted by Dame Studie. But, having defined Ymaginatif as "Imagination or Fancy" in the same notes, Skeat also created our difficulty with the interpretation of Ymaginatif. If Ymaginatif were "Fancy," then all of Ymaginatif's theological learning would be fanciful, and the following visions would be unrelated to Ymaginatif.[4] Some students of the B-text used and still use "Fancy" to admire the strange beauty of Will's vivid images in limited passages of the *Vita*, and, therefore, continued and continue to interpret the B-text as a "series of detached pictures, a collection of separate visions, a compilation of distinct arguments,"[5] supposing that the addition of Ymaginatif in the B-text exercised no real influence upon the psychological and theological structure of the B-text from Passus 14 to Passus 20. Should we continue to interpret Ymaginatif as "Fancy," we would understand neither the medieval depth psychology of Ymaginatif nor his prominence in the structure of the B-text. The brief discussion of Ymaginatif in the recent *Companion to Piers Plowman* explains our predicament: we accept Ymaginatif's prominence in the B-text and reject Ymaginatif as the hypostasis of "Imagination or Fancy;" but we cannot explain   how   Ymaginatif   answers   Will's   theological

---

[2] "Introduction," *The Vision of William Concerning Piers the Plowman*, 2, paragr.18, lxxiii–iv.

[3] "Introduction," 2, vii–xxi, lxiv–lxxii.

[4] "Introduction," 2, paragr.9, xxv.

[5] E. D. Hanscomb, "The Argument of the *Vision* of *Piers Plowman*," PMLA, 9(1894), 412.

"purpos."[6]   Since 1914, more and more readers have accepted H.S.V. Jones' definition of Ymaginatif, "spokesman of Reason," in order to relate Ymaginatif to the Reson of Kynde.[7] Instead of a modern psychology of imagination (free association of images in dreams), Jones looked into medieval psychologies of the imagination (representation of images in dream visions), and found a psychology of "imaginatio" in Richard of St. Victor's *Beniamin minor*, translated into ME as "A Tretyse of the Stodey of Wisdom þat Men Clepen Beniamyn."[8] In 1954, however, Randolph Quirk demonstrated that the Victorine term "imaginatio" translates into the ME "ymaginacioun," a term whose suffix "-ioun" signifies the power to represent images in the imagination but not the power to reason by images.[9] Then, he demonstrated that the Latin term, "vis imaginativa," would translate into the ME "ymaginatif," so that "ymaginatif" would signify *both* Ymaginatif's power to make images *and* Ymaginatif's power to deliberate the truth/good or false/bad in the images. Victorine psychology does not fully explain the name "spokesman of Reason."

Quirk's research leads us to two possibilities: first, that the "vis imaginativa" or "ymaginatif" is not a term developed by Victorine interpretations of the psychology of "Augustine" but a term of rare scholastic psychology developed from "Aristotle;" second, that the depth psychology of the "vis imaginativa" is rare in both medieval Latin and ME, i.e., not transmitted, as Quirk says, in the "mainstream of medieval psychology." Joseph Wittig in 1970 and Alastair Minnis in 1981 have shown us that, even if the Victorine expression "rationalis imaginatio" is applied to the psychology of Ymaginatif,[10] such a

---

[6] Ed. John Alford (Berkley: Univ. of California Press, 1988), pp.47–8, 98, where Ymaginatif's meaning and function, if not still disputed, is at least restricted to one question, e.g., the salvation of Trajan (12, ll.210–3, 283–5).

[7] H.S.V. Jones, "Imaginatif in *Piers Plowman*," *JEGP*, 13(1914), 583–4.

[8] Richard of St. Victor's Latin is to be found in *PL*, 196, 1–64. The ME translation, "A Tretyse of the Stodey of Wisdom þat Men Clepen Beniamyn," has been edited by Phyllis Hodgson in *Deonise Hid Diuinite*, EETS, o.s.231 (London: Geoffrey Cumberledge, 1955), 12–46.

[9] Quirk's study of Thomistic psychology and medical physiology (based upon Arabic interpretations of Aristotle) finds that "ymaginatif" refers to "deliberative imagination," i.e., to an ability to reason in the imagination. According to Quirk, Aristotle's "deliberative imagination" is signified by the unusual term "imaginativa" (ME "ymaginatif"), not by the Victorine term "imaginatio" (ME "ymaginacioun"). "Imaginatio," he says, refers to the "reproductive imagination," the power to make images of a thing absent present to the imagination ("Vis Imaginativa," *JEGP*, 53 [1954], 81–2).

[10] Joseph Wittig finds a "rationalis imaginatio" in the *Beniamin minor* ("*Piers Plowman* B, Passus IX–XII: Elements in the Design of an Inward Journey," *Traditio*, 28[1972], 269):

> Rationalis [imaginatio] autem est illa, quando ex his quae per sensum corporeum novimus, aliquid imaginabiliter fingimus (The rational [imagination, as opposed to the imagination in animals] is that [used] when we create

"rationalis imaginatio" has to be explained in the framework of an Arabic-Aristotelian "(vis) imaginativa," in order to account for Ymaginatif's rationality.[11] In 1961, M.W. Bloomfield suggested that the term "ymaginatif" refers to a psychology of prophecy. Ymaginatif's ability to "give rise to true knowledge" through a theory of prophecy "whereby imagination could be elevated" gave Bloomfield the hunch that such a prophetic psychology of the "vis imaginativa" might be found in some Arabic-Aristotelian source, adapted to a Christian psychology of prophecy (Augustine's, for example) and located in some "fourteenth-century English work."[12]

Bloomfield's intuition reaches to the heart of the history of the unusual depth psychology. *Imaginative Prophecy in the B-text of Piers Plowman* will demonstrate that *Piers Plowman* is a "learned work. . . somehow prophetic," by demonstrating that the *PP*-poet modelled his psychology of Ymaginatif upon Avicenna's interpretation of Aristotle's psychology of the imagination, an interpretation accomodated to "Augustine's" psychology. By way of a thirteenth-century, anonymous English tract, the *PP*-poet came to know how Avicenna's prophetic "vis imaginativa" was *first* accomodated to "Augustine's" psychology. This book follows up Quirk's conclusion that the depth psychology is obscure, follows up Wittig's and Minnis's ideas that "Augustine's" psychology is wedded to "Aristotle's," and follows up Bloomfield's hunch that the wedding took place in some English tract.

According to Avicenna's psychology of the "vis imaginativa," both Thouȝt and Ymaginatif are different names for the *same* "spokesman of Reason." "Spokesman of reason" refers to Will's one power of sensory reason, named "Thouȝt" at the beginning of the vision but named "Ymaginatif" at the end of the vision. "Spokesman of Reason" means that Ymaginatif "answers" the "purpos" in the questions to which Will puts Thouȝt, so that Will may discover from Wit whether he be "man" (the animal with human rationality) or "no man" (the animal with animal rationality), as Dame Studie predicts (10, 1.119) and Will outlines

something in the imagination from these which we know through bodily senses).

Alastair Minnis uses "rationalis imaginatio" to erect a very convincing explanation of Ymaginatif's meaning and function in the B-text ("Langland's Ymaginatif and Late Medieval Theories of Imagination," *Comparative Criticism*, 3[1981], 71–103).

[11] In "Elements" (p.266, note 174), Wittig refers to Etienne Gilson's important article about the Christianization of Avicenna's "vis imaginativa" in the *Archives d'histoire doctrinale et littéraire du moyen age*, 4(1929), 56; and Minnis notes the importance of Jean de la Rochelle and Vincent of Beauvais in the transmission of Avicenna's "vis imaginativa" ("Langland's Ymaginatif," 92–3, and notes 74–7; for the Arabic-Aristotelian *Poetics*, see 86, note 53).

[12] *Piers Plowman as a Fourteenth-Century Apocalypse* (New Brunswick, N.J.: Rutgers Univ. Press, 1961), p.172.

his "purpos" (8, ll.124–5, 130–1). Will uses the rare psychology to clarify the intents toward good in his "cors." According to Will's use of Avicenna's depth psychology, Ymaginatif hypostatizes an instinctual rationality in Will, when Will hypostatizes "appetitus" or the natural intent toward the good in all the bodies of all animals; Thou3t hypostatizes the human rationality in Will's sensory mental acts, when Will hypostatizes concupiscence or the unnatural intent toward the good in the human body. As if Will were using both the reasoning of a Freudian "id" in his wits and the reasoning of a Jungian "anima" to clarify the intent in his wits, Will discovers by Passus 13 that his "id" answers the purpose of his "anima."

The Depth Psychology of the "Vis Imaginativa Secundum Avicennam"

As Bloomfield intuited, Ymaginatif's psychological prominence in the B-text can be traced to a thirteenth-century English tract which adapts the psychology of Avicenna's "vis imaginativa" to the psychology of pseudo-Augustine. Around 1230, an anonymous English psychologist and theologian disguised Avicenna's psychology of a prophetic imagination, called "mutakhayyila" in Arabic and "vis imaginativa" in Latin, as "Augustine's" psychology of "imaginatio" in a tract entitled "De potentiis anime et obiectis" (On the powers of the soul and its [objects of knowledge]), edited by Fr. D.A. Callus from three mss in the libraries of Lincoln Cathedral, Balliol College (Oxford), and Worcester Cathedral.[13]

---

[13] "The Powers of the Soul: An Early Unpublished Text," *Recherches de théologie ancienne et médiévale*, 19(1952), 131–70; the three copies are in "*Lincoln Cathedral MS. 221, Worcester Cathedral MS. F. 57*, and *Balliol College, Oxford, MS.207*" ("Powers of the Soul," 131). Amélie-M. Goichon's *Lexique de la langue philosophique d'Ibn Sina (Avicenne)* (Paris: Descleé de Brouwer, 1938) gives Avicenna's Arabic terms and the equivalent Latin terms. On paragraph §242 (p.120), she identifies the Arabic "mutakhayyila" with the "vis imaginativa" (Ymaginatif) *and* "vis cogitativa" (Thou3t):

> MUTAHAYYILA, *imaginative*, se disant de la *faculté imaginative. . .;* "*Imaginativa. . . cogitativa*," i.e., "*cette faculté*" (*vis imaginativa*) "*est appelée mufakkira*" (vis cogitativa) "lorsque l'intelligence l'emploie, et *mutahayyila, imaginative* lorsque l'emploie l'estimative" (p.120).

In the recent critical edition of Avicenna's *Liber de anima* (ed. in two volumes by S. van Riet and G. Verbeke as *Avicenna Latinus: Liber de anima seu sextus de naturalibus, I–II–III* [Leiden: E.J. Brill, 1972] and *Avicenna Latinus: Liber de anima seu sextus de naturalibus, IV–V* [Leiden: E.J. Brill, 1968]), the "Lexique Latino-Arabe" says (*Liber de anima seu sextus de naturalibus, IV–V*, p.300): "(virtus) imaginativa: *mutakhayyila*."

The anonymous Englishman knew Avicenna's psychology from one of two sources: either from the twelfth-century Latin translation of the sixth book of Avicenna's encyclopedia, the *Kitab al-Shifa* (*Liber Sanationis* or *Liber Sufficientia*), known as *Liber de anima seu sextus de naturalibus* (Book of the Soul or Sixth Book of Physics), or from the

According to Fr. Callus, the Franciscan, Jean de la Rochelle, fitted Avicenna's term "vis imaginativa" into "Augustine's" term "imaginatio," by adapting the psychology of imagination in the *"De potentiis anime et obiectis"* to the psychology of the "vis imaginativa secundum Avicennam" in Avicenna's *Liber de anima*.[14] By way of Jean de la Rochelle, Avicenna's "vis imaginativa" entered the mainstream of Christian psychology, disguised as "vis imaginativa" of Augustine (in psychology) or of John of Damascus (in medical tracts on physiology).

According to Fr. V. Doucet, an historian of medieval Franciscan theology, Jean de la Rochelle's colleague and compeer, Alexander of Hales (from Hales Owen in Shropshire), introduced Avicenna's "vis

---

"Compendium de anima," a commentary on the *Liber de anima*, attributed to the translator of the sixth book of the *Kitab al-Shifa*, the Spanish Archdeacon Gundissalinus (ed. by J.T. Muckle as "The Treatise *De Anima* of Dominicus Gundissalinus" in *Mediaeval Studies*, 2[1940], 23–103).

The anonymous Englishman reconciled Avicenna's psychology to psuedo-Augustine's psychology by finding in both authors a common "intellectual light" ("Powers of the Soul," 151, ll.27-9, and note).

[14] That is, in his *Summa de anima* (ed. by Teofilo Domenichelli as *La Summa de Anima di Frate Giovanni della Rochelle* [Prato: Tipografia Giachetti, 1882], p.262, ll.30-1), Jean de la Rochelle first quotes the passage from the anonymous tract which explains the function of the imagination in dreams ("Powers of the Soul," 132, 154, ll.15-6),

> *Aliis* vero videtur quod imaginatio sit conversio ipsius virtutis sensibilis interioris super imaginem tamquam rem (*To others*, however, it seems that the imagination is the conversion of the interior power of sense upon an image as an [extramental] thing).

Then, he accommodates this Augustinized notion of "imaginatio" to Avicenna's psychology of the "vis imaginativa" (*Summa de anima*, p.263, ll.2-8), by quoting verbatim from Avicenna's *Liber de anima seu sextus de naturalibus, I-II-III*, p.6, ll.73-8:

> Iam autem scimus verissime in natura nostra esse, ut componamus sensibilia inter se et dividamus ea inter se [non] secundum formam quam vidimus extra. . . Oportet ergo in nobis sit virtus quae hoc operetur, et haec est virtus quae, cum intellectus ei imperat, vocatur cogitans, sed cum virtus animalis illi imperat, vocatur imaginativa (We know most certainly that in our nature we compare sensibles among themselves and divide them among themselves, not according to an image which we see outside. It is, therefore, necessary that there be a power in us which does this. This is the power called thought, when the intellect commands it; but, when the animal power commands it, the power is called the imaginative power).

Finally, between 1247 and 1259, Vincent of Beauvais not only quotes this passage from Avicenna's *Liber de anima* but also quotes the words preceding it from the anonymous Worcester tract, *"Aliis uero uidetur,* quod imaginatio sit conuersio ipsius virtutis sensibilis interioris super imaginem tanquam rem" (*Speculum Naturale*, Bk.27, ch.10 [Douai: Ex Officina Typographica Baltazaris Belleri, 1624; repr. Graz, 1964] 1, 1924B). In other words, the *Speculum Naturale* establishes that Avicenna's psychology of the "vis imaginativa" had entered the mainstream of medieval psychology through the anyonymous Worcester psychologist and through Jean de la Rochelle by 1259.

The quotation from Avicenna's *Liber de anima, I-II-III* establishes Ymaginatif's meaning and function in the first vision (in 12, l.1, he is the same power as Thou3t, in 8, l.74), his conversion from Arabic psychology into Christian psychology (in the anonymous English tract), and his English provenance.

imaginativa" into the arts curriculum of the University of Paris at the same time as he was introducing the *Sentences* of Peter Lombard into the theology curriculum.[15] The evidence tempts us to conclude that the *PP*-poet revived a Christianized psychology and (mendicant) theological questions as a model for Thouȝt's "purpos" and Ymaginatif's "answer" in the B-text, a psychology developed in England – perhaps near Worcester – and exported to Paris around 1230. But the evidence we are to see in the B-text tells us that the *PP*-poet revived the purely Avicennan psychology, for neither the anonymous Worcester tract nor Jean de la Rochelle nor Alexander of Hales mention the prophetic inner dreams attributed to the "vis imaginativa" in Avicenna's *Liber de anima*. The research of Bale, Skeat, Jones, Quirk, Wittig, Minnis and Bloomfield, combined with the manuscript evidence and the evidence of historical theology, point to an Ymaginatif who is Avicennan, who is prophetic, whose baptism into Christian psychology could have taken place in the environs of the Malvern Hills, and whose theological acuity derives from early Franciscan interpretations of the *Sententiae* of Peter Lombard.

Avicenna's depth psychology well accounts for the interaction of Thouȝt, Wit, Kynde, Ymaginatif, and the Clergie of Kynde and Ymaginatif (11, ll.415–24) in the first vision of the *Vita*. Thouȝt (Avicenna's "vis cogitativa" or power of thought), Ymaginatif (Avicenna's "vis imaginativa" or imaginative power), Wit (Avicenna's "sensus communis" or receiver of information from the five external senses), Will (Avicenna's "appetitus" or the power of desire in the body), and Kynde (Avicenna's "Primum Movens" or First Mover of the "appetitus" in all bodies) would interact only in dreams, for only in dreams could Will's Anima (Avicenna's "anima sensibilis") *picture* Will's intent as something permanently envisioned. From the Firmament of Heaven (Avicenna's "absentia" or the world of invisibles), Kynde would move the desire in Will's "cors." The desire, in turn, would move sensation (Wit), which, in turn, would move thought in men-as-men, which, in turn, would move the imaginative power in men-as-animals. Anima would create the inner dream in order to permit Ymaginatif to show and tell. In the inner dream, Will would look into

---

[15] That Alexander of Hales was a Franciscan and compeer of Jean de la Rochelle, see V. Doucet, "Prolegomena," *Magistri Alexandri de Hales Glossa in Quatuor Libros Sententiarum*, Bibliotheca Franciscana Scholastica Medii Aevi, XII, ed. PP. Collegii S. Bonaventurae (Quaracchi: Collegii S. Bonaventurae, 1951), 23–4, 72. That he came from Hales Owen in Shropshire, see *Ibid.*, 58–61. That he was the first to comment on Peter Lombard's *Sententiae* in the faculty at the University of Paris, see *Ibid.*, 65–6, 102, and also Doucet's "Prolegomena," *Quaestiones Disputatae 'Antequam Esset Frater'*, Bibliotheca Franciscana Scholastica Medii Aevi, XIX–XXI, ed. PP. Collegii S. Bonaventurae (Quaracchi: Collegii S. Bonaventurae, 1960), 6, and notes 1–2.

two sides of the "Mirour of middelerþe," one side at 11, l.9, the other at 11, l.324. At 11, l.406, Will would awake from the inner dream, in order that Ymaginatif interpret it by means of the continuing outer dream. From 11,l.413–12,l.297, Ymaginatif's Clergie would be Avicenna's "disciplina," a self-taught Clergie, not learned from the books of Scripture's husband. In 13, l.1, Will would awake from the continuing outer dream, and interpret the the whole first vision as a means to his "konnynge" taught him by an Avicennan "vis imaginativa."

Seven features of the depth psychology illuminate the structure and meaning of the first vsion of the *Vita*. First, "vis cogitativa" (ME "Thouȝt") and "vis imaginativa" (ME "Ymaginatif") refer to the *same* power. The power both transforms sensations into images and reasons in the imagination:[16]

> Et haec est virtus quae, cum intellectus ei imperat, vocatur cogitans, sed cum virtus animalis illi imperat, vocatur imaginativa (This is the power called thought, when the intellect commands it; but, when the animal power commands it, the power is called the imaginative power).

If Anima (Avicenna's "intellectus") commands the one power, Thouȝt creates images from Will's Wit and reasons in Will's Wit (to repeat, Anima's name, " '*mens* þouȝte,' " in 15, l.25, in the reading of the "R-group" of mss). If the "virtus animalis" in all Kynde commands the same power (Kynde's Reson in 11, l.335), Ymaginatif creates images from Will's Wit and reasons in Will's Wit (the "oon" in 11, l.320). According to Avicenna, Will would need two powers to mediate the information he receives from the twofold intents (human and animal) within the twofold wit (human and animal) in his body: Thouȝt (the "vis cogitativa") and Ymaginatif (the "vis imaginativa"). Both would convert the intents within Wit, in Passus 9 and 11, l.323b, into images in Will's imagination. Both would reason in the images, for both are "craftes" in Will's "cors." Both convert information from Wit into images in Will's imagination; both reason out the meaning of the images; both derive from Will's mental acts either a concupiscent or a natural "konnynge;" both form mental words (concepts) for Will's mental acts.

The two powers become speakers in Will's dreams, just as Will is in the mental act of transforming the sensations of desire in his body into images in his imagination (8, ll.74, 113, 115, 119, 124–5; and 11, ll.320–3). In 8, ll.70–1, just after Will falls asleep,

---

[16] *Liber de anima, IV–V,* p.6, ll.76–8. Adapting Avicenna's psychology to "Augustine's" psychology, Christian psychologists usually added to "vis imaginativa" the phrase "secundum Avicennam." Only Avicenna both identified the "vis imaginativa" with the "vis cogitativa" and attributed naturally prophetic powers to the "vis imaginativa."

> A muche man me þou3te, lik to myselue,
> Cam and called me by my kynde name.

The concerns of Anima excite Will to make a mental act of "þou3te" at 8, l.70, which becomes the speaker " 'þou3t' " in 8, l.74. As a reaction to this act, Will makes Thou3t the "mene" between himself and Wit (8, l.125),

> [To] pute forþ som purpos to preuen his wittes.

As a reaction to Will's act, Thou3t names Will with the name "wil," in the act of introducing Will to Wit in 8, l.129:

> 'Here is wil wolde wite if wit koude [hym teche].'

Reciprocal mental acts and names then create the "purpos" which Ymaginatif is to answer. To prove his "purpos," Thou3t defines Will as a twofold Will and Wit as a twofold Wit in Avicennan terms (8, l.130):

> 'And wheiþer he be man or [no man] þis man would aspie.'

As "man," Will is human will with a human wit; as "no man," Will is the will in all animals with an animal wit. The one name, "wil," hypostatizes two "appetitus" or desires in the rational animal. Thou3t reasons out the human desires in Will. Ymaginatif reasons out the animal desires in Will. But both use Will's one power of sensory reasoning.

While Thou3t proves the questions raised by Will's human Wit, the reasoning is purely human and will is "man." When, however, Ymaginatif answers to Will's "purpos" in 11, l.320, Will is simply named "my name" by Kynde in 11, l.322; and Will sees within his body another Wit in 11, l.323b. From 11, l.320, where the "oon" appears, Kynde commands the same power in a confused Will. At this point, Will's reasoning is purely instinctual, and "will" is named "no man" (8, l.130). Thinking instinctively, Will is named "my name" and, therefore, acts by an appetite or desire he has in common with all other animals. Knowing his wits as an instinctual animal, i.e., a man with an animal Anima, Will would be aware of the hypostasis "oon" by means of his acts of instinctual reason. Will's "cors" would indeed have an innate "craft" for "kynde knowyng." The part of the "craft," hypostatized into Ymaginatif, would enable Will, more as the animal "wil" than as the human "wil," to perform the same four mental acts instinctually: to convert the information from his Wit into images in his imagination; to reason out the meaning of the images; to derive from the mental acts the instinctual "konnynge" of "kynde" (concluded by 13, l.15); and to form mental words for the mental acts. According to

Avicenna, all animals, including man, have such a "vis imaginativa." Their "ymaginatif" instinctually tells them to recognize what is good and what is bad, as infallibly as a lamb recognizes the bad in the image of the wolf (to use the common example).

Second, Anima would create the lower inner dream, in order that Ymaginatif correct Thouȝt:[17]

> Cum occupatur anima sensibus exterioribus. . .ita quod non permittit imaginativam cogitare, sed ut imaginativa impediatur a sua propria actione. . . Saepe enim inter utrumque [scilicet dormitionis et vigiliae] contingit eos in ultimo absentari a sensibilibus et accidit eis quasi dormitatio (When Anima is engaged by the external senses so that Anima does not permit Ymaginatif to think but so that Ymaginatif is impeded from his proper acts. . . For often in between each [namely sleep and waking] it happens that some persons are raised on high away from the sensibles and an intense sleep befalls them).

After Will's concupiscence confuses his thoughts in the inner dream, Ymaginatif shows Kynde's Wit and Reason to Will (11, ll.320–406), to correct the thoughts confused by Will's intent toward concupiscence. After Will awakes from the inner dream, Ymaginatif defends the truth of the inner dream with the clause, " 'Thouȝ I sitte by myself in siknesse n[e] in helþe' " (12, l.2). Ymaginatif does not produce the inner dreams of sickness (hallucinations) but the inner dreams of health (prophetic inner dreams).[18] According to Avicenna, healthy inner dreams occur in a flash, early in the morning.

Third, Ymaginatif's power to create speakers from images and to form the words for Will's "makynges" (12, l.16) would be prophetic and poetic:[19]

---

[17] *Liber de anima, IV–V*, p.16, ll.9–12, p.19, ll.54–6. The "vis imaginativa secundum Avicennam" appears in lower inner dreams, when either the prophet's "anima" or his "vis cogitativa" impede the prophetic activity of the "vis imaginativa" (*Ibid.*, p.17,l.25–p.18, l.40). As soon as Thouȝt, Wit and Anima impede Will's desire to know himself, Ymaginatif's quick appearance straightens out the reasoning in Will's intent (*Ibid.*, p.37, l.66, and p.28, ll.75–8).

Avicenna describes how the same psychology works in higher inner dreams (i.e., 16, ll.19–167); when the prophet sees through the higher mirror of Anima and Anima's higher understanding impedes the prophet's vision, a sublimation of the "vis imaginativa" makes a quick appearance to straighten out the prophet's higher intent (*Ibid.*, p.152, ll.89–90).

[18] *Liber de anima, IV–V*, p.18, ll.38–42.

[19] *Liber de anima, IV–V*, p.19, ll.59–61. In the last tractatus of the *Liber de philosophia prima sive scientia divina* (also ed. by S. van Riet and G. Verbeke in three volumes, *Liber de philosophia prima sive scientia divina, I–IV* [Leiden: E.J. Brill, 1977], *Liber de philosophia prima sive scientia divina, V–X* [Leiden: E.J. Brill, 1980], and *Liber de scientia divina sive scientia divina, I–X: Lexiques* [Leiden: E.J. Brill, 1983]), i.e., in ch. 1 of tractatus 10 (*Liber de philosophia prima sive scientia divina, V–X*, p.529, ll.52–3), Avicenna applies the prophetic psychology of the "vis imaginativa" (explained on p.523, ll.23–30) to Aristotle's *Poetics*. Avicenna claims that God reveals to the prophet in "poetic argumentations" ("poeticis

Multotiens apparet similitudo et videtur eis quod id quod apprehendunt sit locutio illius imaginis veluti verba audita quae tenunt et legunt. Et haec est propria prophetia virtutis imaginativae (Very often the likeness of the thing appears, and it seems to them that what they grasp is the speech of that image, as it were, words heard which they hold and read. And this is the prophecy proper to the imaginative power).

An image ("similitudo") in Will's previous outer dream, e.g., "heþen" in 10, 1.354, or "lele" in 10, 1.355, would become a speaker in Will's inner dream, e.g., Trajan or Lewte, for the reason that Ymaginatif has the power to transform images into speakers whose words Will holds and reads, and whose words make up Will's "makynges" in 12, 1.16.[20] The transformation of images into speakers would be prophetic, for the "vis imaginativa" represents God's Imagination and Speech to the sensory imagination of the prophet. In Avicenna's psychology of prophecy, Ymaginatif would be God's (Kynde's) angel, carrying God's (Kynde's) images into Will's imagination. In Avicenna's psychology of prophetic poetry, the images would be so vivid that the images become speakers who speak words that Will would "hold and read."[21]

Fourth, purely Avicennan psychology would explain both the utter naturality of Ymaginatif's infallibile reasoning and yet Ymaginatif's

---

argumentationibus") and that the prophet reveals to his hearers in the same form of argumentation. It seems plausible that Will's prophetic psychology is assimilated by the written poetics, i.e., by the words and structure of the B-text.

Unless the *PP*-poet read Arabic (i.e., the Arabic of Avicenna's Commentary on Aristotle's *Poetics*), he would have known and used Averroes' Middle Commentary on Aristotle's *Poetics*, translated into Latin by Hermannus Alemannus in 1256, and edited by William F. Boggess as *Averrois Cordvbensis Commentarium Medium in Aristotelis Poetriam* (unpublished doctoral dissertation, Univ. of North Carolina at Chapel Hill, 1965; reprinted by University Microfilms at Ann Arbor, Michigan, §65-14, 314, in 1987). Avicenna and Averroes both use a common source for their respective commentaries on the *Poetics*: Alfarabi's *Canons*.

[20] *Liber de anima seu sextus de naturalibus*, IV-V, p.19, ll.59–61:

> Multotiens apparet similitudo et videtur eis quod id quod apprehendunt sit locutio illius imaginis veluti verba audita quae tenent et legunt. Et haec est propria prophetia virtutis imaginativae (Very often a likeness appears [to the prophets] and it seems to them that what they grasp is the speech of that image, as if the words are heard which they hold and read. And this is the prophecy proper to the imaginative power).

[21] Avicenna explains how his "vis imaginativa" is angelic in a companion passage in his *Metaphysics*, i.e., the *Liber de philosophia prima sive scientia divina*, V–X, tractatus 10, p.523, ll.23–30:

> In cujus viribus animalibus sunt he tres proprietates, scilicet ut audiat verbum dei, et videat angelos transfiguratos coram se in forma quae possunt videri,. . . et fit in auribus vox (And in the senses [of the prophet] are these three qualities: that he hear the word of God and see the angels transformed before him,. . . and that [their] speech be made in his ears).

For a general description of the "vis imaginativa secundum Avicennam" as angelic, see the illuminating remarks of Fazlur Rahman, "Ibn Sina," in *A History of Muslim Philosophy*, ed. M.M. Sharif (Wiesbaden: Otto Harrassowitz, 1963), I, 500.

references to the Holy Spirit (e.g., 12, l.63). Avicenna relates prophecy by the "vis imaginativa" to the Holy Spirit in the last tract of his *Liber philosophia prima sive de scientia divina, V–X*, specifically in his discussion of the preaching of the Promise in the Law.[22]

The *PP*-poet applies three more parts of Avicenna's psychology (Will's self-taught Clergie, the mirror [11, l.9a], Will's development of a satisfying language) to the first vision of the *Vita* in the B-text. The first part, the self-taught Clergie, would explain the inner conflict between Will's innate Clergie and his acquired Clergie. Avicenna says that Clergie ("disciplina") belongs to the "discentes" (the self-taught learners) who learn in inner dreams, but not to those who acquire "disciplina" from outside themselves, i.e. from Dame Studie's cousin and Scripture's husband, Clergie.[23] Had not Dame Studie silenced Wit, had not Will followed Dame Studie's cousin's line of Clergie instead of Scripture's teaching, and had Will not rebuked Kynde's Reson in 11, ll.374–5, Will ought to have achieved a purely natural Clergie taught him by Kynde's Reson in the inner dream, as Ymaginatif explains in 11, ll.414–24. The acquired Clergie, represented by Dame Studie's cousin, is what confused Will, caused the inner dream, and occasioned the appearance of Ymaginatif. According to Avicenna, the "vis imaginativa" shows and tells only to instill in the prophet only self-taught "disciplina" or Clergie.

Avicennan psychology would explain the function of Will's "longynge" and the function of the "Mirour" of "middelerþe" in which Will first sees the images of Fortune (11, ll.8–9) and then sees "forbisnes" of the love of Kynde (11, ll.324–5). In inner dreams, the Avicennan prophet sees the conflicts in his intent reflected on the two sides of one mirror ("speculum").[24] Will's sensory Anima, accordingly, would ravish Will into an inner dream in 11, l.6, and force Will to look into one side of the the "Mirour" called Middlearth (11, l.9), as if into an Avicennan "speculum" which mirrors the confused images of one side of Will's twofold intent, from 11, l.6, to 11, l.319. Mirroring his desires to images of Middle earth perceived through Fortune (i.e., God perceived as the Highest Good for bodies), Will compares the ultimate intent of his human wit to the goods reflected by Fortune. From 11, l.320,

---

[22] *Liber de philosophia prima sive scientia divina, V–X*, tractatus 10, ch.1 (p.523, ll.22–30) and ch.2 (p.533, l.21).

[23] Avicenna would call Ymaginatif's Clergie an "aptitudo" or "subtilitas," because Ymaginatif teaches Will to recognize an innate Clergie (*Liber de anima, IV–V*, p.151, ll.76–83).

[24] *Liber de anima, IV–V*, p.27, l.73 (for the term "speculum") and p.27,l.70–p.28, l.78 (for the psychology of the split inner vision). In the prophetic psychology of Avicenna, higher mirrors and "faces of the soul" perfect the vision of lower mirrors and "faces of the soul" (*Liber de anima, I–II–III*, p.94, ll.8–14); lower inner dreams lead to higher inner dreams.

"middelerþe" reflects exempla, when Will takes wit from Kynde (God perceived as the Highest Good for the bodies of all animals). On Fortune's side of the mirror (11, ll.9–319), Will sees how the reason of Thouȝt leads his human Wit to the confused intents reflected by Fortune and the Sisters Concupiscence (11, ll.12–4); on Kynde's side of the mirror, Will perceives how the intent of Kynde's Reson of Wit contrasts with the intent of Thouȝt's reasoning of human Wit. For Kynde's Reson follows the wits of all animals in Kynde except the wits in human kynde (11, ll.321, 324, 335, 370–2), so that the intents of animals are always the same "in etynge, in drynkynge and in engendrynge of kynde" (11, l.336).

Will's perception of the opposed consequences of the twofold Wit, reflected in both sides of the mirror, forces Will to a fundamental kynde wit about himself named "wil." The kynde wit is this: named "appetite" or "wil," Will stimulates his "kynde knowyng" by a "craft in my cors" toward two intents which should be the same (Kynde's intent ought to be similar to human kynde, as Wit said in 9, l.31) but are not the same (as Kynde's Reson says in 11, ll.399–404). As a result of the comparison between human Wit's intent in Passus 9 of the outer vision and Kynde Wit's intent in Passus 11 of the inner vision, Will finds that the intent in his human wit is flawed and confused because, named "appetitus" or ME "Will," Will himself hypostatizes conflicting desires: one toward innate good, another toward innate concupiscence.

By 11, l.320, Ymaginatif's function is to join the two halves of the mirror in Will's inner dream together, so that Will can see for himself where his concupiscence has stimulated the intents of his reason and wit to deviate from the intents of kynde knowyng and where his natural desire has not stimulated the intents of his reason and wit to deviate from the intent of kynde knowyng. So at first Will speaks rudely to Kynde's Wit (11, ll.370–5), because Will acts concupiscently and thinks only in the terms of the intents of his human wit: Kynde must be at fault for making his human wit flawed. Then the recognition of Kynde Wit's "suffraunce" stimulates Will to "amend" his intent (11, ll.378–82).

The vision in a two-sided mirror thus leads to Will's development of a satisfying speech. For Ymaginatif ministers to Will's development of the speech of "cristene" from Kynde (12, l.65, "loquimur"). When Ymaginatif's showing forces Will to the highpoint of inner conflict in 11, ll.370–4, Will's speech assimilates his perverse desire and his human lack of "kynde wit." Will speaks perversely to Kynde's Reson for the sight seen in 11, ll.331–4, i.e., man's lack of Kynde's Wit (11, l.375):

'Why þow ne sewest man and his make þat no mysfeet hem folwe.'

Then the instinctual Reson in Kynde's Wit corrects Will's thought by correcting Will's speech in the next lines (11, ll.376–7):

> And Reson arated me and seide, 'recche þee neuere
> Why I suffre or noȝt suffre; þiself hast noȝt to doone.'

Kynde's Reson counterclaims that the "Rechelesnesse," produced by Will's misuse of Thouȝt in 11, l.34, has been the cause of Will's lack of kynde wit and rude speech. Will's reckless thought and wit from 11, l.34, to here, is proven by Will's reckless speech. For Will's speech lacks the " 'sufferaunce' " of Kynde (11, ll.377, 379), as Ymaginatif explains " 'sufferaunce' " after Will awakes from the inner dream (11, ll.413–22). Kynde's " 'sufferaunce' " is "cristene," because " 'he (God) suffreþ for som mannes goode, and so is oure bettre,' " says Reson (11, l.382).

Will sees, of course, a different stimulus in the Reson and Wit of all animals than the stimulus in his human Wit which carried him from Passus 9 up to this point at 11, ll.331–41. Specifically, he perceives a different desire in *his* body than he perceives in the bodies of all other animals in Kynde. By 11, l.376–7, Will, of course, knows something about the wit which he developed from Thouȝt's mediation of Wit's information in Passus 9. For, when Thouȝt said to Wit in 8, l.129,

> 'Here is wil wolde wite if wit koude [hym teche],'

and Wit compared " 'wil's' " desire to Kynde's desire in 9, l.30b (" 'at his wille' "), with the words in the next line,

> 'Ac man is hym (Kynde) moost lik of marc and of [shape],'

Will assumed that his desire was the same as Kynde's desire to create good in all bodies, and that his human desire was as good as Kynde's when Kynde created man (9, ll.32–46). By 11, ll.369–72, Will knows that he does not drink, eat and engender as animals do, but that his desire stimulates him to concupiscent acts of drinking, eating and engendering. By 11, l.376–403, Will knows that he has misused the " 'marc and [shape]' " of Wit, because Kynde's Reson tells Will that Will's speech in 11, ll.374–5, found fault with the innate good in the " 'shap' " and the " 'shaft þat god shoop hymselue' " (11, l.397).

What Randolph Quirk rightly calls a rare Latin "vis imaginativa," translated into the rarer ME "ymaginatif," describes how the *PP*-poet disentangled Avicenna's thought from its Christian adaptation. Although the Avicenna's "vis imaginativa" was adapted into the Christian psychology of Augustine in an anonymous tract, complete

24

only in the copy of *Worcester MS F. 57*, near the Malvern Hills,[25] the poet restored what the anonymous tract omitted: the identity of the "vis cogitativa" with the "vis imaginativa" and the psychology of inner dreams. If the *PP*-poet developed the B-text of the *Vita* from the end of A-text in the environs of the Malvern Hills (and not Lincoln or Oxford), it is even possible that he adapted the psychology of Ymaginatif and the structure of two inner dreams from the copy of Avicenna's *Liber de anima seu sextus de naturalibus in Worcester MS Q 81*.[26] Although we are not at all sure that the ms was in Worcester in the fourteenth century, these features of Avicenna's psychology of the "vis imaginativa,"

1. the two different names, Thouȝt and Ymaginatif,
2. the inner dream in 11, ll.60–406
3. Ymaginatif's creation of prophetic speakers,
4. natural prophecy by the Holy Spirit,
5. Will's self-taught Clergie,
6. the two sides of the mirror of "middelerþe" (11, ll.9a, 324),
7. Will's development of a natural language,

do explain much of the complex structure in the first vision of the *Vita*.

The Perfection of the Depth Psychology of the "Vis Imaginativa Secundum Avicennam"

Although this volume can only introduce it, Avicenna's psychology of the perfection of prophecy by the "vis imaginativa" accounts for Will's mental acts in the B-text, from Passus 13 to Passus 20. According to Avicenna, the "vis imaginativa" is sublimated into the powers of a "sanctus intellectus" (a prophetic Anima), after the two lower appetites

---

[25] According to Fr. Callus ("Powers of the Soul," 137–8), the Worcester tract contains material not found in the copies of the tract in Oxford and Lincoln. For instance, material in the Worcester tract explains Piers Plowman's description of the "Tree" of "Trinite" in 16, ll.29–52. The "potentia, scientia, voluntas" at the end of the Worcester tract (p.170, ll.17–8) are three powers in Anima which Piers Plowman props up with divine " 'potencia' " and " 'sapiencia' " and " 'liberum arbitrium' " (free will) in 16, ll.30, 36, 50.
[26] *Worcester MS Q.81* is listed among the mss in the critical edition of Avicenna's *Liber de anima* (*Liber de anima, IV–V*, p.81*) and described by M.T. d'Alverny in "Avicenna Latinus: Codex Wigornensis," *Archives d'Histoire Doctrinale et Littéraire du Moyen Age*, 32(1965), 297–302. There are also copies in Cambridge (*Peterhouse 157, Conv. and Caius College 497 [996]*), and Oxford (*Bodleian 463, Bodleian Digby 217, Merton College 282*). There is a big "if" attached to the poet's possible knowledge of and use of *Worcester MS Q 81*. We are not at all sure that *Worcester MS Q 81* was present in the Worcester Cathedral Library in the fourteenth century.

of the prophetic will (the concupiscible and irascible) are governed by the third appetite (the rational), so that God enables the prophetic Anima to perform four higher functions: to perfect the "vis activa" (the active power), to become a higher mirror in which the prophet sees in a higher inner dream, to perfect the prophet's ability to preach the Law in vivid images, and to grant him a "virtus sancta" (an infallible power to discern right from wrong).

To begin the elevation of Ymaginatif's power in himself, Will perfects two branches of the appetite signified by his lower name, "appetitus," in Passus 13 and 14: the concupiscible branch to possess, and the irascible branch to be angry. In purely Avicennan psychology, Will amends his wit and reason by correcting his concupiscible appetite to covet and his irascible appetite to become angry with Kynde's Wit; in Christian adaptation (Passus 13 and 14), Ymaginatif stimulates Will to the Christianized virtues which counteract Will's concupiscence and irascibility: poverty (against concupiscence) and patience (against irascibility).

While the prophet perfects his concupiscible and irascible appetite, the lower power of prophecy in the "vis imaginativa" is being elevated to the higher power of prophecy in "sanctus intellectus," by means of the power which Avicenna calls by the Arabic name "àmali" and which Christians call "virtus activa."[27] Just as the Avicennan prophet perfects the two lower appetites of his human will by practice of the "active power" ("virtus activa") in between lower and higher inner dreams, so Will meets and surpasses " 'Activa uita' " in 13, l.224 ("Actif," in the Kane-Donaldson edition of the A-text in 11, l.183, " 'Actif' ") in between the lower inner dream and higher inner dream. The two signs that Will has surpassed Haukyn's power by the end of Passus 15 are that Will has perfected his rational appetite (called, in Christian adaptation, "liberum arbitrium," in 16, l.16) and that he prefaces his second inner dream with this exclamation to Anima (16, ll.1–2):

'Now faire falle yow', quod I þo, 'for youre faire shewyng!
For Haukyns loue þe Actif man euere I shal yow louye.'

According to the Christian and Franciscan interpretation of Avicenna, practice of the "virtus activa" would perfect the prophet's concupiscible

---

[27] *Liber de anima, I–II–III*, p.93,l.3–p.94,l.4. In the "Lexique Latino-Arabe" (*Liber de anima, I–II–III*, p. 384²), "(virtus *vel* vis) activa: àmali." In her *Lexique de la langue philosophique d'Ibn Sina (Avicenne)* (p.335, §610, paragr. 18), Amélie-M. Goichon gives the same: "àmila, faculté qui agit, faculté d'agir, active. . . Vis activa."

There being no original sin in Avicenna's thought, prophets do not remedy the effects of sin in themselves, but rather perfect what is already God-given or given by Nature. The "virtus activa" perfects the prophet's "mores," i.e., Avicenna's sense of virtue (*Ibid.*, p.93,l.3–p.94,l.14).

appetite to possess in his practice of poverty, and would perfect the prophet's irascible appetite to be angry in his practice of patience, so that the Christian Free Will would be enabled to perform miracles which prove the truth in his mental and written words, i.e., his preaching of the Law. For Avicenna developed his psychology of a prophetic "vis imaginativa," in order to prove how the prophet's dreams, moral power, and miracles do affect his society: his preaching, reinforced by miracles, converts society to observance of the Law of God. Will's exclamation to Anima means that Will perceives the perfection of the "active power" in Haukyn, i.e., the miraculous provision of food and cure of diseases (Haukyn's potential power in 13, ll.240–59, but Piers Plowman's actual power in 16, ll.103–16).[28]

Accordingly, after Will learns Kynde's "konnynge" in 13, l.15, Ymaginatif's power is partially perfected in Will's practice of patience and poverty in Passus 13 and 14, so that Will achieves "kynde knowyng" by 15, l.2, after long practice; but Will's names " 'fre liberal wille' " in 15, l.150, and " '*liberum arbitrium*' " in 16, l.16, signify Will's ability to perform the miracles shown by Piers Plowman in the higher inner dream, after Will has perfected Haukyn's power in the practice of patient poverty out of which grows charity (16, ll.1–2; see 12, ll.61–3). This miraculous power is intended to reinforce the preaching of a Law, held in common by " 'pharisees and Sarȝens, Scribes and [Grekes]' " (15, l.605). That is, Will is to discover within himself Haukyn's potentially miraculous power, actualized by Piers Plowman's miracles (16, ll.103–18), in order that Will preach the words of Anima's sermon, outlined at the end of Passus 15, in ll.605–613, to all men. Will preaches the acts of charitable free will to all men, by practising the mental acts of free will in the continuing outer dream (16, l.168–17, l.356). "*Actiua vita*" in 13, l.224b (Avicenna's "vis activa") or "þe Actif man" in 16, l.2, guides Will to two perfections. First, he (it) has potentially the power to perform miracles, if his speech is true. Second, Actif ("vis activa") perfects the prophetic speech taught by Ymaginatif ("vis imaginativa").

According to Avicenna, Will's perfection of his "vis imaginativa" (Ymaginatif) by the "virtus activa" (Haukyn) would enable him to achieve what Avicenna calls "ᶜaql qudsi" or, in Latin, the vision of "sanctus intellectus" (holy intellect) in his "anima."[29] In such a vision at

---

[28] *Liber de anima, IV–V*, p.65,l.48–p.66,l.51; p.66, l.59:
 [Anima nobilis] sanet infirmos et debilitet pravos,. . . et pro voluntate eius contingant pluviae et fertilitas. . . Et haec etiam est una de proprietatibus virtutum prophetalium ([The noble soul] cures the ill and weakens the depraved,. . . and at its will, rains and fertility come. . . And this is also one of the properties of the prophetic powers).

[29] *Liber de anima, IV–V*, p.151, ll.84–8, and p.153, n.17: "L'intellect saint, ᶜaql qudsi."

15, ll.161-2, Will would use Avicenna's higher mirror to envision charity and Christ within himself, the higher "Mirour" supplied by the power of Anima, according to Christian interpretation of Avicenna:[30]

'Ac I seiȝ hym neuere sooþly but as myself in a Mirour:
[*Hic*] *in enigmate, tunc facie ad faciem'*
(Here in a glass darkly, then face to face).

Having perceived his higher intent in the "Mirour" of Christ or charity within himself by seeing through Anima, Will would know the third branch within his appetite: the rational branch or, according to Christian interpretation, free will. Thus Will's recognition of himself as rational appetite would be signified by Anima's change of Will's name in 15, l.150, and again in 16, l.16: " 'fre liberal wille' " or the Latin " 'liberum arbitrium' " (free will).

Will's change of name would then be assimilated by Anima's higher speech, i.e., by the image "tree" (16, ll.4-17). In Avicennan psychology, "Will" or "appetitus" is comparable to a tree, because, "rooted" in "anima," the human will grows into a tree made up of three branches: the concupiscible and irascible and rational appetites. Thus the name "Free Will" is comparable to a tree in which the highest branch, the rational appetite (free will, according to Christian interpretation), governs the two lower branches, the concupiscible and irascible

Amélie-M. Goichon gives *"Àql qudsi, intelligence sainte. . . intellectus sanctus"* (*Lexique de la langue philosophique d'Ibn Sina (Avicenne)* p.230, paragr.7).

Vincent of Beauvais Christianizes Avicenna's "sanctus intellectus" into Augustine's "visio intellectualis," adapting Avicenna to Augustine's commentary on *Genesis* (*Speculum Naturale*, Bk.26, ch.75 [Douai-Graz, I, 1885C]).

[30] Franciscans took Avicenna's famous doctrine of the "two faces of Anima" (*Liber de anima, I-II-III*, Bk.1, ch.5; p.94, l.8), i.e., that Anima's lower face is the "virtus activa" and Anima's higher face is the "virtus contemplativa," and turned it into Avicenna's teaching that Anima has a lower mirror and a higher mirror (*Liber de anima, I-II-III*, pp.44*-5*; *Liber de anima, IV-V*, pp.44*-5*, 99-101; Louis Gardet, *La Pensée Religeuse d'Avicenne* [Paris: J. Vrin, 1951], pp.151-152). J. Rohmer shows how Jean de la Rochelle developed the doctrine from this passage in Gundissalinus' *Compendium de anima* ("Sur le doctrine franciscaine des deux faces de l'âme," *Archives d'Histoire Doctrinale et Littéraire du Moyen Age*, 2 [1927], 74-6):

> Hic oculus animae qui est intelligentia in contemplationem creatoris intendit. . . ipsa intelligentia tanta claritate divini luminis perfunditur ut in ipsa intelligentia sic irradiata lux. . . tamquam forma in speculo resultare videatur. Ipsa enim intelligentia creaturae rationalis quasi speculum est aeterni luminis de qua Apostolus 'Videmus nunc per speculum' (This eye of the soul, intelligence, intends toward contemplation of the Creator. This intelligence is suffused with such a brilliance of Divine Light that the irradiated Light is seen to leap in the intelligence, as though an image were leaping in a mirror. For the intelligence of the rational creature is, as it were, a mirror of eternal Light of Which the Apostle speaks: "We see now through a mirror").

appetites perfected by poverty and patience.[31] Because Free Will is rooted in Anima, Anima describes the "Tree" of Free Will in Avicennan terms: " 'Pacience hatte the pure tree' " in 16, 1.8; but, because Free Will is also rooted in the Charity of the Holy Spirit (16, ll.50-2), Piers Plowman perfects Ymaginatif's powers by showing the same tree as the "Tree" of "Trinite" in 16, 1.63 (according to the Christian interpretation of Avicenna).[32]

At this juncture in the Christianization of Avicenna's paradigm for the perfection of prophecy in the "vis imaginativa," Anima has the power to command the "vis imaginativa" to invoke a higher inner vision. As soon as Will says to Anima (16, ll.1-2),

'Now faire falle yow', quod I þo, 'for youre faire shewyng!
For Haukyns loue þe Actif man euere I shal yow louye,'

Piers Plowman is about to perfect Ymaginatif's power of showing (in order to create Will's higher speech) and Haukyn's power of miracles (in order to prove that Will's higher speech is true). Just as Anima's showing of Charity sublimates Will into Free Will and Ymaginatif into Piers Plowman (16, 1.17), so, after the vision of "sanctus intellectus," the Avicennan prophet's Anima commands the "vis imaginativa" to invoke a higher inner dream.[33] Thus, Piers Plowman shows Free Will that the universal Tree of Trinite requires an act of Divine Free Will to prop it up (16, ll.88-9),

Filius by þe fader wille and frenesse of *spiritus sancti*
(the Son by the Will of the Father and the Freedom of the Holy Spirit),

so that Divine Speech assimilates the Act of Divine Free Will (16, 1.90),

---

[31] *Liber de anima*, IV-V, p.56,1.6-p.57,1.7:
> Huius autem virtutis voluntatis rami sunt virtus irascibilis et virtus concupiscibilis (The branches of the power of will are the irascible power and the concupiscible power).

[32] That is, according to the anonymous Worcester tract (D.A. Callus, "Powers of the Soul," 170, ll.17-8). On the "Tree" of "Trinite" in 16,ll.29-52, the powers of Anima named "potentia, scientia, voluntas," are propped by Piers' props of divine " *'potencia'* " and " *'sapiencia'* " and " *'liberum arbitrium'* " (free will) in 16, ll.30, 36 and 50. The divine-human powers signify that the one divine grace of free will in Anima is propped by the attributes of the Three Persons in the One Trinity of God, such as they are perceived by men before the Incarnation and revelation of the Trinity of Persons.

[33] *Liber de anima*, IV-V, p.151,1.88-p.159, 1.90:
> Emanet aliquid ad imaginativam quod imaginativa repraesentat etiam secundum exempla visa vel audita verba, eo modo quo praediximus (Something emanates to the imaginative power. And the imaginative power represents it likewise with the exempla seen and the words heard, in the manner mentioned before).

"In the manner mentioned before" refers to the prophetic power of the "vis imaginativa secundum Avicennam" in lower inner dreams.

And þanne spak *spiritus sanctus* in Gabrielis mouþe,

so that the miracles of Piers-Jesus prove the Truth in the Divine Speech in the *plenitudo temporis* envisioned in 16, ll.103–18 (16, l.93):

Til *plenitudo temporis* [tyme] comen were.

The intent, signified by the name "Free Will," and the showing of the Act of Divine Free Will would give Free Will the power to perform the miracles potentially in Haukyn, in order to convert all "cristene" Anima's to the Law, i.e., the sermon outlined by Anima (15, ll.605–13). Piers Plowman thus perfects Ymaginatif's power in the second inner dream, both by showing the historical and sacramental origins of Charity in Divine Free Will (16, ll.88–90) and by using the Act of Divine Free Will to actualize Haukyn's miraculous power to perform miracles (16, ll.103–18), in order that Free Will preach the Law by practice of the Law within himself.

From 16,l.167–17,l.356, Free Will's mental acts preach the Law of Charity, i.e., ' "*Dilige deum & proximum*,' " by overcoming the scandal in the same Law (16, l.157a), namely that the " '*Dilige deum & proximum*,' " practised by Jews, Christians and Saracens creates hatred rather than charity. In Will, from 16, ll.26–49, the confusing interaction of the one "feiþ" of Abraham and the disparate hopes of *Spes* in diverse practices of the one " '*Dilige deum & proximum*' " causes severe doubts in Will, until the Charity of the Samaritan historically and sacramentally does and explains what the power of Free Will is, from 16, ll.51–137: to love all men as "euenecristene," no matter what sect or Law they practise. Thus, Free Will develops from his higher psychology in Passus 15 the power to love all men as Piers-Jesus did, and develops the words to preach the Christ Who comes in the human nature of Piers Plowman-Jesus. Free Will perceives the unity of Piers Plowman with Jesus in miraculous works (16, ll.103–18), not in order to confuse the two but in order to show that the power of the Holy Spirit (common to Christians, Saracens and Jews) makes both the "crist" and "cristene." In the continuing outer dream, Free Will practises what the term "cristene" means: all those "anointed" (Gk. "christos") by the Holy Spirit in the Law, i.e., Jesus, Piers Plowman, Will and all other "euenecristene."

Piers Plowman's Clergie, " '*Dilige deum*' " (13, l.127a), thus becomes Free Will's Dobet, practice and sermon. Will's practice and preaching of that Clergie as Law, from the psychology self-developed from Passus 13–17, would convert universal ("catholic") society to observance of this perfect Law of God. Miracles would follow: men would be healed, fed and observe the Spirit of the "catholic" Law rather than the letter of the sectarian Laws of Christians, Jews, Saracens and pagans. Thus, the

Christianized perfection of Avicenna's psychology of the "vis imaginativa" well explains that Anima stimulates Free Will to preach the sermon in 15, ll.605–13, by the practice of mental acts from 16,1.168–17,1.356, so that men will convert to the Law of Piers Plowman's Clergie, " '*Dilige deum*,' " and be rewarded for their observance of that Law in their earthly dealings with one another. In the B-text, the added visions in the *Vita* develop higher significations of the name "Will," both by developing more dialectic in the mental acts to signify the higher name and by developing a higher assimilative language to parallel the language of the B-text to the mental acts.

In Passus 18–20, the *PP*-poet applies Free Will's perfection of Avicenna's prophetic psychology to the problems of mendicancy. According to Avicenna, inner dreams supply the prophet with such forceful images that his living and preaching will perform miracles.[34] That is, higher inner dreams enable the prophet to so perfect his rational appetite (the will) that the vivid images stemming from the inner dream will convert his readers or hearers to the Law of God as soon as the prophet preaches to them; and as a result of their practice of the Law, God will miraculously grant their societies food, health and peace. If the higher inner dream gives Free Will the power to confirm his preaching by the performance of miracles, if Piers Plowman not only perfects Ymaginatif but gives Will the vivid images for a sermon of charity (suggested by Anima at the end of Passus 15, in ll.609–13) and performs the miracles that Anima spoke of (15, ll.446–515, 590–5), and if the dialectic of Faith, *Spes* (Hope) and the Samaritan (Charity to all men in the Law) sharpens the focus of Anima's suggested sermon, then Will is being perfected to preach to all men, i.e., to Christian, Saracen, Jew and Greek (Eastern Christians). Passus 18 gives Will the forceful images to preach; and, in Passus 19, at 215–6, Will finally receives the Avicennan "virtus sancta" which would enable him to preach without moral concerns about his food, clothing and shelter. For Grace gives him the baptized Avicennan "qudsi," or, in Latin, the "virtus sancta," or in ME, the "tresour" given to his " 'fyue wittes,' " and a craft to practise (19, ll.228–49).[35] At this highpoint of the *Vita*, Free Will receives the gift

---

[34] "Tractatus 10," *Liber de philosophia prima sive scientia divina, V–X*, p.527,1.8–p.530,1.78.
[35] *Liber de anima, IV–V*, p.153, ll.15–8:
> Et hic est unus modus prophetiae qui omnibus virtutis prophetiae altior est. Unde congrue vocatur virtus sancta, quia est altior gradus inter omnes virtutes humanas (And this is the one type of prophecy which is the highest of all the powers of prophecy. Whence it is fittingly called the "holy power," because it is the highest achievement among all the human powers).

"Lexique Latino-Arabe," *Liber de anima, IV–V*, p.318: "sanctus: *qudsi*." Amélie-M. Goichon gives "Q[uwwa] qudsiya, faculté sainte. . . virtus sancta" (*Lexique de la langue philosophique d'Ibn Sina (Avicenne)*, p.336, paragr.23).

which would allow him to live, preach, and perform miracles without the "encumbrance" of Conscience, spoken of by holi chirche said in 2, l.51, and reiterated by Grace in 19, l.220. Like the Avicennan prophet, Free Will ought to awake from his dreams, ought to live the life revealed to him in dreams, and ought to preach that life to his family and countrymen, after he receives this "virtus sancta." If he uses his "virtus sancta" well, his preaching will be effective. His words will convert all hearers or readers. They will conform themselves, their families and their nations to the Law of God. God, in turn, will perform miracles for them. He will reward them with health, food, and peace, whether they be Christian, Saracen, Greek (Christian) or Jew.

From 19, l.335b (Pride's attack) to the last line of the B-text, however, Free Will and Conscience envision a society where the members of Piers Plowman's church, i.e., the "cristene" anointed by the Holy Spirit from each "couenant" (19, ll.186), do not observe the Law of Christ at 19, l.394, " '*Et dimitte nobis debita nostra &c'* " (And forgive us our debts [as we forgive our debtors]). Pride attacks the two weaknesses of this Church of Piers Plowman (19, ll.348–50):

> 'Conscience shal noȝt knowe who is cristene or heþene,
> Ne no manere marchaunt þat wiþ moneye deleþ
> Wheiþer he wynne wiþ right, wiþ wrong or wiþ vsure.'

In the first attack, these "cristene" and "heþene" become so confused that the "cristene" do not practise the Law of Christ.

In the second, Free Will awakens to Nede (20, l.1–50) who so encumbers his Conscience that Free Will cannot practise the "virtus sancta" without encumbrance of Conscience. Nede claims that Will's mendicant Conscience may take food, clothing and money at need, but not go into debt (20, ll.10–20). Nede justifies the practice with the same words that Rechelesnesse used in 11, ll.37–8 (20, l.33), " '*Homo proponit & deus disponit'* " (Man proposes and God disposes). Mocking Free Will's perfection of Ymaginatif's powers with " 'wenyng is no wysdom, ne wys imaginacioun' " (20, l.33), Nede himself hypostatizes the contradiction of Avicenna's definition of waking:[36]

> Vigilia est dispositio in qua anima imperat sensibus et virtutibus moventibus exterius cui non est necessitas (Waking is the disposition where Anima both commands the senses and powers moving exteriorly, and has no need).

Awake, Will confronts Nede, cannot be free, and is returned to the Rechelesnesse which plagued him before he met Ymaginatif. At the end

---

[36] *Liber de anima, IV–V,* p.33, ll.59–61.

of the B-text, Anima's sermon is not to be preached, nor men converted to the Law, nor miracles to be performed.

The same dialectic which began the *Vita* also ends it: the dialectic between Thou3t and Ymaginatif. Awake, Will's Thou3t would overpower Will's Ymaginatif and lead to a reckless intent; asleep, Will's Ymaginatif would lead to a carefully thought out intent. After 20, l.386b, Will, therefore, awakes into a crisis where he knows what he ought to do but cannot do. For Anima's Thou3t will overcome Ymaginatif and trap Will into thinking about the needs of his body for food, clothing, and housing, as Nede says (20, ll.6-7):

> '[Coudes]tow no3t excuse þee as dide þe kyng and oþere:
> That þow toke to þi bilyue, to cloþes and to sustenance.'

So attacked, Will's Conscience asks Kynde to bring him out of care (20, l.201). Kynde responds, " 'konne som craft' " (20, l.207); and defines the craft (20, l.208): " 'Lerne to loue, and leef alle oþere.' " And Will asks *the* question debated by mendicants (20, l.209):

> 'How shal I come to catel so to cloþe me and to feede?'

The rest of the vision describes the destruction of the unity of Conscience for needs of income ("fyndyng," in 20, l.383a). Will's lack of self-taught Clergie confuses him not only in Passus 10-11 but again at Passus 20 (as Ymaginatif prophesies in 11, ll.430-4).

The presence of this Avicennan psychology in the manuscript collections of every library in Europe sufficiently proves that this psychology of Ymaginatif in the B-text indeed entered the mainstream of medieval psychology,[37] but disguised as "Augustine's" psychology of vision and prophecy. The evidence in *Worcester MS F 57* and in *Worcester MS Q 81* seems to indicate that Ymaginatif both entered the maintream of Christian psychology in the environs of the Malvern Hills and restored a dignity to natural reasoning in the environs of the Malvern Hills.[38]

---

[37] In preparation for the critical edition of *Avicenna Latinus*, M. T. d'Alverny surveyed the holdings of the libraries of the Europe for copies of Avicenna's *Liber de anima*. She published her findings, entitled "Avicenna Latinus" in eleven articles in *Archives d'Histoire Doctrinale et Littéraire du Moyen Age* (28[1961], 281-316; 29[1962], 217-233; 30[1963], 221-72; 31[1964], 271-286; 32[1965], 257-302; 33[1966], 305-327; 34[1967], 315-343; 35[1968], 301-335; 36[1969], 243-280; 37[1970], 327-361; 39[1972], 321-341), as S. van Riet notes (*Liber de anima, IV-V*, p.VI).

[38] Skeat, *Introduction*, 2, liv, says that
> the reader should be aware also of being much influenced by the mention of Malvern Hills. One great merit of the poem is, that it chiefly exhibits London life and London opinions, which are surely of more interest to us than those of Worcestershire.

If the Christian psychology represented by Ymaginatif may have originated near

Imaginative Prophecy in the B-text of Piers Plowman

The two following chapters apply Avicenna's psychology of the "vis imaginativa" (ME "ymaginatif") to the meaning and function of Ymaginatif in the B-text of the *Vita*. The first chapter explains Ymaginatif's prominence in the first vision of the *Vita* in terms of seven features of Avicenna's psychology of the "vis imaginativa:"

1. the "vis imaginativa" (ME "ymaginatif," in 12, 1.1) is the same as the "vis cogitativa" (ME 'þouȝte," in 8, 1.70),
2. when conjoined to "appetitus" (ME "wil") in sleep, the "vis cogitativa" and the "vis imaginativa" not only produce speech but also create visions of awe ("merueillouseste metels" in 8, 1.68a, 11, 1.6a; "wonder" in 11, 1.347a; "merueilled" in 11, 1.360),
3. the "vis imaginativa" appears in sleep and inner dreams (8, 1.67–13,1.1),
4. the "vis imaginativa" prophesies in inner dreams by converting images into speakers (11, ll.6–406),
5. the "vis imaginativa" produces shame in Will (11, 1.405b),
6. the "vis imaginativa" appears and disappears suddenly (11, 1.320, 12, 1.297b),[39]
7. in between the sudden appearance and disappearance, the prophet learns an innate syllogistic ("konnynge" in 13, 1.15).[40]

The second chapter takes up to the transmission of Avicenna's psychology from Spain to England, where, during a period of controversy, it was disguised as the prophetic psychology of "Augustine" in a process known as "Augustinisme Avicennisant" (the Augustinizing of Avicenna). This chapter suggests how perfection of the

Worcester or Oxford, most of the psychological interest in Ymaginatif is to be traced to Worcester or Oxford.

[39] *Liber de anima, IV–V*, p.28, ll.76–8:
> cito aderit comparatio quae est necessaria inter absentiam et animam et inter virtutem imaginativam, et videbitur subito visum (quickly will the comparison be present, a comparison necessary among the world of invisibles and Anima and the imaginative power. And the thing seen will be seen suddenly).

[40] Ymaginatif's sudden appearance as "oon" in 11, 1.320, and sudden disappearance in 12, 1.297 (as well as Piers Plowman's sudden appearance in 16, 1.21 and disappearance in 16, 1.168), signify two effects of the "vis imaginativa secundum Avicennam" in the prophet: first, that all which occurs in the lower or higher inner dream occurs in a flash of insight, secondly, that the prophet learns by an innate syllogistic signified by the sudden appearance and disappearance. The innate syllogistic is the prophet's "genius," an aptitude to "syllogize;" the prophet is said to provide the middle term of a syllogism in an instant because of the power of his "vis imaginativa" (*Liber de anima, IV–V*, p.151, 1.79, and p.152, ll.95–9).

naturally prophetic powers in the Augustinized "vis imaginativa secundum Avicennam" parallels Will's perfection of the naturally prophetic powers in Ymaginatif, from Passus 13–19 of the B-text.

Students of the B-text may be so accustomed to the traditional interpretations of Ymaginatif and the structure of the B-text as to be overwhelmed by this long introduction to the complex artistry of the *Vita*. Nevertheless, they cannot deny that Avicenna's psychology of the lower functions of the "vis imaginativa" explains how Thouȝt and Ymaginatif respectively begin and end the first vision, how Will's "purpos" develops from his interactions with Wit, Dame Studie, Clergie and Scripture, and how Ymaginatif's showing and telling answers the "purpos."[41] Avicenna's psychology also explains why the

---

[41] A well-known scholastic axiom binds Will's theological "purpos" and Ymaginatif's "answer" to the Avicennan psychology: "powers of knowledge are revealed through acts of knowledge, and acts of knowledge are revealed through objects of knowledge" ("potentiae distinguuntur per actus, et actus per objecta"). The axiom comes from commentaries on Aristotle's *De anima*, Bk.2, ch.4; 415a, ll.16–23, here tersely expressed by Thomas Aquinas (*Quaestiones Disputatae: De Anima*, quest.1, art.13, sed contra) but even more tersely by Alexander of Hales: "per actus cognoscuntur potentiae, et actus per obiecta" (*Quaestiones Disputatae' Antequam Esset Frater'*, quaest.31, membr.2 [Bibliotheca Franciscana, XIX, 539, ll.19–20]). Alexander of Hales summarizes Avicenna's interpretation of Aristotle (*Liber de anima, I–II–III*, Bk.1, ch.4, pp.67–79). Thomas Aquinas summarizes Averroes' Commentary on Aristotle, edited by F. Stuart Crawford as *Averrois Cordvbensis Commentarium Magnum in Aristotelis De Anima Libros*, Corpus Commentariorum Averroes in Aristotelem, VI, pt.1 (Cambridge, Mass.: The Medieval Academy of America, 1953), p.179,l.1–p.180,l.52.

The axiom means that Will innately knows "objects of knowledge" (i.e., Dowel) before he makes "acts of knowledge" (i.e., comes to know Dowel) and, therefore, comes to be aware of the "powers of knowledge" (i.e., Thouȝt, Wit, Dame Studie, etc.) while in the process of making "acts of knowledge" from "objects of knowledge." For example in 8, ll.70–4, Will, asleep and attempting to know an "object of knowledge" called "Dowel," makes an act of knowledge called "þouȝt;" therefore, Will comes to be aware of "þouȝt" while in the process of making an act of knowledge from his attempt to know Dowel kyndely. At 8, ll.125–31, Will puts Thouȝt to a "purpos," i.e., to know the same "object of knowledge" called Dowel, and makes an act of knowledge called "wit;" therefore, Will comes to be aware of the power of knowledge called "wit" while in the process of making an act of knowledge from an object of knowledge called Dowel.

Throughout Passus 9, the power of knowledge named "Wit" defines the object of knowledge called Dowel; in Passus 10, Wit's wife, Dame Studie, applies Will to the study of the same object of knowledge (Dowel) by her power as the speaker "studium." The hypostasis of Christian "studium" ("the continuous and vehement Anima applied and occupied with some thing, accompanied with an immense Will"), according to pseudo-Vincent of Beauvais (*Speculum Doctrinale*, Bk.1, ch.24 [Douai-Graz, 2, 21E]),

> Est namque studium assidua & vehemens anima ad aliquem rem applicata,
> magna cum voluntate, occupata,

Dame Studie is the hypostasis of Will joined to his Anima. If, however, she hypostatizes Avicenna's "studium," Dame Studie would signify Will's innate ability to combine two terms of a syllogism in a flash of insight provided by the "vis imaginativa" (*Liber de anima, IV–V*, Bk.5, ch.6; p.152, ll.92–9). Dame Studie, then, would apply Will to the vehement examination of Thouȝt's and Wit's information but would also predict Ymaginatif's "answer." Will acquires such vehemence from her that she predicts Ymaginatif's

the first vision of the *Vita* contains an inner dream enveloped by an outer dream, and why Ymaginatif's "answer" is infallibly rational but "cristene." The psychology of the perfection of the "vis imaginativa secundum Avicennam" accounts for the hypostases as Actif and Pacience in Passus 13 and 14, for Will's perfection of two of his appetites by the practice of patience and poverty in the same Passus, for Will's perfection of his third appetite (or himself) in Passus 15, for the second inner dream and for the perfection of Ymaginatif by Piers Plowman. The Christianization of the psychology accounts for Will's vision through a higher "Mirour" in 15, l.162, for Will's preaching at 15, ll.605–13, for his vision through Piers Plowman in Passus 16, for his preaching-by-practice of loving "euenecristene" (17, l.137), and for the interaction of Abraham, *Spes* and the Samaritan (an interpretation of the second inner dream). The pschology explains why Ymaginatif is infallible only in dreams and, therefore, why Nede wakes Will up and returns him to problems with Rechelesnesse.

Students of *Piers Plowman* as literature may not be aware that this study only skims the rich primary sources of medieval psychology, cited at the end of this book. Students of *Piers Plowman* as historical psychology may not be aware that this study applies rather than quotes the rich literary criticism.[42] The bibliography of psychological works is intended to introduce students of literature to the primary sources. The line index is intended to spare readers from reading more than they wish. Having read this introduction, readers may use the index to find the interpretation of the line(s) and the primary sources which interest them.

"answer" to the "purpos" Will develops from the thought given by her husband (10, l.119).

Her cousin, Clergie, signifies both Avicennan and Christian "disciplina;" Clergie's wife, Scripture, signifies Saracen and Jewish and Christian revealed truth (10, ll.352–74). The names, "Thouȝt," "Wit," "Dame Studie," "Clergie," "Scripture," "oon" "ymaginatif," "Kynde," signify specific mental acts of Will who learns the object of knowledge, "Dowel," from innate and acquired powers of knowledge.

[42] See the latest summation of work dealing with *PP* in *Piers Plowman: A Reference Guide*, by Vincent DiMarco (G.K. Hall: Boston, Mass., 1982), and *An Annotated Critical Bibliography of Langland*, by Derek Pearsall (Univ. of Michigan Press: Ann Arbor, 1990).

Chapter One

The Meaning and Function
of Ymaginatif

We usually speak of the meaning and function of Ymaginatif as if Ymaginatif were independent of the other hypostases in the first vision of the *Vita*. Also, we usually separate Dame Studie's prophecy of Ymaginatif (10, l.119), " 'Ymaginatif herafterward shal answere to [youre] purpos,' " not only from his psychology but also from the "purpos" to which Will puts Thou3t (8, ll.124–5):

> But as I bad þo3t þoo be mene bitwene,
> [To] pute forþ som purpos to preuen his wittes.

The B-text does not make these separations. Ymaginatif's psychology is bound up with the psychology of the other hypostases, for Dame Studie prophesies that Ymaginatif will answer the "purpos" to which Will puts Thou3t and the other hypostases.

It being axiomatic in scholastic psychology that "powers of knowledge are revealed through acts of knowledge, and acts of knowledge are revealed through objects of knowledge," accordingly, the psychology of the "vis imaginativa secundum Avicennam" is bound to Ymaginatif's answer which is bound to the psychology of the other hypostases which is, in turn, bound to the "purpos" of Thou3t. Although a power of knowledge innate to Will, Ymaginatif reveals himself to Will only at 11, l.320, after Will's other powers of knowledge have been revealed by acts of knowledge which, in turn, are revealed by objects of knowledge, i.e., the questions involved in knowing Dowel kyndely. All the acts, powers and objects constitute the "purpos" to which Will puts Thou3t. Before Ymaginatif answers Thou3t's "purpos," Will must develop that "purpos" by several powers of knowledge which come from several acts of knowledge which, in turn, are revealed in several objects of knowledge.

From 8, l.125 to 11, l.319, Will's objects, acts and powers of knowledge explicate the implications in the "purpos" of Thou3t: to prove "his

37

wittes'' (8, 1.125). So Will proves his wits by putting Thou3t to the mediation of Wit's objects of knowledge. Subsequent acts of knowledge by means of Wit and Thou3t lead Will to other faculties of knowledge: to Dame Studie, who, in turn, leads to more objects, acts and other faculties, Clergie. Clergie's objects and acts lead Will to another faculty, Scripture, whose objects of knowledge lead Will to an act of rebellion (10, ll.377–481) and to the confusing speakers and thoughts of the inner dream. By study – Dame Studie – of such objects and acts of knowledge, Will comes to know two types of faculties of knowledge: his innate faculties of knowledge, i.e., Thou3t, Wit and Ymaginatif, and his acquired faculties of knowledge, i.e., Clergie, and Scripture. After his theological rebellion (10, ll.377–481), Will's objects and acts of knowledge become speakers in the inner dream (11, ll.6–406), i.e., the speakers Fortune, the sisters Concupiscence, Elde, Rechelesnesse, Fauntelte, holynesse, the friar, Conscience, Lewte, Scripture, Trajan and the speaker after Trajan (11, ll.7–319).

In Avicennan terms, Anima drags in other hypostases ''ad libitum'' (at Anima's pleasure) to represent the Thou3ts of Anima after Will's rebellion against Scripture; and, in the inner dream, Ymaginatif has the power to convert the thoughts into speakers. Since Thou3t represents Anima's rationality in Will's sensory imagination, and since Anima has the power to create inner dreams, when Anima ''imagines an intent permanently seen,''[1] then Ymaginatif answers Thou3t in an inner dream. In the first part of the inner dream (11, ll.7–319), Ymaginatif makes Will's confused thoughts into the speakers Fortune, the sisters Concupiscence, Rechelesnesse, etc.; and then, as ''oon,'' he himself breaks into the debate, in order to have Will perform another ''comparison among the world of invisibles and Anima and the interior imaginative power'' (11, 1.320–406). In the mental acts after 11, 1.323b, Will compares his intents in the images of human wit and reason (ll. 331–4) to the intents in the images of Animal Wit and Reson (ll.335–68). The method of the comparison is dictated by the psychology: Avicenna would require Will to compare images ''among the world of invisibles and Anima and the interior imaginative power.'' This chapter demonstrates how Will's objects, acts and faculties of knowledge in the first vision of the *Vita* parallel Avicenna's psychology of the operations in the sensory ''anima.''

In light of this psychology, Will's objects, acts and faculties of knowledge elucidate the ''purpos'' of Thou3t (8, ll.124–5): to ''prove'' the ''wit'' in the information which Will receives from Wit in Passus 9. The ''purpos'' is developed from 8, 1.125, to 11, 1.319. Ymaginatif

---

[1] Avicenna, *Liber de anima,* IV–V, p.27, ll.65–70, quoted *passim* throughout this paragraph.

answers from 11, l.320, to the end of the first vision. That is, Ymaginatif shows Kynde's Reson. Kynde's Reson really answers the complex "purpos," erected by Anima's spokesman for human sensory reason (Thouȝt). Ymaginatif's showing of Kynde's Wit and Reson proves a Wit different than the wit proposed by Will's Thouȝt, because Ymaginatif represents Universal Reson Who wills and reasons with a different Kynde Wit than that with which Will reasons and desires. The meaning and function of Ymaginatif is correlative to the psychology of Thouȝt. The two are bound together, in order that Will prove, by different sources of reasoning, the true/good and the false/bad in the "entente" of his human wit (8, l.131), as he proceeds to reason out complex objects of theological knowledge. This chapter takes up only the psychology of Thouȝt and Ymaginatif, according to the first half of the axiom, "powers of knowledge are revealed through acts of knowledge." Explication of the second half would bury the psychology in a lengthy discussion of fourteenth-century theology.

Seven Functions of the "Vis Imaginativa Secundum Avicennam"

Seven interrelated activities of the "vis imaginativa secundum Avicennam" account for the psychology of Ymaginatif in the first vision of the B-text:

1. the "vis imaginativa" (ME "ymaginatif," in 12, l.1) is the same as the "vis cogitativa" (ME "þouȝte," in 8, l.70),

2. when conjoined to "appetitus" (ME "wil") in sleep, the "vis cogitativa" and the "vis imaginativa" not only produce speech but also create visions of awe ("merueillouseste metels" in 8, l.68a, 11, l.6a; "wonder" in 11, l.347a; "merueilled" in 11, l.360),

3. the "vis imaginativa" appears in sleep and inner dreams (8, l.67–3,l.1),

4. the "vis imaginativa" prophesies in inner dreams by converting images into speakers (11, ll.6–406),

5. the "vis imaginativa" produces shame in Will (11, l.405b),

6. the "vis imaginativa" appears and disappears suddenly (11, l.320, 12, l.297b),

7. in between the sudden appearance and disappearance, Will learns an innate syllogistic ("konnynge" in 13, l.15).

1. The identity between Thou3t and Ymaginatif (8, l.70; 11, l.320)

In Avicenna's physiology of the sensory soul (''anima vitalis''), the ''vis cogitativa'' is the same faculty as the ''vis imaginativa.'' Vincent of Beauvais summarizes the physiology, as it is represented in the first vision of the *Vita*:[2]

> Porro imaginativa sive cogitativa est secundum Avicennam vis ordinata in media concavitate cerebri, potens componere aliquid de eo quod est in imaginatione cum alio et dividere secundum quod vult, quam virtutem manifestat sic. Scimus certissime in nostra natura esse ut componamus sensibilia inter se, & dividamus ea secundum similitudinem formae quod videmus extra, oportet ergo ut in nobis virtus sit quae hoc operatur, & haec virtus in quantum imperat ei intellectus noster vocatur cogitativa, in quantum vero illi imperat virtus animalis vocatur imaginativa (Then, the imaginative power or power of thought is, in Avicenna's opinion, a power located in the middle ventricle of the brain. [The power] is able to compare something of that which is in the imagination with another thing, and to divide [it], at will. Avicenna shows how the power works in the following explanation. We know for certain that there is in our [human] nature the activity of comparing and dividing sensibles according to the similarity of form which we see outside [ourselves]. There must be, therefore, a power in us which does this. When commanded by our intellect [to compare and

---

2 *Speculum Naturale*, Bk.27, ch.10 (Douai-Graz, 1, 1924B), which excerpts either directly from Avicenna's *Liber de anima*, IV–V, p.6, ll.73–78, or (more likely) indirectly from Jean de la Rochelle's *Summa de anima* (Domenichelli, p.262,l.30–p.263,l.8.), which, in turn, borrowed from the anonymous Worcester commentator (Callus, ''Powers of the Soul,'' p.132), as we have seen (''Introduction,'' note 15). Parts of the formulation are to be found in Jean's *Tractatus* (p.76, ll.238–42).

The first sentence of Vincent's excerpt repeats Avicenna's *Liber de anima*, I–II–III, p.89, ll.46–8):
> Quae [imaginativa seu cogitans] est vis ordinata in media concavitate cerebri. . ., et solet componere aliquid deo eo quod est in imaginatione cum alio et dividere aliud ab alio secundum quod vult,

but omits two of Avicenna's heterodox ideas, one contained in the previous sentence and another within the quote itself. The previous sentence contains this heterodox teaching of Avicenna (*Liber de anima*, I–II–III, p.89, ll.44–45):
> Post hanc est vis qui vocatur imaginativa comparatione animae vitalis, et cogitans comparatione animae humanae (After this is the power which is called the imaginative power in respect to the vital soul, but the power of thought in respect to the human soul).

Avicenna refers the name ''imaginativa'' to the sensory rationality in the sensory soul (''anima vitalis'') of all animals, including man. All animals have an ''anima vitalis'' physiologically located in both the heart and the cerebellum (*Liber de anima*, I–II–III, p.82, l.40, p.139, l.19). Since man has both an ''anima vitalis'' and an ''anima humana,'' then the one power has two different names: ''imaginativa'' when it is guided by the ''anima vitalis,'' or ''cogitans'' when it is guided by the ''anima humana.'' To Christian *theologians*, the two names seem to imply that there are two souls within man. So, following the psychology and physiology of Thomas Aquinas (*Summa theologiae*, ''Prima Pars,'' quest.78, art.4, corpus), Vincent of Beauvais drops this sentence. For Thomas Aquinas argues that the ''anima humana'' is the one substantial form of man. Therefore, the ''vis cogitans'' suffices for both functions in the human soul.

divide images], the power is called thought; but, when commanded by the animal spirit, it is called the imaginative power).

When Will sensorily reasons in the middle ventricle of his brain, the one sensory reasoning in the middle ventricle has two different names, because the middle ventricle of his brain uses two different sources to reason in the senses: either the "vis imaginativa" of Will's animal Anima or the "vis cogitativa" of Will's human Anima. Only the "command" to compare and divide the intents of the images separates the reasoning of Ymaginatif from the reasoning of Thou3t. If Anima ("intellectus noster" or Anima as " *'animus'* " in 15, l.24) commands Thou3t to compare and divide images in the middle ventricle of Will's brain, then the sensory reasoning power is called Thou3t (8, 1.74). If Kynde (the celestial "virtus animalis" in 11, 1.321) commands Ymaginatif to compare and divide images in the middle ventricle, the same sensory reasoning is called Ymaginatif ("oon," in 11, 1.320).

When Thou3t perceives the occult true/false or good/bad in the images received from the human Wit in Will's "anima vitalis" (i.e., the spirit both in Will's heart and in the middle ventricle of Will's brain, as Wit describes it in 9, ll.57–8), then Thou3t judges true/false or good/bad in the intent of the images. Thou3t judges by the standards of the human Anima, and Will desires to shape his intent to Thou3t's "purpos." When Ymaginatif perceives the occult true/false or good/ bad in the images received from the animal Wit in Will's "anima vitalis," then Ymaginatif judges the occult true/false or good/bad in the animal Wit in Will's body. Ymaginatif judges by the standards of the animal Anima, and Will shapes his intent to Ymaginatif's answer. Wit names the standard of true/good or false/bad perceived by both Thou3t and Ymaginatif, when, in 9, 1.31, he says that man is most like Kynde in "marc and shafte" (9, 1.31, in the "F-group" of mss). That is, man, like Kynde, has an innate will to intend the good and to avoid the evil.

Both Thou3t and Ymaginatif "reason" according to the etymology "ratio:" both apply the "patterns" ("rationes") of "same-as" (comparing sensory data to the objective standard) and of "different-from" (dividing sensory data, according to the objective standard). Thou3t and Ymaginatif differ only in the source of their sensory powers and in their objective standards of true/good. Thou3t's power and standard originate in Anima; Ymaginatif's power and standard originate in Kynde, although both standards of true/good are innate to Will's kynde as the *rational* (the standard of Thou3t) *animal* (the standard of Ymaginatif). Will kyndely knows how to compare and divide images by the power of comparison and division common to all animals in Kynde, i.e., by an innate ME "konnynge" of "Kynde" (13, l.15). The *PP*-poet's "vis imaginativa" is Avicennan, though, as we shall see, Avicennan with an admixture of pseudo-Augustine. It is certainly not Thomistic. Thomists refused to separate the "vis imaginativa secundum Avicennam" from the "vis cogitativa" in man.[3]

The identity between Thou3t's Reson and Ymaginatif's Reson vaguely unifies the first vision of the *Vita*, although the physiology of the Reson in Thou3t is not as prominent in the B-text as the physiology of the Reson in Ymaginatif (compare the " 'Reson wolde it neuere' " or " '*humana racio*' " of Dame Studie and Clergie in 10, ll.119, 256, to the numerous references to Kynde's or Ymaginatif's Reson in 11, ll.335, 370-6, 387, 414-5, 420, 429, 438). The one sensory Reson, hypostatized by Thou3t and by Ymaginatif compare and divide the intents in the images stemming from Wit. Since Wit or the "sensus communis" is located in the brain in Will's "cors" where Wit receives all the images from the external senses, the five fair sons of the first wife of Inwit (9, l.19), then Will uses the sensory reasoning of Thou3t to compare

---

[3] In the *Summa theologiae*, "Prima Pars," quest.78, art.4, corpus, Thomas Aquinas allows to the human "vis imaginativa" only the power of comparing and dividing images, but not the power of reasoning in the senses. His position is similar to Averroes' teaching (*Commentarium Magnum*, Bk.3, ch.11, 434a, l.6 [ed F. Stuart Crawford, p.529, ll.2-3]).

Thomas defines the soul ("anima") not as the "perfectio" of the body (as Avicenna does) but as "forma" united to the body. "Anima intellectiva" is the form of the body, united as form is to matter (*Summa theologiae*, "Prima Pars," quest. 76, sed contra). There being not three souls in man (vegetative, sensitive and rational) but only one soul, considered as "principium intellectivum" (*Summa*, "Prima Pars," quest. 76, arts. 1 and 3), the "principium intellectivum" is united to the body as a "species intelligibilis" which unites with the two "subjects" of corporeal knowledge, the "possible intellect" and the "phantasmata" (images) which are in the organs of sensory knowledge (*Ibid.*, quest.76, art.1, corpus). Thomas allows for no reason within the sensory powers apart from the reason in the "principium intellectivum," that is, the reason in the *human* anima. There is no *humanly* rational "vis imaginativa" in Thomas Aquinas.

When Thomas takes up the question of sensory knowledge of the intentions in the senses not perceived by sensory organs ("Necessarium est ergo animali quod percipiat huiusmodi intentiones quas non percipit sensus exterior" [*Ibid.*, quest. 78, art.4, corpus]), he disposes of a "vis imaginativa" in man. In animals other than men, the power is called the "vis aestimativa;" in men, it is called the "cogitativa" or "ratio particularis." To the human "vis imaginativa," Thomas attributes only the power comparing and dividing images (*Ibid.*):

> quae [potentia] componit et dividit formas [imagines] imaginatas. . . Sed ista operatio non apparet in aliis animalibus ab homine, in quo ad hoc sufficit virtus imaginativa (the faculty compares and divides imagined forms [images]. . . But this activity does appear in animals other than man. In man the imaginative power suffices for this).

Since Thomas allows no rational activity in the senses apart from the reason in the "principium intellectivum," we are to infer that the discrimination involved in the "composition and division of images" comes from the "vis cogitativa," not from the "vis imaginativa."

and divide the images which Wit presents to him at the beginning of the first vision of the *Vita*. Being the hypostasis of Anima's sensory reasoning, Thou3t is as innate to Will as his *rationality* is to his animality. From 11, l.320, Ymaginatif as "oon" begins to dispute with Will's previous comparison and division of images received from Wit. The same sensory reasoning, now called Ymaginatif, compares and divides the intents in the images which the Wit of Kynde presents to Will from the point where Kynde comes and "bad me wit for to take" (11, ll.321b, 323b). Will's standard of true/good is still as innate to him, but as innate as his *animality* is to his human rationality. So the objective standard of Wit and Reson is represented as being outside of Will, i.e., in the Wit and Reson of Kynde mediated by Ymaginatif. By 11, ll.370-4, where Will's human Thou3t rebukes the Wit and Reson in Kynde, the opposition between the two hypostases of Will's one sensory reasoning proves that there are contrary "purposes" within Will's body, within his external wits, within his interior Wit, within his sensory reasoning, and, therefore, within his initial "entente" in 8, l.131. Although both Thou3t and Ymaginatif receive images from Wit, each shapes Will to a contrary intent by a different standard of reasoning.

We agree that Ymaginatif is a reliable "spokesman for Reason." Now we begin to understand why he is reliable. The source of the Reson in Ymaginatif guides Will's sensory movements toward the kynde knowyng of Dowel more reliably than the source of the Reson in Thou3t, by means of a standard both within Will ("konnynge") and outside of Will (Kynde's Wit and Reson). Thou3t leads Will's Wit astray, because Thou3t's standard is within only the human Anima. Ymaginatif reliably speaks for Reson, because he returns Will's Wit to an awareness of Kynde's Wit.

Nevertheless, the meaning and function of Ymaginatif in the first vision still confuse Will (and us), until Avicenna's psychology reveals that the real guides who lead Will to know Wit kyndely are " '*mens þou3te*' " in Anima (15, l.25, in the "R-group" of mss) and the "konnynge of Kynde" (Avicenna's "virtus animalis" in the ME of 13, l.15). Will (and we) are not aware of the true guides until 13, l.15 and 15, l.25. It is Anima and Kynde who actually "command" the sensory reasoning hypostatized by Thou3t and Ymaginatif. In the first vision, the B-text intends to parallel only the beginnings of Will's search for kynde knowyng within himself, not the achievement of it by 13, l.15, or the perfection of it in Passus 15. From Passus 8–12, Will intends to know only about the good in the animality of his kynde and about the evil in the human animality of his kynde. From a fundamental wit of good and evil innate to his own corporeal kynde, Will knows everything else. Literally "quicquid est per se scit" (whatever is he knows through himself), according to Avicenna's psychology.[4] And literally, "nil cognitum nisi prius fuerit in sensu" (nothing known except in the senses).

Very literally and pictorially, Will follows the logic of his human sensory reason to conclude and object that Kynde's Reson does not follow many acts of human sensory reson (11, 1.374-5):

> 'I haue wonder [in my wit], þat witty art holden,
> Why þow ne sewest man and his make þat no mysfeet hem folwe.'

Will sees the logical "non-sequiturs" ("ne sewest") in human acts. For the fact that Kynde's Reson does "not follow" from human acts, it "follows" that the Reson in Kynde makes mischief for man, i.e., the mischief represented in Will's Thouȝt from the beginning of this vision up to this point. Having compared images by means of the Reson shown by Ymaginatif, Will now sees "that Reson took reward and ruled alle beestes saue man and his make" (ll.370-1b, in the "F-group" of mss). Will blames Kynde's Reson, instead of blaming the deviant desire in himself and all other men: a deviant desire which put Thouȝt to a deviant "purpos." At last, Will finds the " 'craft in my cors' " he requested of holi chirche in 1, 1.139, i.e., the perception of a good and evil stimulus within himself as hypostatized "desire" or "appetite." But he comes to this craft or konnynge in his "cors" by the tortuous way of a *Visio* and by way of a continuing interior debate, re-presented among Wit, Thouȝt and Ymaginatif, each of whom serve the higher powers of Anima and Kynde, not revealed until later (11, 1.323b, 15, 1.23).

Therefore, Ymaginatif's function as "spokesman for Reason" emerges from a conflict, a conflict between the good explicated by the sensory reasoning of Anima (Thouȝt) and the good explicated by the sensory reasoning of Kynde (Ymaginatif), after a "purpos" and "answer" have been set for both of them by Dame Studie. Since Will limits the "purpos" of the "mene bitwene" himself and Wit only to differentiate "Dowel fro dobet and dobest from hem boþe" (8, 1.126; see 1.128-9), then Will has already limited Thouȝt's "purpos": to prove only the good in his original "entente" (8, 1.131). By 11, 1.319, however, the good "entente" in the proof has been confused by Will's deviant desire, such that Thouȝt and the hypostases stemming from Thouȝt reason to a "purpos" denied by Kynde's Reson. Reson's contradiction signifies something wrong in Will's initial "purpos." Will has overemphasized the good in Thouȝt, commanded by Anima, and has excluded the good

---

[4] *Liber de anima*, IV-V, p.151, ll.82-3.

in Ymaginatif, commanded by Kynde. For, in Passus 8, Will does not propose that Thou3t prove the distinction of Dowel from "Dobad" or Dobet from "Doworse" or Dobest from "Doworst." Will's reasoning by Thou3t excludes fifty percent of the "konnynge" present in his Anima: the discernment of evil. Therefore, Will's limitation of Thou3t to only the good "purpos" embroils him in theological arguments about the origins of evil outside of him and inside of him, i.e., about the effects of Adam's sin in himself.

The hypostatized extensions of Thou3t, the two sets of married couples (Wit and Studie, Clergie and Scripture) represent more arguments over these objects of knowledge, one spouse seeing something good and being contradicted by the other spouse. Dame Studie's study opposes her husband's wit and Will's act of knowledge, after Will uses Wit and Thou3t to think through objects and acts of their knowledge. According to her, the objects of knowledge communicated to Will by Wit are so much "wisdom" cast to hogs (10, ll.3–16, 140–6). Similarly, Scripture thinks that Will has misunderstood the objects of knowledge communicated to him by her husband Clergie. Dowel is not " '*dominus* and kny3thode' " (10, ll.336–48) but baptism into patient poverty (10, l.346). Although the married couples extend Will's thoughts to objects of learned knowledge necessary for Will's kynde knowyng, their self-arguments also elucidate the confusion in Will's thoughts. According to axiom, the topics or "objects of knowledge" ought to reveal "acts of knowledge" so that the "faculties of knowledge" keep a logical consistency. By the time Will begins to rebel against Scripture in 10, l.377, Will's "purpos" is already at cross purposes. Will cannot choose the good he desires, because his "coueitise" or "likyng" puts his faculties of kynde knowyng, his acts of knowledge and his objects of knowledge at cross purposes. Extensions of Will's Thou3t do hint at the evil in Will's use of kynde wit, but Will has proposed to use Thou3t to prove only the good in human Wit.

The infallibility of the "spokesman of Reason" answers the "purpos" prophesied by Dame Studie by showing (11, ll.320–406) and by telling (11,l.414–12, l.297). On the one hand, Ymaginatif's answer shows the truth in Scripture's rebuke of Will: " '*Multi multa sciunt et seipsos nesciunt*' " (11, l.3). Will knows many theological objects of knowledge but nothing about the good and evil in his own desire. The showing of the Wit and Reson in Kynde proves that Will knows nothing about the evil in his own kynde wit. On the other hand, Will's contradictions of Scripture's Clergie in 10, ll.377–481, do contain " 'sooþ of somme' " (12, l.159a), because Ymaginatif upholds an innate power in "lewed" men like Will, a power to be saved more easily than learned men (12, ll.157–8). In Passus 12, Ymaginatif's "purpos" becomes more subtle. He distinguishes that academic learning which *teaches* about the good or evil in human kynde from that self-learning which *experiences* the good and evil in human kynde. Against the learned theologians, Ymaginatif upholds the teaching power of the animal instincts within man, e.g., the konnynge to swim compared to the konnynge to repent, or konnynge to say ritual words compared to the konnynge to be released from prison (12, ll.160-95). With the learned theologians, Ymaginatif upholds the power of learned Clergie to teach men of instinct (12, ll.70-158). The showing and telling of the other source of reason in Will's senses, Ymaginatif's Reson, informs Will of the evil and the limitations of Wit and Thouȝt in the human Anima (12, l.235).

The consequences of the one sensory reasoning in Will's middle ventricle lead Will to a theological and moral morass, represented in the inner dream by the collision of the ''purpos'' of one hypostasis and the ''answer'' of another. By the time that Will's animal Reson, the Reson in Kynde represented by Ymaginatif (11, l.335), confronts him, Will's reasoning by Thouȝt has led him to one set of consequences hypostatized in the inner dream: to the concupiscence in the sisters Concupiscence, to his anger with the friars' concupiscence over the costs of his burial and suffrage (11, ll.13-32, 43, 50-60, 63-83), to the conflicts among Lewte, Scripture, Trajan and the speaker after Trajan (11, ll.84-319). From 8, l.74, Will has followed the one sensory reasoning, hypostatized by Thouȝt and extensions, until he reaches the point in 11, l.319, where the reasoning of the speaker after Trajan angrily returns to patient poverty as a cure for ignorant clergy. The speaker praises the very patient poverty which Will objected to, when Scripture spoke of it in 10, l.346, in opposition to Will's Dowel of '' *'dominus* and knyȝthode.' '' Because Thouȝt's ''purpos'' has brought Will to this quandary by 11, l.319, the very next line, 11, l.320, introduces the other source for Will's sensory reasoning: the reasoning of Kynde's minister, Ymaginatif. The inner dream continues, but Ymaginatif as ''oon'' changes the source of Will's one sensory reasoning (11, ll.321-3):

> And slepynge I seiȝ al þis, and siþen cam kynde
> And nempned me by my name and bad me nymen hede,
> And þoruȝ þe wonders of þis world wit for to take.

The Reson in Kynde (11, ll.335, 370) bids Will to take another view of his ''wit,'' from the perspective of the Wit of Kynde in the acts of all animals except the human animal (11, ll.328-68). Will objects: this Wit does not ''follow'' (''sequitur'') human kynde. Reson responds, '' 'recche þee neuere' '' (11, l.376b), referring Will back to Rechelesnesse's '' 'recche þe neuere' '' and to the morass of human thought from then on (11, l.34). Reson's '' 'recche þee neuere' '' confronts Will's eye with visual evidence of a poverty and patience within all Kynde, called " 'suffraunce' " (11, 1.379) and defined as follows (11, 1.382):

'Ac he (god) suffreþ for som mannes goode, and so is oure bettre.'

Will does take Wit, Kynde's Wit. Through this source of Reason in his animality, Will compares and divides out the kynde of the body of man from the kynde of the bodies in all Kynde, according to *the* standard of Reson and sufferance (11, 11.369-79), i.e., Kynde's Reson and Sufferance. The bodies in all Kynde except those in the human kynde are guided by the innate good in the Reson of Kynde. Will sees immediate evidence of the "sequitur's" in Nature. Nature has sufferance while some men repent. This Reson and Wit must be infallible, because it is Kynde's. Ymaginatif's Wit and Reson must be infallible, because Ymaginatif is the angel of Kynde's Reson and Wit.

Although Ymaginatif is, therefore, "not only the spokesman of Reason but. . . gifted with a vision of joy and sorrow to come," according to H.S.V. Jones' definition,[5] he is an Avicennan "spokesman of Reason" who prophesies the "joy and sorrow to come." Avicennan "joy and sorrow" are the logical and moral emotions or reactions in Will which follow upon Will's sight of all Kynde through Ymaginatif. Joy and sorrow ("gaudium et tristitia") are the products of Will's concupisicible and irascible desires, when Will is the hypostasis of the power of desire ("virtus desiderativa"):[6]

Tristitia. . . de accidentibus irasicibilis. . . Gaudium. . . pecuniam cupere et cibos appetere et concupiscere coitum. . . sunt ex virtute bestiali concupiscibili. . . Virtus autem desiderativa sequitur has virtutes praedictas: cum enim intenditur eius vis, desiderat (Sorrow [is one] of the accidents of the irascible appetite. Joy,. . .[and] to desire money and to desire food and to desire sexual intercourse are [all] from the power of the bestial concupiscible appetite. . . For the power of desire follows these aforementioned powers. For, when the power of desire is intended, it desires).

Named "desire," Will would have three appetites for and toward the good/true: the concupiscible appetite, the irascible appetite, and the

---

5 "Imaginatif in *Piers Plowman*," *JEGP*, 13(1914), 584. Avicenna, however, treats "joy and sorrow" ("gaudium et tristitia") as "mores" (i.e., habitual activities), not as virtues (*Liber de anima, IV–V*, p.58,1.26–p.59,1.36; p.67, 11.70–75). Avicenna's "mores" are a long way from the Christian virtues of patience and poverty. According to Avicenna, human kynde does not inherit the effects of Adam's sin, so that patient poverty does not remedy the effects of Adam's sin. Avicennan "mores" signify the medicinal and physiological benefits of patience and poverty, not the remedial value of them. Avicennan "Joy and sorrow" signify the *natural* perfection of the concupiscible appetite to possess and the irascible appetite to be angry. Avicennan prophets perfect the *natural* appetites to possess and to be angry.
6 *Liber de anima, IV–V*, p.58,1.26–p.59,1.38, *passim*.

rational appetite.[7] The three appetites of the "bestial" Will desire the concupiscible good and the irascible good and the rational good. Will's perfection of the concupiscible branch within himself produces joy if he is poor (as he is in Passsus 13 and 14), although the loss of land and lordship also produces sorrow in the same appetite if he is poor and "reccheles" (as he is in 11, 1.34). Will's concupiscence to possess or to be poor causes both joy and sorrow, depending upon the "purpos" to which Will puts his intent: to possess patient poverty joyfully (" 'Ioye to pacient pouere,' " in 14, 1.285) or to possess it recklessly ("pouerte. . . putte me lowe," in 11, 1.62). Will's irascibility to love or to hate can cause either joy or sorrow, also depending upon the "purpos" to which he puts his intent: to speak angrily against Kynde's perspective (11, ll.374–5) or to speak patiently in accord with Kynde's perspective (11, ll. 416a–421). This "spokesman of Reason" naturally inculcates in Will a desire for patient poverty much more motivating than Scripture's call for Will's "baptism" into patient poverty (10, 1.346).

2. *Ymaginatif's power to produce "awe" (11, ll.6, 324, 374) and patient speech (11, ll.395–6)*

Avicenna's "vis cogitativa" and "vis imaginativa" create awe in Will ("merueillouseste metels" in 8, 1.68a, 11, 1.6a; "wonder" in 11, 1.347a; "merueilled" in 11, 1.360). Will's mental reactions, "I hadde wonder" (11, 1.347), "Muche merueilled me" (11, 1.360), and "Manye selkouþes I seiȝ" (11, 1.364), are the results of an Avicennan psychology of the "animal spirit," not the results of a Miltonic "animal spirit" (quoted by Samuel Taylor Coleridge):[8]

> Man's nourishment, by gradual scales sublim'd, To *vital* spirits aspire: to *animal*: To *intellectual*! – give both life and sense, Fancy and understanding: whence the soul Reason deceives. And reason is her being, Discursive or intuitive.

Such an "animal spirit" would transform Ymaginatif into the "Fancy" whose "Reason" deceives "the soul." Quoting Leibniz after this quotation from Milton, Coleridge refers to a "principium" (beginning) of the "vires" (powers of the soul), something like the "formal power" ("formale") which the scholastics simply call "imaginatio." Had the *PP*-poet used "ymaginacioun" ("imaginatio") instead of "ymaginatif," Will's awe would foreshadow a Romantic awe of Kynde. Should we continue to interpret Ymaginatif as a Coleridgean "Imagination" or

---

7   *Liber de anima*, IV–V, p.56,1.6–p.57,1.9.
8   S.T. Coleridge (*Biographia Literaria*, ch.13), who quotes from *Paradise Lost*.

"Fancy" in the " '*animal*' " spirit,[9] we would misunderstand what is meant by Thou3t, by Ymaginatif and by Will's awe. The "purpos" to which Will put Thou3t deceives Will. Ymaginatif's "answer" tells Will the truth. Will's awe arises from an unexpected revelation of a truth about himself from an "animal spirit" ("virtus animalis") within himself, i.e., from Ymaginatif as "oon."

Although Will's awe is the affect of a sensory, Galenic animal spirit, Will's awe is medieval and Avicennan. That is, his awe arises from the very act of reason where he discovers the power of Ymaginatif as "oon." In 11, ll.325–30, and 335–62, under the influence of the "oon," Will sees a Reson following ("sewe") the acts of every beast in Kynde with logical "sequitur's" (it follows). The result is an awe ("admiratio") of what Avicenna calls the instinctual "arts" of all animals, especially of birds:[10]

> Cetera vero animalia, et praecipue aves, habent artes: construunt enim casas vel nidos et praecipue apes, sed hoc non fit adinveniendo nec meditando, sed instinctu insito, unde non variatur nec differt; plura autem ex his fiunt ad meliorandum dispositiones suas aut propter necessitatem specialem, non propter necessitatem singularem (But animals [other than man] and especially birds have arts. They build houses or nests, especially the bees. They do not do so by adventitious knowledge or study but by innate instinct. Hence, there is no variance nor difference. Many of these [activities] are done to better their conditions or for the need [to preserve] their species, but [none are done to preserve] themselves).

Instinct gives all animals the "arts" ("artes") to ameliorate their living conditions, for all animals instinctually create their "artes," in order to overcome the difficulty of living in conditions of natural necessity.

Having looked from Kynde's perspective, i.e., down from the "sonne" to the "see" and then to the "sond" (11, l.327), Will first espies "briddes and beestes" next to their mates (11, l.328), and then "man and his make" (11, l.331a). He compares the results of the acts of man and his mate (11, ll.332–4),

> Pouerte and plentee, boþe pees and werre,
> Blisse and bale boþe I sei3 at ones,
> And how men token Mede and Mercy refused,

to the results of the acts of all other animals (11, ll.335–6):

> Reson I sei3 sooþly sewen alle beestes,
> In etynge, in drynkynge and in engendrynge of kynde.

---

[9] Skeat considers him to be "Imagination or Fancy" (note to C.XV.l.1) and, accordingly, would place him in the among the Galenic "*vital*" or "*natural*" and the "*animal* functions" (note to B.IX.l.55).
[10] *Liber de anima*, IV–V, p.73, ll.53–8.

First, he concludes that no animal sexually pursues his mate after conception (11, ll.337–44), "saue man oone" (11, l.344b, in the "F-group" of mss). Then, he concludes that birds build nests better than carpenters build houses (11, ll.349–50). Then, he marvels at the birds who cannot fly well ("me merueilled moore," 11, l.351a): they automatically know how to hide their eggs from human and animal predators (11, ll.351–5, 362).[11] Then, in 11, ll.356–62, he marvels that other birds conceive their young in trees and build their homes in trees, in order to protect their young and their species, and not to protect themselves. His awe comes from Avicenna's description of the contrast between the houses of birds and the houses of men:[12]

> in eis [casis] autem quae faciunt homines, plura fiunt propter necessitatem singularem et plura ad meliorandum dispositionem ipsius singularis (in the homes which men make, many are made for personal necessity and many to ameliorate a personal condition).

Will's "awe" is not the result of the worship of Nature. Rather, Will marvels that the arts of the birds are designed to preserve the species and not themselves. Even though Nature subjects animals to need ("necessitatem"), animals use their innate instinct to preserve their species ("necessitatem specialem"), but not to preserve themselves ("necessitatem singularem"). That is, the natural needs shared by man and beast, e.g., the need to eat, to drink, to reproduce, differentiate man from beast. The "arts" of man and his mate use food, drink, sexuality and housing to protect themselves but not their species. The "arts" of all other animals use the same conditions of natural need, in order to protect their species.

Avicenna's physiology and psychology account for Will's awe – and for his different perspective on the problem of Mede (11, l.334):[13]

> Ex proprietatibus ergo hominis est ipsa necessitas quae eum induxit ad discendum et docendum et alia necessitas quae eum induxit ad dandum et recipiendum secundum mensuram iustitiae et deinde aliae necessitates, veluti facere conventus et adinvenire artes. Cetera vero animalia, et praecipue aves, habent artes: construunt enim casas vel nidos et praecipue apes, sed hoc non fit adinveniendo nec meditando, sed instinctu insito, unde non variatur nec differt; plura autem ex his fiunt ad meliorandum dispositiones suas aut propter necessitatem specialem, non propter necessitatem singularem; in eis autem quae faciunt homines, plura fiunt propter necessitatem singularem et plura ad meliorandum dispositionem suam ipsius singularis (Of the properties of man, then, is one necessity

[11] *Ibid.*, p.73, ll.55, and 53–60.
[12] *Ibid.*, p.73, ll.58–60.
[13] *Ibid.*, p.73, ll.49–60.

which has led him to learn and to teach, and another necessity which has led him to give and to receive according to the measure of justice; and still other necessities, such as to make agreements and to discover the arts. Other animals, however – especially birds – have arts. They build houses or nests: especially the bees. But this is not done by discovery or by meditation; rather, by innate instinct. Hence, it does not vary nor differ. Several of these are done to ameliorate their conditions or because of necessity for their species, not on account of their individual necessity. In those which men do, several are done for individual necessity and several for the amelioration of the condition of the individual [man]).

Men have three necessities: to learn and teach, to give and receive, and to join together and learn the arts. If Nature teaches man the wit to form a human society (''conventus'') to protect the human species, then men discover the adventitious arts (''adinvenire artes'') to protect the society and species with food and housing. From this instinct, comes the wit to ''give and receive according to a measure of Justice.'' From this, in turn, follows formal learning and teaching, i.e., what is called adventitious learning (Latin ''disciplina'' or ME ''Clergie''). Instincts toward natural Justice create the arts of human Mede and human Mercy just as naturally as birds build nests to preserve their species.

Will's comparison and division of the instinctual arts of birds with the reasoned arts of men explains Will's unromantic awe:[14]

> De proprietatibus autem hominis est ut, cum apprehenderit aliquid quod rarissimum est, sequitur passio quae vocatur admiratio (One of the properties of man is that, when he perceives something very rare, there follows the emotion called awe).

Will's ''rare'' perception is that the animals have more Reson and Justice than man. Animals, not men, know the use of Mede (11, ll.334–5), because animals care more about the preservation of their species in conditions of natural necessity. The rare insight and awe come from a visual contrast of the wit in animals with the wit of the human animal, in the images Will studies from 11, ll.345–62.

It first awes Will that no human wit or Thou3t is employed to preserve the human species in conditions of need, i.e., needs for food, clothing and shelter (a concept which was enunciated by holi chirche in 1, ll.17–25, and which will be hypostatized into Nede in 20, l.4). Then, Will is awed by the sight that all ''men token Mede and Mercy refused'' (11, l.334). ''Men token Mede and Mercy refused'' not only proves that Theologie's definition of Mede was correct (2, l.119),

'For Mede is muliere of Amendes engendred,'

---

14 *Ibid.*, p.73, ll.61–2.

when Peace presented a complaint to Parliament (4, 1.47) who decided
that Mede was be used *in society* for "amends" and Mercy (4, ll.90–103).
The sight also proves that Will himself took Mede and refused Mercy in
11, ll.53–9, when Will used Mede for his personal salvation but refused
Mercy to the friar for his salvation. For Coueitise of eiʒes advised Will to
use his money to buy salvation from the friars in 11, ll.53–9; then, old
and poor and refused, Will refused Mercy to the deceitful friar
(11, ll.86–106).

Visual evidence of the lack of Wit in his human kynde and in all
human kynde changes Will's awe to anger (11, ll.369–72):

> Ac þat moost meued me and my mood chaunged,
> That Reson rewarded and ruled alle beestes
> Saue man and his make; many tyme [me þouʒte]
> No Reson hem [ruled, neiþer riche ne pouere].

Under the showing of the "oon," Kynde's Wit provides Will with ample
"forbisenes" or "ensamples" of Kynde's concern for the preservation
of each species (11, ll.325–6):

> I was fet forþ by [forbisenes] to knowe
> Thorugh ech a creature kynde my creatour to louye.

These "forbisnes" oppose the friars' "forbisne" for Will's personal
preservation (8, ll.48–50):

> 'Ay is þi soule saaf but [þow þiselue wole
> Folwe þi flesshes wille and þe fendes after,
> And] do deedly synne and drenche þi[selue].'

By 11. ll.325–6, Will sees the contradiction of the Thouʒt intended in 8,
1.131: " 'And werchen as þei þre wolde; th[i]s is his entente.' " Lines
325–6 contradict the Wit Will was taught in Passus 9, 1.31: " 'man is hym
moost lik of marc and of [shape].' " The "forbisnes," thoughts and acts
of Will's human kynde intend not to love the Creator but to love the
human individual.

The Reson shown by the "oon" forces Will to grant what he is most
unwilling to grant: reason follows the acts of every animal except the
rational animal. The human wit's intent for the personal rather than for
the societal is that which separates the kynde of the rational animal from
the Kynde of all other animals, for (11, 1.335):

> Reson I seiʒ sooþe sewen alle beestes.

Since every animal except man acts in order to ensure the survival of the
whole species in conditions of natural necessity, human acts create
unnatural necessity by ensuring the survival of the individual rather

than of the species. For human wit acts only to ensure that there is poverty for many and affluence for a few, peace for a few and war for many, pleasure for a few and misery for most, "Mede" for a few and no "Mercy" for many (11, ll.331–4).

No Romantic awe or "Fancy" deceives Will's human reason. Medieval awe is produced by the visual logic of a rational Ymaginatif. Will recognizes that his human desire and human reason have deceived him. What Will desired Wit and Thou3t to teach him about Kynde (9, l.31),

'Ac man is hym moost lik of marc and [shape],'

is false. So Will now desires that Kynde's Reson be responsible for the "mysfeet" in human wit (11, l.374–5):

'I haue wonder [in my wit], þat witty art holden,
Why þow ne sewest man and his make þat no mysfeet hem folwe.'

But Kynde's Reson, responding to Will's accusation of "mysfeet," counterclaims that Will own acts created "mysfeet." Reson recalls Will to his Rechelesnesse in 11, ll.34–41 (11, ll.376–377):

And Reson arated me and seide, 'recche þee neuere
Why I suffre or no3t suffre; þiself hast no3t to doone.'

Reson's " 'recche þee neuere' " parallels Rechelesnesse's " 'recche þee neuere' " (11, ll.375, 34). Reson's statement, " 'You do not care why I suffer or not,' " amply articulates the universality of Kynde's (God's) sufferance, a sufferance which opposes the purposeless suffering of Rechelesnesse's " 'Folwe forþ þat Fortune wole' " (11, l.35), thought by Will. The Reson in Kynde perceives Kynde's purpose: sufferance to preserve every species, including an unwitty human species.

Until 11, ll.376–7, Will has not perceived that his poverty is a sufferance which imitates the sufferance of Kynde (God). Rather, Will has perceived his poverty as a lack of personal Mede (enough money to buy salvation) and personal Mercy (God's or the friar's Mercy would would allow him entrance into Heaven without payment either for his misdeeds or suffrage). According to his Thou3t and desire, his lack of Mede is the result of personal Fortune (11, l.7ff.), not the result of a human sufferance imitating Kynde's "suffraunce" to preserve mankind (11, ll.377–82). Although Kynde's intent, "suffraunce" for the preservation of every species, comes close to Will's ultimate intention to preserve himself eternally (by patience and poverty and charity to all men), Will cannot now see that Kynde cares for the preservation of human kynde. What kind of human thought would perceive personal sufferance as an attractive good rather than a tolerated evil, unless the thought is directed toward a more universal concern?

Up to 11, ll.379–81, Will's personal Fortune appears to be a virtuous "rechelesnesse," because Will is poor (11, ll.34–38) and because Rechelesnesse invokes God to " 'doon his wille' " to an old and poor Will. (Nede will tempt Will with the same reasoning in 20, ll.33–5.) But celestial Reson counterclaims (and will counterclaim in 20, ll.210–11) that Will's recklessness and sufferance have no purpose unless they parallel Kynde's societal purpose: to preserve the species by the Wit of sufferance. Personal patience and poverty serve no purpose unless they are intended for societal purposes, i.e., for preservation of the human species. Kynde's intent surpasses Will's present intent toward concupiscent salvation. If " 'god' " as God or Good suffers and suffers, even though He or It might " 'amende in a Minute while al þat mysstandeþ' " (11, l.380–1), then God or Good " 'suffreþ for some mannes good.' " God's or Good's suffraunce of the evils of some man leads to the better. " 'And so is oure bettre,' " says Reson (11, l.382b). The suffraunce of God or Good leads beyond "god" (if translated as "good") to the "bettre." Will will preserve himself if he looks beyond his concerns for personal fortune to societal concerns: learning the "arts" of preservation, teaching them, forming societal alliances to preserve the human species, providing for the use of Mede and Mercy. Such thinking is the foundation of Ymaginatif's natural Clergie and natural theology.[15]

Kynde's Reson simply points out a simple fact about animal arts. The instinctual arts of animals are followed by no "Rechelesnesse," such as follows Will after 11, l.34. The wits of Animals do not perceive Kynde as if He were "Fortune" (11, l.7), and their wits do not suffer from the effects of the Sisters Concupiscence (11, ll.13–33, 43, 46–60). Will is in awe at the contradiction between Kynde and human kynde, and in anger because of the sight. Kynde's Reson responds that men are reckless about the preservation of the species, and that all other animals suffer because of unnecessary necessity created by human recklessness (11, l.382).

Kynde teaches Will patient speech, when Reson rebukes Will's "tongue" (11, ll.387–91b):

---

[15] The *Book of Privy Counseling* (EETS, o.s., 218 [138, ll.10–2]) gives the same psychological dialectic, called by the mystics the "discretion of spirits." That is, men follow the search within "kindely wittys" in order to reach a "wit" of human "kind" – that each and every person is a "foule stinking wreche by synne." The *PP* has substituted the naturality of Arabic-Aristotelian psychology for the mysticism of pseudo-Dionysius and Augustine, in order to prove the same thing: Will does not know how to discern the good in his wits from the evil in his wits.

'Forþi I rede', quod reson, '[þow] rule þi tonge bettre,
And er þow lakke my lif loke [þyn] be to preise.
For is no creature vnder crist can formen hymseluen,
And if a man myȝte make [laklees] hymself
Ech a lif wolde be laklees.'

Before Will faults Kynde, Will ought to assay his life. If "no creature can form himself," then "every life would be faultless, if man might create himself faultless." If Will were faultless, then his tongue would be faultless. Will's rebuke of Reson thus signifies a natural "lack" in Will's kynde, i.e., Will's " 'shap' " and " 'shaft' " (11, l.397); the natural lack contradicts that Will is "moost lik" Kynde in "marc" and "shafte" (9, l.31, in most mss).

Therefore, Will's speech in 11, ll.370–4, contradicts the "purpos" for which Kynde created speech and created by Speech (9, ll.32–46): the communication of infinite desires. Other animals, says Avicenna, have only instinctual desire; they need only instinctual and indistinct speech to communicate their desires. Men, driven by infinite desires,[16] have invented the conventions of speech to express the infinity of their desires. Speech is created to help men to live in society,[17] to provide themselves with food and clothing,[18] to support the four communal crafts ("artes") of agriculture ("agricultura") of baking ("panem praeparet") of weaving ("texat") and of commerce ("mercimonii de peregrinis regionibus").[19] Avicenna says:[20]

> Necessarium fuit homini habere naturaliter potentiam docendi alium sibi socium quod est in anima eius signo aut opere. . .. Ergo natura fecit ut anima ex sonis componeret aliquid per quod posset docere alium (It was necessary for man to have naturally the power to teach another human companion what is in his soul by sign or act. . . Therefore, Nature made it that the human soul composed something of sounds by which it could teach another human soul).

Kynde invented human speech so that men could teach other men how to overcome mutual necessities, not so that Will can complain about the " 'mysfeet' " of man and blame it on Kynde. Will's use of speech has not followed the intent for which human speech was created. He has not taught others the crafts for survival; he has complained about the human condition created by human beings, and has carried the complaint to the source of all natural Reson and natural speech. His misused speech

16 *Liber de anima, IV–V,* p.72, ll.45–7.
17 *Ibid.,* p.69, l.10–p.70,l.14.
18 *Ibid.,* p.70, ll.16–22.
19 *Ibid.,* p.70, ll.22, 25–6.
20 *Ibid.,* p.71, ll.29–30; p.72, ll.41–2.

parallels his *unnatural* desire. Therefore, Ymaginatif's powers involve not only the creation of awe but also the creation of patient speech. The science of the "vis imaginativa secundum Avicennam" teaches the use of speech in conditions of necessity.

So Kynde's Reson does not hesitate to alter the words of Scripture to make a natural revelation out of His concern for the human species, so that Will's speech may become more patient. In 11, 1.383, Kynde drops the word "humanae" in *I Peter* 2:13, "subiecti estote omni humanae creaturae propter Deum" (be subject to every human creature on account of God). Instead of the usual politico-theological interpretation of the verse,[21] Kynde says to Will, " 'Be subject to *every creature* for the sake of God.' " Kynde's care aims Will at a natural obedience that all animals have while they live in conditions of the natural necessity. Reson's gloss reveals a truth naturally known.

Politically and theologically interpreted, "be ye subject to every human creature" means that the "body politic" (the state or church) was composed of three classes: the rational or regal or judgmental (located in the head of the body politic), the irascible or military or knighthood (located in the heart of the body politic), and the concupiscible or communal or crafts pertaining to the mechanical arts (located in the genitalia of the body politic). Revealed Scripture would ordinarily mean that each man should be subject to his or her political superior "for the sake of God." Reson's gloss contradicts this conventional wisdom. If there is a penance in this subjection, Reson implies, the supernatural worth of the penance is questionable: *I Peter* 2:13 has been used to manipulate men into thinking that their political or ecclesiastical obedience is penitential. Reson could "care" ("recche") less about the political or ecclesiastical interpretations of *I Peter* 2:13. Whether the body politic obeys the primacy of the temporal powers of the State or the spiritual powers of the Church matters not a whit to

---

[21] For the political interpretation of *I Peter* 2:13, see Marsilius of Padua, *Defensor Pacis*, Bk.2, Ch.5 (ed. and transl. Alan Gewirth as *Marsilius of Padua: The Defender of Peace* [New York: Columbia Univ. Press, 1956], 2, 130–40), and the explanation (Gewirth, 1, 100–1). For the Latin text, see C.W. Previte-Orton, *The Defensor Pacis of Marsilius of Padua* (Cambridge: Cambridge Univ. Press, 1928), p.157, ll.14–9.

Reson de-glosses *I Peter* 2:13, to make an important change in the theology of sufferance, ordinarily stated, e.g., by Robert Bradwardine (*De causa Dei contra Pelagianum*, Bk.1, ch.31 ([London: Apud Ioannem Billium, 1618, rpt. Minerva, 1964], p.275A): "who resists the power resists the ordination of God," "ordination" backed up with *I Peter* 2:13, "subiecti estote omni *humanae* creaturae propter Deum." The Archbishop repeats Boniface VIII's gloss ("Unam sanctam," *Extravagantes Communes*, Bk.1, title 8, ch.1 [Friedberg, 2, 1246]):

> Quicumque igitur huic potestati a Deo sic ordinatae resistit, Dei ordinationi resistit,

which means that obedience to the God the King and to God's temporal "duces" is salutary. All human creatures must be subject to papal power. Kynde's Reson de-glosses Boniface VIII's pretensions to wisdom and to non-concupiscent possession.

Kynde. Reson deliberately ignores the glosses of *I Peter* 2:13 in, e.g., Marsilius of Padua's *Defensor Pacis* or Robert Bradwardine's *De causa Dei contra Pelagianos*.

Reson's gloss of *I Peter* 2:13 traces political disorder to the unregulated appetites of man (the rational [located in the head], the irascible [located in the heart], and the concupiscible [located in the genitalia]). The evil in man's societal relationships are the result of the evil in every man's appetites. Reson insists that all men are subject to Nature and to the necessity of the human condition. Men must cooperate as a species in order to survive. Reson returns the politico-theological gloss of *I Peter* 2:13 to the natural "Averroism" in the opening chapters of the *Defensor Pacis* (Bk.1, chs.3–5). The species of man survives by sufferance. " 'Be subject to every creature,' " Reson says, in order to teach Will to imitate the Reson of the other animals in Kynde. Will must learn to tolerate the conditions of human necessity, created for the human kynde and by the human kynde. Will must use his Reson to tolerate poverty, plenty, joy, woe, peace and war. To preserve the human species, Will must learn "suffraunce for some mannes goode," in imitation of Kynde's "suffraunce" for some good of man or some man's good. Such "suffraunce" gives a new sense to Mede, because such "suffraunce" amends. Reson, therefore, reteaches Will the meaning of Theologie's slogan, " 'Mede is muliere of Amendes engendred' " (2, ll.115, 119–20). The alteration of Scripture implies to Will that there is a *natural* penance practised by all Kynde, including men, while some men amend (11, l.382).

Since poverty tempers the concupiscible appetite and patience tempers the irascible appetite, the Reson in Kynde by this very tag phrase tells Will that patience and poverty are practised by every animal except man. Even Kynde Himself suffers while man amends. This second function of the "vis imaginativa secundum Avicennam," the teaching of arts for survival in conditions of necessity, is, of course, an important resolution to the problem of Mede and an important stimulus for Will to learn that patient poverty necessary to his salvation and the salvation of all men. His salvation is related to the salvation of the human species. His individual trek towards the kynde knowyng of Dowel becomes more societal in Passus 13 and 14 and much more universal in Passus 15–20. Will's awe at the order and sufferance in Kynde begins, of course, the "science" which Ymaginatif's Clergie teaches Will in Passus 12 (ll.64 ff.).

Unlike the friar's theological "forbisne," Kynde's natural "forbisnes" force Will to the "kynde knowyng. . . to conceyuen wordes" he sought from within himself, in 8, l.57. Will uses another Wit, the Wit of Kynde represented by Ymaginatif, to "look," and thus he "learns better"

(8, ll.57–8). Through the Thouȝt and Ymaginatif in his sensory Anima, Will so imagines an intent permanently seen that he

1. changes the source of his one sensory reasoning,
2. produces the kynde concepts,
3. which produce the natural words of the B-text,
4. which define the "oon" (11, l.410) as Ymaginatif (12, l.1),
5. who changes Will's intent.

By the standard of Kynde's Wit and Reson both inside of himself and outside of himself, Will innately differentiates the good and evil in human kynde wit from the good in Kynde's Kynde Wit. The rational acts of Kynde's minister, the awe produced by Kynde's minister's showing, and the patient speech learned from Kynde's minister teach Will about the powers of the "oon" whom Will begins to recognize within himself.

3. The "vis imaginativa" appears in sleep and inner dreams (8,l.67–13,l.1)

A third activity of the "vis imaginativa secundum Avicennam" explains why the opposition between the Reson in Thought and the Reson in Ymaginatif occurs only in Will's sleep, i.e., from 8, 1.68, to 13, l.1. In waking, Thouȝt always overcomes Ymaginatif, because the human Anima always impresses the human will with the Thouȝt of food, clothing and shelter, i.e., the stimuli in Will-as-concupiscible-appetite. The two powers of the one sensory reasoning are able to oppose each other only when Will sleeps. According to Avicenna, the interior powers are necessary to Anima, in order that Anima receive the emanations from the world of invisibles in two ways, as an imagination of an intent permanently seen in them and as powers dragged into a dream "ad libitum," so that Will may compare the images from the viewpoint of the world of invisibles, of Anima and of Ymaginatif.[22] While Will sleeps and learns his intent, Anima's Thouȝt and Will and Wit and the other hypostases who appear before 11, 1.320, imagine the intent; after 11, 1.320, Ymaginatif imagines the same intent.

Only in sleep can the "vis imaginativa secundum Avicennam" counteract the intent imagined by the "vis cogitativa:"[23]

> Aliquando autem anima praevalet super eam [imaginativam] in suis actionibus quae continuantur ei de cognitione et cogitatione, et hoc duobus modis: uno, cum dominatur imaginativae et subicit eam ad componendum formas et disuiungendum secundum quod appetit anima

---

[22] *Liber de anima, IV–V*, p.27, ll.65–70.
[23] *Liber de anima, IV–V*, p.16,l.15–p.18,l.36, passim.

vehementer; unde non licet imaginativae agere quod debebat agere naturaliter, sed trahitur ad partem ad quam trahit eam anima rationalis; alio, cum revocat eam ab imaginationibus quae non assimilantur rebus extrinsecis et retrahit eam ab his falsificando eas; unde non multum licet effigiare eas et repraesentare. . . Sed remoto utroque impedimento sicut fit in hora dormiendi, tunc imaginatio potest niti et converti ad formalem et iniungere ei [imaginativae] operari, et earum adunatio confortatur simul, et actio formalis fit manifestior, et formae quae sunt in formali praesentantur. . . et videntur quasi habeant esse extrinsecus (Sometimes Anima overpowers the imaginative power by activities continued in it [the imaginative faculty] from knowledge and thought. Anima does this in two ways. First, Anima dominates the imaginative power and subjects it so that the imaginative power compares and divides images according to Anima's vehement desires. Whence, the imaginative power is not permitted to do what it ought to do naturally; but the rational Anima drags it off in the direction where Anima draws it. Secondly, Anima recalls the imaginative power to imagining things unlike things outside the mind, and draws it from assimilating things to falsifying things. Whence, the imaginative power is not permitted to make a likeness of the images or make them present again. . . But when both impediments are removed as happens in the time of sleep, then the imagination can increase its strength, be turned to the activity of making images, and command the [imaginative power] to function. Then the union of the imagination with the imaginative power strengthens both, and the image-making activity becomes more evident, and the forms which are in the imagination are made present. . . And they [the images] are seen as if they have an extramental reality).

Concerns about the salvation of his Anima intrude into Will's sleep (8, ll.50–6, 67–9), for Will worries about the concluding words of the friar's "forbisne" (8, ll.48–50):

> 'Ay is þe soule saaf but [þow þiselue wole
> Folwe þi flesshes wille and þe fendes after,
> And] do deedly synne and drenche þi[selue].'

Asleep in 8, l.68, he is impressed by Anima's conflicting desires: that Anima be "saaf" yet that no "flesshes wille" kill Anima by deadly sin. Then in ll.70–1, Anima's guide to reasoning in the senses calls Will by his "kynde name," i.e., by the name "desire" or "appetite." Will sees "a muche man me þouȝte, lik to myselue." "Me þouȝte" translates both the Modern English "it seemed to me" and "it thought me," indicating that Anima is the "it" who appears by the minister hypostatized as " 'þouȝt' " in 8, l.74. Will's thoughts are so "lik" Thouȝt that the verb "þouȝte" is hypostatized into the person Thouȝt, as soon as Will thinks, even though the source of the thoughts is not known to Will until Passus 15.

Although the source of the reason in Thouȝt is not mentioned, it need not be mentioned. From the friar's "forbisne" (8, l.48), Anima's vehement desire to be "saaf" carries over into Will's sleep and impresses Anima's concerns by way of Thouʒt, Anima's minister of sensory reasoning in Will's body. Will's concern about the "flesshes wille," also from the "forbisne" (8, 1.49), also carries over into Thouʒt's mediation of Wit's information in Passus 9, while Will sleeps. Hence, Wit, mediated by Anima's Thouʒt and Will's will for the flesh, defines Anima's Castle both as " 'man wiþ a Soule' " (Anima) and as " 'caro' " (the castle of sinful flesh), in 9, 11.50–1. Anima's and Will's conflicting concerns, "salvation" but salvation with the "flesshes wille," are the sensory reasoning and desire which guide the mental acts through the other hypostases toward an open rebellion with Scripture at 10, 1.377. By means of Thouʒt and Wit, Anima's and Will's conflicting desires begin to falsify the good and true in the intents of the images of the kynde knowyng of Dowel, until Ymaginatif appears. Anima's and Will's concerns turn Will (named "rational appetite") upside down, so that Will (named "concupiscible appetite" and "irascible appetite") ultimately turns Wit to wretchedness because of concupiscence (11, 1.45). Obviously, Will needs to receive a different reason and different wit of his kynde than that which he received from Wit through Thouʒt's mediation, prompted by Anima's desires.

But such a perception occurs only when the impediments of Thouʒt are removed. While deep sleep removes Anima's Thouʒt, i.e., in the first part of the inner dream, the sensory reasoning of Thouʒt becomes incoherent, forgetful, skipping from one image to another, as the B-text parallels the incoherence from 11, 1.6,[24] because the one sensory reasoning is being conjoined to the celestial Imagination by the "vis imaginativa." After the impediment of Thouʒt is removed, Will sees his permanent intent:

> Est igitur necesse comparationem esse inter absentiam et inter animam et inter virtutem interiorem imaginativam (There is, then, a necessary comparison among the world of invisibles and Anima and the interior imaginative power).

Ymaginatif ("virtutem interiorem imaginativam") now governs the one sensory reasoning and communicates infallible information from the celestial spheres ("absentiam"). In such sleep, Will sees that faculty not only *outside* of himself but also *above* him. For the "oon" whom Will meets in 11, 1.320, summons a celestial Kynde who also calls Will by his name (11, 1.322), not, however, by the "kynde" name that Thouʒt called Will (8, 1.71). In such sleep, Will named "desire" or "appetite" is not an animal in "kynde," but a rational animal whose vehement desires are

---

24 *Ibid.*, p.22, 11.97–03; p.27, 1.70.

temporarily suppressed. Kynde calls Will by the generic name "Will," because Will, like all human wills, desires the good naturally and innately, though vehemently and concupiscently and irascibly because of his human rationality. As soon as Kynde bids Will "þoruʒ þe wondres of þis world wit for to take" (11, 1.323), Will uses "wit" as all animals use "wit" to reason out information received from their senses. According to this feature of the psychology, 11, ll.335–8, 343–4,

> Reson I seiʒ sooþly sewen alle beestes,
> In etynge, in drynkynge and in engendrynge of kynde.
> And after cours of concepcion noon took kepe of ooþer,
> As whan þei hadde ryde in Rotey tyme anoon [reste þei] after;
> Boþe hors and houndes and alle oþere beestes
> Medled noʒt wiþ hir makes, [saue man allone],

now mean that Will literally sees. "I seiʒ" signifies the sight literally. That is, Will compares and divides images according to the Wit and Reson in Kynde. Will sees Reson "sewen" or "following." The acts of animals evidence an immanent reason; hence the logic of "sequitur," "follows." Reson in Kynde "follows" in the acts of all creatures except in the acts of man. Animals act with logical "sequitur's," not the "non-sequitur's" of human animals. Will takes wit of a different logic and sensory reason within the middle ventricle of his brain by the mediation of Ymaginatif. From a different source in the one sensory reasoning, Will now perceives the reason for the non-sequitur's in all his Thouʒt, in all his faculties of knowledge, his acts of knowledge, and his objects of knowledge. Will's eating, drinking and reproducing are led by "flesshes wille," i.e., Will so defined by the friar in 8, 1.49. The Will or desire in the concupiscent and irascible appetites leads sensory Reson. Will is not the rational appetite, the rational desire in sensory reason. Will is not governed by sensory reason but by the lower branches of the Avicennan will: concupiscence and anger. Will has been comparing and dividing images with a series of "non sequiturs," following his appetites to possess and to be angry. Up to 11, 1.335, Will named "desire-as-concupiscence-anger" has been "leading" this one sensory Reson instead of following it.

4. *The "vis imaginativa" prophesies in inner dreams by converting images into speakers (11, ll.6–406)*

The opposition between the Reson in the Thouʒt of the human Anima and the Reson in the Ymaginatif of all animals in Kynde brings us to the fourth and most unusual function of the "vis imaginativa secundum Avicennam," represented only in the B- and C-texts of *Piers Plowman*, and, as far as I know, only in *Piers Plowman*. In Will's sleep, Ymaginatif prophesies naturally, by means of inner dreams:[25]

> Contingit autem aliquibus hominibus quod haec virtus imaginativa sit creata in illis fortissima et praevalens. . . Isti habent in vigilia quod alii in somnis, sicut postea dicemus: haec enim est dispositio dormientis dum apprehendit visiones, ut certificentur ei. . . Saepe enim inter utrumque istorum [idest vigiliae et somni[26]] contingit eos in ultimo absentari a sensibilibus et accidit eis quasi dormitatio;. . . multotiens apparet similitudo et videtur eis. . . quod sit locutio imaginis veluti verba audita quae tenent et legunt. Et haec est propria prophetia virtutis imaginativae (In some men the imaginative power has been made very powerful and predominant. . . Such men have in waking what others have in sleep, as we shall discuss a little later: the mental state of a sleeper who, while seeing visions, has certitude. . . Sometimes between states [of waking and sleeping] they are taken out of their senses to experience a quasi-sleep;. . . many times the appearing image is seen by them as an image which speaks, as it were, in spoken words which they hold and read. And this is the essence of the prophecy of the imaginative power).

Anima, of course, causes the inner dream at 11, ll.5–7a:

> And in a wynkynge [worþ til I weex] aslepe.
> A merueillous metels mette me þanne,
> [For] I was rauysshed riȝt þere.

Then, in the first part of the inner dream (11, ll.7–319), i.e., "inter utrumque [idest vigiliae et somni]" or "quasi dormitatio," Will is ravished ("absentari a sensibilibus") into a sight of the Mirror of Middle Earth (11, l.9). Now the images of Will's previous concerns in the outer dream become the hypostases of the inner dream: the "speech of an image" ("locutio imaginis"), e.g., Will's concern about "lele" transforms into the speaker Lewte. Hypostatized concerns speak and interact with one another from 11, ll.10–319. The words of the hypostatized concerns are words which Will "holds and reads," i.e., the words of the "makynges" which we readers read in 12, l.16, but also

---

[25] *Ibid.*, p.18,l.46–p.19,l.62.

[26] The explanation "scilicet dormitiones et vigiliae" was added to numerous Latin manuscripts, apparently because of the influence of the Archdeacon Gundissalinus' compendium *De anima*. See the *Liber de anima*, *IV–V*, p.19, n.54, and the compendium *De anima* (ed. J. T. Muckle, "The Treatise De anima of Dominichus Gundissalinus," *Mediaeval Studies*, 2[1940], 77, ll.20–21.

The *PP*-poet must have had first hand acquaintance with either Gundissalinus' compendium *De anima* or with Gundissalinus' translation of Avicenna's psychology. Neither Jean de la Rochelle nor Vincent of Beauvais nor the anonymous Worcester psychology mention the inner dreams caused by the "vis imaginativa secundum Avicennam."

the "þou3te" for the next vision in Passus 13, ll.4, 21a. Then, Ymaginatif breaks into the inner vision, in order to establish "a necessary comparison among the world of invisibles and Anima and the interior imaginative power," so that Will may indeed see his intent permanently envisioned. Then, as soon as Will awakes from the inner dream (11, l.406), Ymaginatif as "oon" (11, l.410) interprets Will's inner dream for the rest of the outer dream (11,l.410–12,l.297). Then, when Will awakes from the continuing outer dream in Passus 13, l.1, the summary from ll.4–20 certifies the truth Will has learned from the first vision of the *Vita*. He summarizes his concerns (13, ll.5–13): the failure of Fortune, the threats of Old Age, the concupiscence of the friars, the ignorance of the clergie (see 11, ll.316–8), and its consequences (11, l.13).

In the inner dream, Ymaginatif himself is prophetic, and his conversion of concerns into speakers is prophetic:[27]

> Ex his autem ille excellentior est qui est aptus ad ordinem prophetiae, et hic est ille in cujus viribus animalibus sunt hae tres proprietates, scilicet ut audiat verbum Dei, et videat angelos transfiguratos coram se in forma qua possint videri; iam autem ostendimus qualiter fiat hoc et ostendimus quod, ante eum cui fiat haec revelatio, transformantur angeli; et fit in eius auribus vox quam ipse audit, quae est ex parte Dei et angelorum, et audit eam quamvis non sit verbum hominis nec animalis terreni, et hic est cui datur spiritus prophetiae. Et sicut id quod primum fit a principio usque ad gradum materiae fuit intelligentia, deinde anima, postea corpus caeleste, sic hic esse incipit esse a corporibus, postea ad animas, deinde ad intelligentias (From among men, he is most oustanding who is fitted for the order of prophecy. And he is the person in whose animal powers are these three properties: namely, that he hear the word of God, that he see angels transfigured before him in a shape in which they can be seen – we have already shown how this is done[28] and shown that the angels are transformed in the presence of him to whom the revelation devolves –, that there come in his ears a speech which he hears, – speech which is from God and the angels –, and that he hears the speech, although it is not the word of man nor of an earthly animal. And this person is he to whom is given the spirit of prophecy. And, just as that which first comes to be from the beginning all the way to the state of matter was [first] an intelligence, then an Anima, then a Celestial Body, so this act [of prophecy] begins begins to act from bodies, then to Anima's, and then to Intelligences).

Thus, in the deep sleep when Will's thoughts are in disarray, Ymaginatif appears as "oon" not only to continue the disputation but to resolve the disarray of Will's thoughts (11, ll.320–3):

---

[27] *Liber de scientia divina, V–X*, tract 10, ch.1, p.523, ll.22–34.
[28] Avicenna refers to the *Liber de anima, IV–V*, p.19 (quoted under note 25), p.66 (the prophet's control over matter, such that he performs miracles), and p.153 (the prophet's holy intellect and holy power).

> Ac muche moore in metynge þus wiþ me gan oon dispute,
> And slepynge I sei3 al þis, and siþen cam kynde
> And nempned me by my name and bad me nymen hede,
> And þoru3 þe wondres of þis world wit for to take.

Ymaginatif is the angel of Kynde, the "oon" of 11, ll.320 and 410, transformed into a speaker seen by Will as "ymaginatif" in 12, l.1. He both shows Kynde's images in Will's imagination and speaks the Speech of Kynde's Reson in Will's ears (11, ll.376b–404), although he is not an "earthly animal." From him Will begins to learn prophecy from his own "cors" ("a corporibus"), whereby he begins his ascent to prophecy by Anima in Passus 15.

Ymaginatif's power to represent and to reason recalls Will's intent ("hede," and "[mynne] on þyn ende" in 12, l.4) to the Wit which governs the intent and actions of all animals possessed of Anima. Will's human Anima does not govern Will's wit and reason now, Kynde governs Will's animal wit and animal reason. Will emerges from the inner dream with a certitude about Dowel. He is first asked by Ymaginatif as "oon" what Dowel is (11, ll.410–1, in the "F-group" of mss),

> And as I caste vp myne ei3en oon loked on me and asked
> 'What þyng þat Dowel is'; 'ywis, sire, y not y,'

and then told what Dowel is (11, ll.413–20, in the "F-group" of mss):

> Than seyd he, 'haddist þou suffred þo þou on slepe were,
> Thow sholdest haue knowe it of clergie & conceyued it by resoun.
> For Reson wolde haue reherced þee ri3t as Clergie seide.
> *Philosophus esse si tacuisses*
> (You would have been a philosopher had you kept your mouth shut).
> Adam, whiles he was heere, he had paradis at his wille,
> And whan he mamelede on his mete, he menede to knowe
> The wisedom of his god & he was put from blisse.
> And ri3t so ferde Reson bi þyn rude speche.'

Dowel is to suffer (not to concern oneself about " 'mete' ") and to speak patiently. Thus Ymaginatif is naturally prophetic and infinitely endowed with four powers from Kynde:

1. to be Kynde's angel,
2. to hypostatize concerns from outer dreams into speakers in inner dreams,
3. to certify the truth of outer dreams by inner dreams,
4. to certify dreams vividly, both when the natural prophet awakes from them and when he is in them.

The first four meanings and functions of Ymaginatif in the first vision of the *Vita* are primarily psychological:

1. Ymaginatif's Reson opposes Thouȝt's human reason because Ymaginatif's Reson has the infallible konnynge of Kynde for its source;
2. Ymaginatif produces "awe" and patient speech in Will;
3. Ymaginatif overcomes Thouȝt only in sleep and inner dreams;
4. Ymaginatif's Reson in inner dreams is not only prophetic but certifiably prophetic both in continuing outer dreams and in waking.

Fifth, sixth, and seventh functions of the "vis imaginativa secundum Avicennam" allow us to perceive the structure of Will's first vision from 11,l.320–13,l.15:

5. the "vis imaginativa" produces shame in Will (11, l.405b),
6. the "vis imaginativa" appears and disappears suddenly (11, l.320, 12, l.297b),
7. in between the sudden appearance and disappearance, the prophet learns an innate syllogistic ("konnynge" in 13, l.15).

5. *Ymaginatif's power to produce shame (11, l.405)*

Quite *naturally*, then, Will "cauȝte. . . colour anoon and comsed to ben ashamed" (11,l.405). His shame is the result of the fifth function of the "vis imaginativa secundum Avicennam." As soon as Will recognizes the truth in Kynde's Wit, the Reson in Kynde and in Ymaginatif cause Will's shame. Will's sensory irrationality – the conflict between the Reson in Thouȝt and the Reson in Ymaginatif – has a physiological etiology, described in John of Trevisa's ME translation of Bartholomaeus Anglicus' *De proprietatibus rerum*:[29]

> þe forhede is þe seete of schame. . ., and þat is for he is nye þe vertue ymaginatif. By þe vertu ymaginatif þinges þat ben. . . vnsemeliche, ben sodenliche ibrouȝt to the dome of resoun.

Ymaginatif brings Will's unseemly words and objections to the judgment of Will's human Reson now infused with the Reson in Kynde. The Reson in Will's Thouȝt grasps suddenly the truth spoken by the Reson in Kynde. The contrast between the Resons is literally brought

[29] M.C. Seymour, *On the Properties of Things: Trevisa's Translation of De Proprietatibus Rerum* (Oxford: Clarendon Press, 1975), p.188, ll.25–29. See Avicenna's explanation in the *Liber de anima*, IV–V, p.75, ll.85–87.

("ibrouȝt") to Will's forehead by the ministrations of Ymaginatif. The psychology of shame is societal,[30]

> Et propter utilitatem societatis est ei proprium ut, ex omnibus actionibus quas solet agere, sint quaedam actiones quas non liceat agere: quod docetur dum est puer et coalescit in eo, et a pueritia consuescit audire quod has actiones non licet agere, ita quod conceptio horum fit ei quasi naturalis (For the use of society it is proper to man that, of all the acts he is accustomed to do, there are some which he is not permitted to do. This he is taught while he is a child and it grows in him; from childhood he is used to hearing that he is not allowed to do these things. The conception of these becomes, as it were, natural to him);

but the physiology of shame is an "animal affect:"[31]

> Hoc autem quod homo percipit alium percipere se fecisse aliquid ex his quae illicitum est facere, sequitur passio animalis quae vocatur verecundia, et hoc etiam est de humanis proprietatibus (When one man sees that another person has watched him doing something which is wrong to do, then there follows the affect of the animal soul which is called shame. This also is one of the properties of man).

The physiology of shame is based upon a standard of conduct, practised by all animals while they protect their young. That is, all animals instinctually love and protect their offspring; if the instinct is violated, the result is shame.[32] Will realizes the "unseemliness" of his thoughts, of his selfishness, of his concern for personal salvation, and of the violation of a morality taught him in childhood but retaught by Kynde. The physiological effect awakens him to confront the same "oon" who began the dispute in 11, l.320. Ymaginatif awakens Will from the inner dream by shaming him (11, l.405).

6. *Ymaginatif's sudden appearance (11, l.320) and disappearance (12, l.297b)*

A text already seen readily explains the sixth function of the "vis imaginativa secundum Avicennam." Ymaginatif appears and disappears because[33]

> Cito aderit comparatio quae est necessaria inter absentiam et animam et inter virtutem imaginativam, et videbitur subito visum (Quick will be present the comparison [of images], necessary between the soul and the world of invisibles and [between these two] and the imaginative power, and the sight will be seen suddenly).

---

[30] *Liber de anima, IV–V*, p.74, ll.65–9.
[31] *Ibid.*, p.75, ll.85–7.
[32] *Ibid.*, p.74,l.71–p.75,l.84.
[33] *Ibid.*, p.28, ll.76–78.

"Absentiam," we recall, refers to the world of invisibles – the celestial spheres – from which Ymaginatif derives his imaginative power. Once the impediment of the Thouȝt of Anima has been removed,[34] Ymaginatif joins the images of the celestial spheres first to himself and, derivatively, to Will's animal Anima. Will sees the truth of self-knowledge instantaneously ("cito," "subito"), and Ymaginatif disappears.

In order that Kynde's intent be "permanently seen" by Will, Will enters a vision at 8, 1.68–9,

> The merueillouseste metels mette me þanne
> That euer dremed [driȝt] in [doute], as I wene,

until the "purpos" to which he puts Thouȝt deepens the vision at 11, l.6–7,

> A merueillous metels mette me þanne,
> [For] I was rauysshed riȝt þere. . .,

so that, having learned from Ymaginatif's showing, he exits from the deeper vision (11, ll.406a),

> And awaked þerwiþ,

and concludes the first vision (13, 1.1),

> And I awaked þerwiþ, witlees nerhande.

The interior faculties of knowledge, Thouȝt (in 8, 1.70–4) and Wit (in Passus 9) come, in order to tell Will about the world of invisibles, i.e., about himself, about the triad of "Do-," about Anima, and about Kynde. Then, at the pleasure of the soul (i.e., Anima by means of Thouȝt), the other faculties of knowledge come at the pleasure of the soul: Dame Studie, Clergie, Scripture, Fortune, the sisters Concupiscence, Elde, Conscience, Rechesnesse, the friar, Lewte, Scripture, Trajan and the speaker after Trajan. The sudden apparition of Ymaginatif as "oon" in 11, 1.320, signifies that Thouȝt and the other powers of Anima have been impeding the "necessary comparison among the world of invisibles and the sensory soul and the interior imaginative power" from the beginning of the outer dream up to 11, 1.320. When the "impedences" of Wit and of Thouȝt are "removed," says Avicenna, then "quick will be the comparison among the world of invisibles, and the sensory soul and the imaginative power," we recall. In other words, the whole series of mental acts, assimilated from Passus 8, 1.68, to the end of Passus 12, is supposed to happen in a flash. "The

---

34 *Ibid.*, p.28, 1.75–6: "cum vero aliquid eorum [intellectus] removebitur."

seen will be seen suddenly,'' says Avicenna. So Ymaginatif disappears, after he has taught Will the Clergie of Kynde's Wit, i.e., the "konnynge" of Kynde (13, 1.15). What Avicenna represents as happening in a flash is re-presented in the first vision in the very slow motion of scholastic discourse from 8, 1.68, to 12, 1.297.

7. In between the sudden appearance and disappearance, the prophet learns by an innate syllogistic ("konnynge" in 13, l.15)

In this Avicennan process of sudden, ecstatic and self-taught prophetic learning, Ymaginatif forces Will to learn from himself by a prophetic logic, peculiarly Avicennan. The "vis imaginativa secundum Avicennam" illumines Will and moves Will. Illumined, Will combines two concerns, as if the concerns were the extreme terms of a syllogism, with a "middle term" supplied by his own kynde wit ("ingenium"). The syllogistic occurs in a flash:[35]

> Manifestum est quod intelligibilia quae studet homo acquirere, non acquirit nisi cum habuerit terminum medium in syllogismo. Hoc autem medius terminus invenitur. . . proprio ingenio (ingenium autem est actus rationis, cuius propria vi invenitur medius terminus; subtilitas autem est supra ingenium) (It is obvious that the intelligibles which man studies to acquire he cannot acquire unless he shall first have the middle term in a syllogism. The middle term is discovered in his own genius [genius is an act of reason; by reason's own power is the middle term discovered. Subtlety, however, is above reason]).

Will learns the "intelligibles" from the celestial Wit of Kynde. In Christian interpretations of this passage, the "intelligibles" are either "self-evident propositions" or "the impression of the first truth, according to which are impressed in us the judgment of Truth about the beginnings of the sciences."[36] In other words, Will is learning about the application of the "prime principles of good and evil," already implanted in him by Kynde, i.e., an innate knowledge to discern good from evil. Ymaginatif teaches Will's kynde wit how to syllogize from innate "prime principles of good and evil" to the concrete practice of the prime principles. When Will "sees" the *application* of his innate logic (the innate sense of good and evil) to all the objections he threw at Scripture in Passus 10, ll.377–481, and sees that Ymaginatif's Clergie has answered the objections in Passus 12, then Will leaps from the concern

---

[35] *Ibid.*, p.152, ll.91–96.
[36] The first definition is drawn from Gundissalinus' compendium *De Anima* (Muckle, p.85, ll.20–1); the second from Jean de la Rochelle's *Tractatus* (Michaud-Quantin, p.91, l.750): "impressio prime veritatis, secundum quod nobis impressa sunt iudicia veritatis circa principia scientiarum."

of the first vision, knowyng kyndely by Kynde Wit, into the concern of
the next vision, the practice of knowyng kyndely by kynde wit. Patient
poverty remedies the evils of rude speech and concupiscence. Will's
own "genius" or "subtlety" makes the leap from one concern, one
moral and artistic intent, and one topic of argument into another.

As if combining two terms of a syllogism – Ymaginatif's Clergie, and
the practice of patient poverty –, Will makes the transitive act of
knowledge from Passus 12 to Passus 13. He combines Ymaginatif's
Clergie, one term, with the practice of patient poverty, the other term,
by supplying the middle term from his innate kynde knowyng. The
innate syllogistic (the knowledge of good and evil) supplies, as it were,
the middle term of Will's syllogism. The middle term unites the learning
from Ymaginatif's Clergie (in Passus 11 and 12) with the practice of
patient poverty (in Passus 13 and 14).[37] The combination of both terms
and Will's practice of patient poverty leads to Will's conclusive kynde
knowyng of Dowel in Passus 15, 1.2. Separate concerns in separate
prophetic visions are connected by prophetic "middle terms," suddenly
supplied by the innate power of a prophetic "vis imaginativa secundum
Avicennam."[38]

---

[37] Avicenna borrowed the notion of "solertia" from Aristotle's *Posterior Analytics* (Bk.1,
ch.34; 89b, ll.10–11): "quick wit, the faculty of hitting upon the middle terms
instantaneously." Gundissalinus' compendium *De anima* repeats Avicenna's definition of
"solertia" verbatim (Muckle, *Mediaeval Studies*, 95,l.32–96,l.15); Jean de la Rochelle's
Tractatus paraphrases them (Michaud-Quantin, p.94, l.847 ("per viam syllogismi. . ."). F.
Rahman paraphrases from another of Avicenna's works (*Avicenna's Psychology* [London:
Geoffrey Cumberledge, 1952], p.36, ll.12–3):

> Intuition. . . is an act of mind by which the mind itself immediately perceives
> the middle term.

[38] The innate syllogistic underlies Avicenna's psychology of natural prophecy (F.
Rahman, "Ibn Sina," *A History of Muslim Philosophy*, ed. M.M. Sharif [Wiesbaden: Otto
Harrassowitz, 1963], I, 499; *Avicenna's Psychology*, pp. 36–7, 94–5; and *Prophecy in Islam:
Philosophy and Orthodoxy* [London: George Allen & Unwin, 1958], pp.31, 66–7; also L.
Gardet, *La pensée religeuse*, p.123).

Hence, one of the earliest of the Christian commentators on Avicenna, William of
Auvergne, disputes that "solertia" proves natural prophecy (*De anima*, Opera Omnia
[Paris: Andreas Pralard, 1674, rpt. Minerva, 1963], 2, 122[2]):

> Amplius prophetici splendores multo maiores sunt ac sublimiores
> apprehensionibus, & secundum errorem istum sunt in animabus pro-
> phetarum ab intelligentia agente, quemadmodum illuminationem
> intelligibilem animarum nostrarum fieri ponunt irradiatione intelligentiae
> agentis. Quapropter nec studium, nec inventio, nec ars inveniendi necessaria
> sit irradiationibus videlicet propheticis. . . Secundum istos vero sola
> applicatio animarum nostrarum ad intelligentiam agentem, aut econverso
> necessaria est, & sufficit ad adquisitionem apprehensionum, et cognitionum
> intelligibilium. . .
>
> Amplius qualiter intelligunt quia intellectus est in nobis principium
> scientiae. . . Qui igitur ponunt intellectum in nobis esse principium
> scientiarum, proculdubio ponunt ipsum esse principium agens, sive
> effectivam scientiarum. Hoc autem evidentissimum est in dispositione, vel

There is no doubt that the "konnynge" Will learns from Ymaginatif and Kynde upon awakening in 13, 1.15, was understood to refer to an innate syllogistic. In a chapter devoted to "quick wit" in his "De dialectica," pseudo-Vincent of Beauvais gives the customary examples of "quick wit" from Aristotle's *Posterior Analytics*, Bk.1, ch.34 (89b, ll.10–6):[39]

> *Solertia est subtilitas quaedam medii inveniendi, in non perfecto tempore*; idest subito; ut si quis vidit quod luna semper habet splendorem ad solem, statim intellexit propter quid hoc sit, scilicet quod id illustratur a sole. Aut videns pauperem disputantem cum diuite, cognouit quoniam accomodatum est; omnis enim causas medias videns, cognouit & ultimas (Cunning is a kind of subtlety of finding the middle term, in quick time; that is, suddenly. As if one sees that the moon glows in relation to the sun and immediately understands why this is so – that it is illuminated by the sun. Or [as if one], looking at a poor person in dispute with a wealthy person, knew that they came to terms. For everyone, seeing the mediate causes, knew the causes on either side).

Interpreting this passage in terms of his prophetic psychology,[40] Avicenna would attribute Will's quick wit to the "agent intellect," i.e., to either Kynde or the Celestial Anima within Will's sensory Anima. Will's quick wit is nothing more than his innate "konnynge," the

> habitu quem aristoteles vocat solertiam in libro posteriorum; vocat namque solertiam promptitudinem inveniendi medium (Furthermore, prophetic splendors are greater and more sublime than apprehensions [of the human mind]. According to that error [of Avicenna, the prophetic splendors] are in the souls of the prophets by the workings of the agent intellect. They posit that the illumination of the intelligibles in our souls is the product of the illumination by the agent intellect. Because of that, neither study, nor invention nor the skill of invention is necessary for prophetic illuminations. According to them, only the application of our souls to the agent intellect, or the application of the agent intellect to our souls, is necessary and suffices for acquisition of apprehensions and knowledge of the intelligibles.
>
> Moreover, this is how they understand that that [agent] intellect is in us the origins of the sciences. . . They, therefore, posit that that intellect is in us the origin of the sciences; indeed, they posit it to be the active principle of origin, effective of the sciences. The idea becomes most evident in the disposition or habit which Aristotle calls "solertia" in his *Posterior Analytics*. Aristotle calls "solertia" the quickness of finding the middle [term]).

39 *Speculum Doctrinale*, Bk.3, ch.55 (Douai-Graz, 2, 252A).
40 *Liber de anima*, IV–V, p.153,l.10–4:
> Possibile est ergo ut alicuius hominis anima eo quod est clara et cohaerens principiis intellectibilibus, ita sit inspirata ut accendatur ingenio ad recipiendum omnes quaestiones ab intelligentia agente, aut subito, aut paene subito. . . cum ordine qui comprehendit medios terminos (For the fact that Anima is illustrious and uniting to its Principles of Intellectibility, it is, therefore, possible that the Anima of some man is so inspired that it is inflamed by cunning to receive all the questions from the Agent Intellect, either suddenly or almost suddenly. . . together with the order in which the middle terms are comprehended).

cunning already innate but recognized only by Kynde's and Ymaginatif's activities in the inner dream. In 13, 1.13, Will's summary of the first vision immediately opposes the "konnynge" to the "vnkonnynge" he learned from ignorant and covetous Clergie, really the "vnkonninge" reasoned out by his own Wit and Thouȝt and the other hypostases.

The good konnynge takes an innate but abstract kynde knowyng, i.e., the so-called "prime principles of morality" within Will, and applies them to concrete moral judgments. The concrete moral judgments concern the "objects of knowledge" or topics Will throws at Scripture in Passus 10, when he rebels. In the inner dream, Will reasons out the thoughtful rebellion up to 11, 1.320, under the influence of Thouȝt. When Will sees the Wit in Kynde, Will's knowledge of his own human kynde is immediate but lacks articulation. When, in Passus 12, Ymaginatif supplies Will with the Clergie to articulate Will's intuition of Kynde Wit, then Will has the konnynge to leap in a flash to the practical knowledge of patient poverty. The konnynge remains within Will after Ymaginatif's disappearance.

If Dame Studie also hypostatizes Avicenna's "studium,"

> Manifestum est quod intelligibilia quae studet homo acquirere, non acquirit nisi cum habuerit terminum medium (It is obvious that the intelligibles which man studies to acquire he cannot acquire unless he shall first have the middle term in a syllogism),

then quite naturally Dame Studie prophesies Ymaginatif's "answer." Ymaginatif's *poetic* logic supplies the middle term which makes Will move from his first vision to the next by supplying the proper words which motivate Will's occult intent. Ymaginatif's poetic logic is the power proper to the "imaginative syllogism," the poetic device of Ymaginatif.

Readers of Will's mental text wonder how Will made the leap from the recognition of the Clergie of Kynde's Wit (Passus 11 and 12) to the practice of patient poverty (Passus 13 and 14) to the certainty of kynde knowyng (15, 1.2). Avicenna would answer that Will's kynde knowyng is, as it were, the simple and certain recognition of the middle terms, the unexpressed interstices between the three visions. The connections which resolve the prophet's concerns, expressed in dreams, are, as it were, the middle terms in syllogisms. In the first vision, Will has concerned himself with the kynde knowyng of Dowel, term "A" of the syllogism; in Passus 13 and 14, he concerns himself with the practice of patient poverty, term "C" of the syllogism. Will's first inner dream, under the guidance of Will's animal Anima and Ymaginatif, provides Will with the middle term: the vision of the practice of naturally patient poverty, i.e., the vision of the sufferance of all animals in Kynde. Will, the human animal, innately recognizes the middle term "B" of the syllogism. Dowel is, therefore, " 'to se muche and suffre moore' " (11, l.412). In the next imaginative syllogism in Passus 13 and 14, term "A" is Will's practice of naturally patient poverty, and term "C" is the kynde knowyng of Dowel (15, l.2). Both terms are conjoined by the middle term "B," i.e., by a power hidden in *Actiua vita* or Haukyn. Will's imaginative genius allows him to make quick connections between the poetic assimilation of long, drawn out concerns.

Every one of the seven psycho-physiological processes of a "vis imaginativa secundum Avicennam" come upon Will in a flash. Ymaginatif has never been idle (12, l.1). He has been present as the twin of Thou3t since 8, l.74, although Will never paid any attention to him until Fortune, Rechelesnesse, and the sisters Concupiscence forced him to. We readers can only assume that the *PP*-poet has assimilated the mental acts of the one sensory reasoning, hypostatized by Thou3t and Ymaginatif in the tedious slow motion from 8, l.74, to the end of Passus 12, in order to call attention to the power of instinctual, natural Reson. Ymaginatif says, "I sitte by myself" (12, l.2), because he is not strictly speaking part of the catalogue of Anima's powers (defined in Passus 15, ll.23-39). He belongs to the sensory, animal soul in Will and in all animals. Although he is with Will "in siknesse or in helþe" (in the reading of the "F-group" of mss), Will's human Anima might well be shamed by his power. Although the imaginative power itself is susceptible of hallucinations, produced by maladies or strong emotions, nevertheless Will's rational Thou3t and Dame Studie have perhaps dismissed the promptings of Ymaginatif too soon: as the " 'frenetike wittes' " of " 'fooles' " (10, l.6).

This unique psychology,[41] described as the seven functions of a "vis imaginativa secundum Avicennam," attributes a rationality and

---

[41] Avicenna's psychology of the "vis imaginativa" is unique and does cut through the numerous problems related to other theories of the "vis imaginativa," applied to the meaning and function of Ymaginatif in the B-text. For the difficulties, see M.W. Bloomfield (*Fourteenth-Century Apocalypse*, p.230, n.2 and n.5), Britton J. Harwood ("Imaginative in *Piers Plowman,*" *MAE*, 44[1975], 249), M.W. Bundy, *The Theory of Imagination in Classical and Mediaeval Thought* (University of Illinois Studies in Language and Literature, XII, sec.2-3 [Urbana, 1927]), and H.A. Wolfson's valuable study, "The Internal Senses in Latin, Arabic, and Hebrew Philosophic Texts," *Harvard Theological Review*, 28[1935], 69-133.

Though Averroes speaks of a "vis imaginativa" in his commentaries on Aristotle's *Parva Naturalia* and *De anima*, he does not mention the opposition between the "vis imaginativa" and the "vis cogitativa." Averroes says, rather, that the two faculties cooperate in the production of dreams ("Averrois Cordubensis Compendium Libri Aristotelis De Sompno et Vigilia," *Averrois Cordubensis Compendia Librorum Aristotelis Qvi Parva Naturalia Vocantur,*

appetency to the animal part of the human imagination: sensory but infallible; sensory but prophetic, sensory but perfective, sensory but capable of patient speech. The infallibility, prophecy and perfection of Ymaginatif reside both in Will's human, sensory imagination and in Kynde's divine, sensory Imagination. Such an infallible, prophetic and perfective sensory reason is not to be found in any of the medieval psychologies of imagination we have used so far to account for Ymaginatif's meaning and function.

We have doggedly used the *Benjamin minor* to explain the psychology of Ymaginatif, even though the *Benjamin minor* describes the reason why Ymaginatif cannot be derived from either the psychology of the *Benjamin minor* or any work related to it. The *Benjamin minor*, denigrates not only "imaginatio" but says that "useless thoughts" run riot in the imagination:[42]

> Si enim imaginationis evagatio quae fit per inutiles cogitationes prius non reprimitur, absque dubio sensualitatis appetitus immoderatus minime temperatur (Unless the wandering of the imagination, occasioned by vain thoughts, be first repressed, without doubt the unrestrained appetite of sensuality will be minimally controlled).

Vain thoughts, such as those Will received from Thou3t, do disrupt the processes of the imagination ("evagatio imaginationis"). And Will's vain Thou3t does disrupt the power of Ymaginatif from 8, 1.74 to 11, 1.320. Vain thoughts introduce the very sensuality ("sensualitatis appetitus") which the friar's "forbisne" pointed to (" 'flesshes wille,' " 8, 1.49) and the Reson in Kynde pinpoints, the " 'fondynge of þe flessh and of þe fend boþe' " (11, 1.401). Sensuality is the first movement of

---

Corpus Commentariorum Averrois in Aristotelem, VII, 79,1.61–80,1.65, ed. Emily L. Shields and Harry Blumberg [Cambridge, Mass.: The Medieval Academy of America, 1949]):

> Et ideo comprehendit homo in sompno futura. . . Et ista virtus cogitativa iuvat presentando illud quod habet de ymagine illius rei et colat ipsam ymaginativa, ut sit preesens in virtute cogitativa (And on that account man grasps the future in a dream. . . And the power of thought helps by making present that which it has of the image of the thing, and the imaginative power draws it up so that it [the image] is present in the power of thought).

Averroes allows for prophetic dreams ("Sompnia sunt..in rebus futuris. Iste modus dationis. . .est a re divina et ex perfecta sollicitudine circa homines. Prophetia intrat hunc modum dationis" ["Ibid.," p.102, ll.49–53]), and attributes dreams to the imaginative power ("somnia debent attribui virtuti ymaginative" ["Ibid.," p.98, ll.64–5]); but nowhere (that I know of) does Averroes mention inner dreams or the conflict between the "vis cogitativa" and the "vis imaginativa" in inner dreams. Furthermore, there is a good possibility that Averroes did not allow for a "vis imaginativa" as an independent faculty of sensory reasoning. Wolfson ("Internal Senses," 108) thinks that Averroes collapsed Avicenna's "vis estimativa" and "vis imaginativa" into the one faculty understood by the Latin West as "imaginatio."

42 *PL*, 196, 19B.

Will's human senses toward sin. Sensuality signifies the "will of the flesh" or a "fondynge," a temptation not quite sinful, but not quite good. Ymaginatif cannot hypostatize the Victorine "imaginatio," because animal reasoning is not possessed of sensuality. Although Ymaginatif quite clearly speaks for Reson, as H.S.V. Jones says, nevertheless, Ymaginatif does not reason like a Victorine "imaginatio" reasons (as Jones also says).[43]

Jones pays no attention to the term "sensuality" in the Victorine psychology of the imagination. The fourteenth-century ME translation of the passage quoted in the *Benjamin minor*, "A Tretyse of the Stodey of Wisdom þat Men Clepen Beniamyn," describes what sensuality does to Thouȝt and to Will's "imaginacioun:"[44]

> Bot ȝif þe ianglyng of þe imaginacioun, þat is to sey þe inrennyng of Veyne þouȝtes, be first refreyned, wiþoute doute þe lust of þe sensualyte may not be attemperid.

Sensuality "iangles" the imagination because sensuality causes the "inrennyng of Veyne þouȝtes." Thouȝt cannot restrain Will's "veyne þouȝtes" and temper them, because Thouȝt is controlled in part by Anima's concerns. So sensuality corrupts the reason in the imagination, when Will is awake, and weakens the reason in the imagination, when Will is asleep. Were Ymaginatif's Reson derived from "A Tretyse of the Stodey of Wisdom þat Men Clepen Beniamyn," Will's corruption would have begun at the beginning of his first vision, when Thouȝt mediated the knowledge Will received from Wit. Now Ymaginatif has no sensuality and has "never been idle." The psychology of Ymaginatif is not, then, at all the psychology of the the "imaginacioun" or "imaginatio" in the *Benjamin minor*. Ymaginatif does hypostatize sensibility (the power of the senses to sense objects), the sensory (the power of the senses to sense exteriorly or interiorly), and sensation (the powers of sensing themselves); for senses, sensation, sensibility and the sensory have all been created good. They are all " '*valde bona*' " as

---

[43] H.S.V. Jones, "Imaginatif in *Piers Plowman*," *JEGP*, 13(1914), 584. Jones's source and view still hold; see Derek Pearsall, *"Piers Plowman": An Edition of the C-text* (London: Arnold, 1978), p.234, n.1.

[44] The "Tretys" has been edited by Phyllis Hodgson (London: Geoffrey Cumberledge, 1955) as part of *Deonise Hid Diuinite* (*EETS*, o.s. 231, p.28, ll.15–19). For the same sentiment, see also p.13,l.10–p.14,l.7. Other works of the same school or authorship, e.g., the *Cloud of Unknowing* and the *Book of Privy Counselling* (ed. Phyllis Hodgson [London: Oxford Univ. Press, 1944], *EETS*, o.s. 218) deny any reliably rational function to the imagination. See the *Cloud of Unknowing*, p.22, ll.15–19. *Privy Counselling*, p.152, ll.6–7, recommends that "ymagynatiue resons ben fast bounden & utterly voidid" so that the novice may make spiritual progress. In the tracts, "ymaginatiue" and "ymaginacioun" are not only confused but are always related to sensuality.

Kynde says (11, l.398). Ymaginatif has been created "exceedingly good." Sensuality. however, has not been created "exceedingly good."

Our belief that Ymaginatif is a "spokesman of Reason" is misrepresented by our source for the psychology of Ymaginatif, the *Benjamin minor*. We have not been able, however, to uncover any other source to account for Ymaginatif's reliable rationality in sensory knowledge. Quirk's brief but intense study of the Latin sources for the "vis imaginativa" concluded that the "deliberative function. . . in Langland's Imaginatif was not transmitted (except incidentally. . .) through the mainstream of mediaeval psychological learning."[45] Ymaginatif's rational functions are not only rare in Middle English but somewhat inaccessible, even in the Latin explanations of the "vis imaginativa secundum Avicennam," precisely because Ymaginatif, without sensuality, does reason in Will's sensory imagination.

If Passus 11 and 12 of the B-text do assimilate the acts by which Ymaginatif

1. compares and divides the intents of Will's images,
2. curbs Will's concupiscences or sensuality,
3. discriminates between the true/ good and the false/ bad sensorily and infallibly,
4. prophesies in both inner and outer dreams the "joy and sorrow to come" out of the conflict between kynde knowyng and concupiscent knowyng,
5. compares Will's Wit to Kynde's Wit,
6. causes awe and shame in Will and
7. teaches patient speech,

then the *Benjamin minor* does not account for any of the seven functions in the Reson hypostatized by Ymaginatif. The *Benjamin minor* serves, rather, as an explanation of Will's acts which lead up to and cause the inner dream. "*Concupiscencia carnis*" and "*Coueitise of eiȝes*" infect Will's Thouȝt from the beginning of his inner dream (11, ll.13ff.), from the beginning of the vision, when "flesshes wille" within Anima carries over into Will's first dream (8, ll.48–9) and is represented by the verb in Will's response to Thouȝt (8, l.113):

'More kynde knowyng I coueite to lerne.'

If we use the *Benjamin minor* as a paradigm not to explain the rationality in Ymaginatif but to call for a rationality without sensuality, we ask different questions about Ymaginatif's meaning and function than we

---

45 " 'Vis Imaginativa,' " 82.

usually have asked. Why and how does the reason in Ymaginatif oppose Will's concupiscence or sensuality?

A Christianization of the psychology of the "vis imaginativa secundum Avicennam" would answer the question. The Reson in Will's Ymaginatif opposes the reason in Will's Thouȝt. Purely natural and animal Reson opposes the human, concupiscent reason, located in the middle ventricle of Will's brain. If Ymaginatif is not subject to the sensuality or the concupiscence of the human Anima, Ymaginatif must, then, hypostatize a reason in the one sensory reasoning power, not subject to the sensuality of the human Anima. Ymaginatif's divine, infallible and animal rationality would emanate from a Kynde Who suffers no effects from Adam's sin, no sensuality from "*Concupiscencia carnis*" or "Couveitise of eiȝes." Ymaginatif's Reson could not be toppled, because his Reson emanates from the Reson in Kynde in the celestial spheres, his powers originate in the "Virtus Animalis" of all Kynde, and his images represent the images of the divine Imagination. The *Benjamin minor* tells us that we must look for Ymaginatif's powers in a psychology of the sensory imagination other than that handed down in the mainstream, since this Victorine psychology cannot explain Ymaginatif's lack of sensuality.

Chapter Two

The "Vis Imaginativa Secundum Avicennam" and the Naturally Prophetic Powers of Ymaginatif

The "Vis Imaginativa Secundum Avicennam" and the Mainstream of Medieval Psychology

Although Avicenna's psychology of a prophetic "vis imaginativa" flooded the Christian-Latin West after 1150,[1] the "deliberative function. . . in Langland's *Imaginatif* was not transmitted (except incidentally) through the mainstream of mediaeval psychological learning."[2] Repeated censures of Avicenna's prophetic psychology and Aristotle's *De anima*, in 1210, 1215, 1231, 1270 and 1277,[3] prevented the transmission of the deliberative function in Avicenna's "vis imaginativa."

The censure of 1270 in the *Errores philosophorum* tells us why Ymaginatif's deliberative function is rare, and why his prophetic functions are rarer. While Christians were warmly embracing Avicenna's psychology of a prophetic "vis imaginativa," they were

---

[1] See note 37 in the "Introduction." The "mainstream of medieval psychological learning" includes much more than the Christian commentaries on Aristotle's *De anima*, e.g., the commentaries of Thomas Aquinas or Albertus Magnus, listed by C. Lohr ("Medieval Latin Aristotle Commentaries," *Traditio*, 23[1967], 313–413; 24[1968], 149–245; 26[1970], 135–216; 27[1971], 251–351; 28[1972], 281–396; 29[1973], 93–197).

[2] Randolph Quirk, "Vis Imaginativa," *JEGP*, 53(1954), 82.

[3] "Avicenne et les décrets de 1210 et de 1215," R. de Vaux, *Notes et textes sur l'Avicennisme Latin aux confins des XIIᵉ–XIIIᵉ*, Bibliothèque Thomiste, XX, (Paris: J.Vrin, 1934), 45, n.2; Pierre Mandonnet, *Siger de Brabant et l'Averroïsme Latin au XIIIᵉ siècle*, 2 ed. (Louvain: Institut Supérieur de Philosophie de l'Université, 1911), Pt.1, pp.15–26 and notes. From 1215 to 1277 (when Robert Kilwardby forbad English students to read commentaries on Aristotle's works and the works themselves), Arabic interpretations of Aristotle were taught in England (William Courtenay, *Schools and Scholars in Fourteenth-Century England* [Princeton, New Jersey: Princeton Univ. Press, 1987], p.279 and note 20).

heatedly protesting the naturality and quasi-pantheism of such a psychology:[4]

> Quod prophetia est naturalis. Ulterius erravit [Avicenna] circa prophetiam. Bene enim dixit circa prophetam. . . quod propheta audit verbum divinum et quod vidit vel saltem videre potest 'angelos transfiguratos coram se in forma qua videri possunt.' Sed male dixit, quia visus est velle prophetiam esse naturalem, et voluit quod secundum ordinem, quem habet anima nostra ad animas supercaelestes et ad intelligentiam ultimam, derivatur ad nos prophetia (That prophecy is natural. Again Avicenna erred on the subject of prophecy. He spoke correctly about prophecy when he [intended to say] that a prophet hears the word of God and that he sees, or at least can see, 'angels transfigured before him in visible form.' But he spoke incorrectly because he seems to have meant that prophecy is natural and that prophecy is transmitted to us according to a relation that our souls have to supercelestial souls and the highest intelligence).

In the censures of 1277, the Archbishop of Paris approved Avicenna's psychology of the ''vis imaginativa'' and even quoted the appropriate words, ''angels transfigured before him in visible form,'' from Avicenna's *Metaphysics*,[5]

> In cujus viribus animalibus sunt he tres proprietates, scilicet ut audiat verbum dei, et videat angelos transfiguratos coram se in forma quae possunt videri (And in the senses [of the prophet] are these three qualities: that he hear the word of God and see the angels transformed before him),

the passage being a gloss of Avicenna's words in the *Liber de anima, IV–V,*

> Et haec est propria prophetia virtutis imaginativae (And this is the prophecy proper to the imaginative power);[6]

but he censured the same two tenets. While Christian *psychologists* were transmitting the ''vis imaginativa secundum Avicennam'' (ME ''ymaginatif''), Christian *theologians* were censuring Avicenna's theory of prophecy.

Thirteenth-century theologians would object to this passage in the *Liber de anima, IV–V,*[7]

---

[4] *Giles of Rome: Errores Philosophorum*, ed. by Joseph Koch and transl. by John O. Riedl (Marquette, Wisconsin: Marquette Univ. Press, 1944), p.32,l.18–p.34,l.3, and note 91; p.36, 1.18; p.39, 1.5. The Latin text has also been edited by Mandonnet (''Tractatus de erroribus philosophorum Aristotelis, Averrois, Avicennae, Algazelis, Alkindi et Rabbi Moysis,'' *Siger de Brabant*, Pt.2, p.13, number 16).

[5] That is, from Avicenna's *Liber de philosophia prima sive scientia divina, V–X*, tractatus 10, ch.1; p.523, ll.23–26.

[6] Bk.4, ch.2; p.19, 1.61.

[7] *Liber de anima, IV–V*, Bk.4, ch.2; p.28, ll.79–82.

> Bonum est ut ostendamus parum principium ex quo provenit aliquid
> praevidere in somnis ex his quae ponemus; non enim firmiter mon-
> strabuntur nisi in philosophia prima (In our explanation, it is good that we
> show an equal principle from which flows foresight in sleep. For our
> explanation will not be firmly grounded except in the Metaphysics),

since it implied this passage in the "Metaphysics:"[8]

> Necessarium est ut virtus animalis sit principium propinquum motui,. . .
> tunc caelum movetur per animam et anima est propinquum principium
> sui motus, et in illa anima renovatur imaginatio et voluntas (The Animal
> Power must be a source [of knowledge] next to [the source of its]
> motion. . . Then heaven is moved through Anima, and Anima is next to
> its source of Motion, and in the Anima are renovated Imagination and
> Will).

The Divine "Virtus Animalis" (the source of the reasoning power of the
"vis imaginativa") is astronomically located next to Its Source for
Intellectual and Voluntary and Imaginative "Motion:" the Divine Soul
in a Body (Kynde). The "vis imaginativa" unites the Divine "Virtus
Animalis" in the tenth and outermost sphere of the universe with the
"virtus animalis" in the prophet. Avicenna's "principle" leads to
pantheism and to the naturality of prophecy.

In terms of Passus 11, Ymaginatif would unite Will's human will and
intellect with Kynde's Divine Will and Intellect in a sphere above
"middelerþe" (11,l.9), by means of a "myȝt" ("motus" or "motion")
common to Kynde's "Cors" and Will's "cors." Will's prophetic sight
would not derive from his separate intellect or will or imagination. In
ecstatic vision, Will would no longer possess his own will, imagination
and intellect. One "Myȝt" would move all the bodies and minds in
Kynde, including Will's. Will would be possessed by what the
theologians call a "unity of intellect:" vision based on the unity of the
physiology in Will's body (motion or "myȝt" in 9, ll.38, 53) with the
Physics in the world around him (motion or "myȝt") and with the
Metaphysics above him (Divine Motion or "Myȝt" in the Firmament of
Heaven). Anima, Will, Imagination, Wit, Reson, Kynde would be
indistinguishable in one act of prophetic vision.

This "principle" would unite Will's foresight in dreams with Kynde's
and Ymaginatif's divine Foresight,[9] because the principle unites Will's

---

[8] *Liber de philosophia prima seu scientia divina, V–X*, tractatus 9, ch.2; p.453, ll.78–9, 454,
ll.86–8.

[9] That is, the "principle" referred to in note 7, i.e., in the *Liber de anima, IV–V*, p.28, ll.79–
82. This passage is preceded by a clause (*Liber de anima, IV–V*, p.28, l.79),

> Sed quia de verbo imaginationis iam pervenimus ad somnia (But because we
> have now arrived at dreams from our words about the imagination),

which relates the "vis imaginativa secundum Avicennam" to prophetic dreams.

"my3t," Kynde's "my3t," and Ymaginatif's "my3t" into a unity of motion. In light of this Physiology (motion or "my3t" in the body), Physics (motion or "my3t" in the sublunary world) and Metaphysics (Motion or "My3t" moving the Firmament of Heaven), Christian theologians would not translate Will's "me [þo] þou3te" in 11, l.324b, into "I thought." They would translate it into "It thought me." The implied subject, "It," would signify the pantheism ("unity of intellect") and naturality of prophecy; for "It" would be either Kynde's or Ymaginatif's motion or "my3t" or Reson, Both performing Will's moving and thinking. Divine Anima, divine Fortune and divine Kynde would all three "ravish" Will up to Adam's Paradise (11, ll.7, 324, 417, in the "F-group" of mss), such that Will would literally look down at "middelerþe" *through* Kynde's Sight.[10] "Praevidere in somnis" (foresight in sleep) means what it says literally. In unity with the Divine and *Animal* Anima, Will would literally foresee in his sleep *through* the Mental Acts of Kynde and Ymaginatif, while his body remains under the "lynde" (8, l.65):[11]

> Dicemus ergo quod omnia quae in mundo sunt praeterita, praesentia et futura, habet esse in sapientia creatoris et angelorum intellectualium secundum aliquid, et habent esse in animabus quae sunt angeli caelorum secundum aliud. Postea autem declarabuntur isti duo modi alias et demonstrabitur tibi quod animae humanae maiorem habent comparationem cum substantiis angelicis quam cum corporibus sensibilibus, et non est illic occultatio aliqua nec avaritia, sed occultatio est secundum receptibilia, aut quia sunt infusa in corporibus, aut quia sunt inquinata ab his quibus deprimuntur deorsum (We will, therefore, say that all the past, present and future in the world has actuality in the wisdom of the Creator and the intellectual angels in one sense. In another sense, all has actuality in souls which are angels of heaven. In due time, these two modes [of actuality] will be clarified for you, and it will be demonstrated to you that human souls are more comparable to angelic substances than to sensory bodies. And in this regard, there is no secrecy nor selfishness. Rather the secrecy is due to the state of the souls receiving, or because the souls are infused in bodies, or because the souls are stained by these which push them downward).

Possessed by a clean Anima (not "inquinata"), Will clearly sees past, present and future *through* Kynde's Providence (etymologically, "foresight"). From 11, l.320, his *animal* Anima has more in common with the "savor" ("sapientia") of Kynde ("Creator") and with angels than with

---

[10] *Liber de anima, IV–V*, p.29, ll.93–4: "id quod videtur est id quod pertinet ad illum hominem vel ad suos vel ad suam terram vel ad suam civitatem vel ad suum clima" (what is seen pertains to that man or to his [family] or to his earth or to his city or to his habitable zone).

[11] *Liber de anima, IV–V*, p.28,l.83–p.29,l.91.

the "savor" of "sensory (human) bodies" with which he originated the vision by means of Anima's Thou3t in 8, l.112 (in the "F-group" of mss):

> & seyde, 'me savoureþ no3t 3yt wel, so me crist helpe!'

Will's literal foresight and wisdom from the wits ("sapientia" or "savor") would be the result of the *unity* of Will's *animal* Anima and imagination with Kynde's *Animal* Anima and Imagination.

Moreover, if Dame Studie is an Avicennan "meditatio" who recognizes Will's "purpos," i.e., to study questions about Kynde's Governance of the world (the effects of Adam's original sin upon human kynde in 10, ll.106–22), she would predict that such a study would lead to such a vision of Providence through Ymaginatif:[12]

> Ille cuius meditatio fuerit de gubernatione mundi videbit eam et instruetur ducatu eius (He whose study has concerned itself with the Governance of the world will see Governance and will instruct himself by its Guidance).

For the "imaginative power represents that which emanates from the heavenly spheres" ("virtus imaginativa . . . representat quod emanat a caelestibus").[13]

Granting that Ymaginatif (the angel of the Lord) speaks *in* the sensory imagination of Will by means of inner dreams,

> And in the senses [of the prophet] are these three qualities: that he hear the word of God and see the angels transformed before him,. . . and that [their] speech be made in his ears,

theologians would nevertheless deny the pantheism or "unity of intellect" implied by the preposition "in" and by the phrase "in the senses:"[14]

> Sed male dixit, quia visus est velle prophetiam esse naturalem, et voluit quod secundum ordinem, quem habet anima nostra ad animas supercaelestes et ad intelligentiam ultimam, derivatur ad nos prophetia (But he spoke incorrectly because he seems to have meant that prophecy is natural and that prophecy is transmitted to us according to a relation that our souls have to supercelestial souls and the highest intelligence).

"In" would refer to four pantheistic mental acts in Will's sensory imagination. First, by means of the angel (Ymaginatif), Kynde's "Virtus

---

12 *Liber de anima, IV–V*, p.29, ll.97–9.
13 *Liber de anima, IV–V*, p.29, l.01.
14 For the specific tenets of Avicenna's psychology, condemned in 1277, see Mandonnet, "Propositions condamnées par Etienne Tempier, éveque de Paris: 1277," *Siger de Brabant*, Pt.2, pp.184–8, numbers 117–8, 122, 140–1, 176–7 (the unity of intellect, the relationship of sensory knowledge to intellectual knowledge in the act of knowing, the agent intellect, and the naturality of raptures, visions, and prophecy).

Animalis'' would unite with Will's ''virtus animalis,'' so that the ''myȝt'' of Wit in Will's animal Anima, explained by Wit in Passus 9 (ll.38, 45, 53), would be in unity with the ''myȝt'' in the ''forbisnes'' of Kynde's Wit in all other animals in Kynde (11, ll.325b, 327–68). In other words, Kynde's angel would convert Kynde's Wit into ''forbisnes'' which appear in Will's imagination. Second, Will would hear and see through a ''vis imaginativa secundum Avicennam'' converted to teach the meaning of '' 'cristes loue' '' (12, l.71a). That is, Ymaginatif as ''oon'' would be the hypostasis of Kynde's angel from 11, l.320 (''wiþ me gan oon dispute''), showing first a vision of Kynde's Wit and then telling about ''cristes loue,'' a Christian theology developed from purely natural vision. Third, the ''forbisnes'' or images of Kynde's Wit and Reson, seen by Will from 11, ll.335–68, would transform into the speaker, Kynde's Reson, Whom Will hears from 11, ll.376–404. Fourth, in such a unity of human and Divine Imagination, Will would compare images of universal human Wit with images of Kynde's Wit, according to a twofold standard of reason *innate* to himself: his human reason communicated by Thouȝt and Kynde's Reson communicated by Ymaginatif (11, ll.331–5). While denying the pantheistic ''myȝt'' or motion and the naturality of prophecy, Christian theologians embraced such acts of the prophetic ''vis imaginativa secundum Avicennam.''

Bloomfield's suggestion, the ''manner whereby imagination could be elevated. . . through the medieval theory of prophecy'' so that imagination ''can give rise to true knowledge,''[15] is a modern restatement of the same approval and the same two problems which theologians discovered in Avicenna's prophetic ''vis imaginativa:'' the naturality of Ymaginatif's prophecy and the manner of the elevation of Will's imagination. Although we tend to agree that

1. Ymaginatif is the spokesman for Reason,
2. Ymaginatif reasons for Will in vivid images,
3. the images are especially vivid in Will's inner dream,
4. the images are the spoken words of Kynde and Ymaginatif,
5. transformed into bodies that Will can see and hear,

we have not been able to account for these functions in terms of a consistent psychology. We have not been able to find the consistent psychology, because it was understood to be part of a theology of prophecy (i.e., Avicenna's *Metaphysics*), repeatedly censured. The physiology and psychology of a naturally prophetic ''vis imaginativa secundum Avicennam'' was and is rare, because the *PP*-poet revived

---

15 *Fourteenth-Century Apocalypse*, p.172.

Avicenna's *theology* of a *naturally* prophetic "vis imaginativa secundum Avicennam" and applied it to the *Christian* theological questions raised in the B-text. That is, the *PP*-poet developed the rare psychology from Avicenna's Physiology (Wit's "myȝt" in Will's "cors"), Psychology (Ymaginatif's "myȝt" in Will's imagination), and Metaphysics (Kynde's "myȝt" in Will's "cors" and imagination), and applied it in such a way that Ymaginatif would answer the concupiscent "purpos" in Will's theological investigations.[16]

It startles us that the "myȝt" in Will's "cors" is prophetic. Such a "myȝt" empowers Ymaginatif to conjoin Will's Wit to Kynde's Wit, and to unite Will's imagination to Kynde's Imagination, in the second half of a prophetic inner dream. Since Will's power to prophesy originates in his animal Anima, then Ymaginatif's "virtus animalis" performs acts above and beyond the powers of the "bisshop" Anima, catalogued in 15, ll.22–39. It is more surprising that, when Will requests a "craft" in his "cors" to know "kyndely" from holi chirche (1, ll.138–9), and, in 9, ll.38, 45, 53, Wit defines the "craft" as a "myȝt" created by Kynde in Will's "cors," the rarity of the request and the unusual definition of it are revealed by the "myȝt" exhibited in Will's body from 11,l.320–12,l.10.

The physiology is rare because, on the one hand, one Motion (ME "myȝt") is shared by the Wit in Kynde, Kynde's angel (Ymaginatif), and Will's human Wit, and because, on the other hand, the Motion opposes the motion in Will's *human* Anima and Will's *human* concupiscence. "Myȝt" would signify Avicenna's objectionable pantheism, were Will not free to rebuke Kynde's Reson (11, ll.374–5). "Myȝt" would also signify Avicenna's objectionable naturality, were not Will raised to Adam's Paradise ("heere," in 11, l.417, in the "F-group" of mss). In the *PP*-poet's application of the psychology, Ymaginatif elevates Will's sensory "myȝt" to the supernatural "myȝt" of Kynde, in order that Will differentiate his "myȝt" from Kynde's "Myȝt," by differentiating his will from Kynde's Will, i.e., by reenacting Adam's sin. The preposition "in" would signify Avicenna's pantheism, were not Will free to separate himself from this "unity of intellect," rebuke Kynde's Reson, and show his *human* and *individual* act of free will.

The psychology is also rare, because, on the one hand, the "light" in Will's faculties of kynde knowyng makes Will *identical* with his objects, acts and power of knowledge, according to Aristotle:[17]

---

[16] The rare psychology carries with it a rare poetic, implied by Will's "makynges" (12, l.26); see "Introduction," note 19.

[17] *De anima*, Bk.3, ch.5; 430a, ll.14–20, passim.

> Mind is what it is by virtue of becoming all things, while there is another
> which is what it is by virtue of making all things: this is a sort of positive
> state like light; for in a sense light makes potential colors into actual colors.
> Actual knowledge is identical with its object.

For example, Will is so "lik" his Thou3t (8, 1.70) as to become "one"
with his thoughts and Will is equally so "lik" his Ymaginatif to become
"one" with Ymaginatif and the Reson in Kynde. More significantly,
Will's sensory Anima, the "witte and wisdom" of the "*sensus*" in
Anima at 15, ll.29–30, is also like the " 'wiasedom and þe wit of god' "
(11, 1.419). Illumined by his faculties of kynde knowyng, Will *could* be
identified with Kynde in a "unity of intellect" because of the identity
between Will's objects of knowledge and Kynde's objects of knowledge
from 11, ll.321b–68. The psychology is most rare, because, on the other
hand, the inner dream proves just the opposite: Will's faculties of kynde
knowyng are not identical with Kynde's faculties of kynde knowyng.
Will's "my3t" and his "objects of knowledge" are not identical with
Kynde's "my3t" and "objects of knowledge." Will's "savor" is not the
same as Kynde's wisdom.

The *PP*-poet resolved the Avicennan problem of the "unity of
intellect" by recourse to the Christian doctrine of free will, i.e., a will
free to rebuke and to fall from the order established by Kynde. Hence,
Will's rebuke of Kynde's Reson in 11, ll.374–5, differentiates Will's acts
of knowing, willing and imagining from Kynde's Acts of Knowing,
Willing and Imagining. Although Will's "powers" of knowledge, e.g.,
Wit, Thou3t, Ymaginatif, are revealed by Will's "objects" of knowledge,
e.g., the human kynde inherited by him from Adam, Will's "powers"
and "objects" of knowledge are not empowered by one "m(M)y3t,"
shared by Will and Kynde in common. Will's "objects" and "acts" of
knowledge do not unify him with Kynde or Ymaginatif, as long as Will,
a son of Adam, is possessed of sufficient Thou3t and Will, inherited
from Adam, to rebuke Kynde. Unlike an Avicennan prophet or an
Aristotelian wit, Will is *free* to choose. At 11, ll.374–4, Will is already the
hypostasis of Christian free will (*"liberum arbitrium"* in 16, 1.16).

When we recognize that the "my3t" of Will allows Will freedom to
choose for himself (and to fall from Kynde's Clergie by 11, 1.416), then
we know why Ymaginatif's "answer" is most important to Will's
"purpos." Wit's "my3t" has convinced Will that man is "moost lik" to
Kynde (9, 1.31); as a result, Will has presumed that the might in his
"cors," the "craft" to know all things, stems from the *identity* of his
body, wits, soul, will and intent with the Body of Kynde. The second
half of the inner dream (11, ll.320–410) forces Will to see *through* Kynde
that the "matere" in Will's body differs from the "matere" in Kynde
Himself and in all of his other creatures (11, ll.402–3):

'For man was maad of swich a matere he may noʒt wel asterte
That som tyme hym bitit to folwen his kynde.'

The matter in Will's body forces Will to use his "myʒt" in a human way. Will's "matere" distinguishes the "myʒt" in Will's human kynde from the "myʒt" in all other Kynde. Therefore, the "powers" of his "cors" and Will's kynde "powers" are not identical with the powers of Kynde. Will " 'moste wo þolie, in fondynge of þe flessh and of þe fend boþe' " (11, ll.401–2), says Kynde. In Avicennan terms, Kynde's statement means that Will's Anima is "stained" and "pushed down" by his body ("inquinata ab his quibus deprimuntur deorsum"). In Christian terms, Will is free to sin, i.e., to choose to rebuke Kynde's Reson, because Will's objects of thought are attached to the "matere" in his body.

Dame Studie's prophecy of Ymaginatif's "answer" to Will's "purpos" is, therefore, well placed in the argument about the effects of original sin on human bodies in 10, l.119 (see 10, l.111). Her prophecy tells us that Will has been studying Wit's Avicennan interpretation of kynde knowyng and falling into a common Avicennan error: that there is no original sin nor any effects from the original sin upon Will's "matere" and kynde.[18] Since Will's "purpos" erroneously presumes that Will is "moost lik" Kynde (9, l.31), Ymaginatif's "answer" most clearly teaches Will that there is no "unity of intellects" whatsoever. For Will lost innocence and became separate from Kynde (11, ll.417–420a), when the "matere" in Will's body made him rebuke Kynde's Reson. Will's very "matere" separates the "myʒt" in his human Wit from the "myʒt" in Kynde's Wit.

On the one hand, Will is *united* with his faculties of kynde knowyng from the "cors" (Wit, Thouʒt, Ymaginatif and Kynde), because "the knower is united with the known in the act of knowing;" on the other, Will is *separate* from the same faculties by the very facts that he "savors" a different wisdom than they savor (8, l.112) and is free to develop a

---

18 According to the censures of 1277, Aristotle's statement in the *"Metaphysics*, Bk.11, man understands and desires the first mover, deceived" Avicenna. Avicenna believed that man is moved by only the good in "celestial bodies. . .[themselves] animated by only understanding and desire" (Mandonnet, *Siger de Brabant*, Pt.2, p.6, number 15). It was not "revealed" to Avicenna that the celestial bodies harm man, that is, that there are demons in the celestial bodies. Unaware of the fall of the angels, Avicenna knew nothing of the evil inflicted on Adam and Eve by bad angels,i.e., original sin. Sensuality descended upon the whole human race, and disrupted the order of the rational, irascible and concupiscible appetites. Avicenna's notion of "illumination" was ignorant of the concupiscence in the concupiscible appetite, the anger in the irascible appetite, and the pride in the rational appetite. Thus Avicenna's "virtues" cannot only perfect human powers. The "virtues" must also "heal" the wounds in human powers. Grace not only illumines but heals the effects of original sin upon the appetites (Mandonnet, *Siger de Brabant*, Pt.2, p.13, number 12, for this censure of Avicenna, and Gardet, *La Penseé Religeuse*, p.172, for an explanation).

"purpos" which rebukes Kynde's Reson (11, ll.374–5). From 11, l.320, then, Ymaginatif's reason is *identical* with the animal reason in Will's sensory imagination, but *opposes* the human, sensory reasoning within Will's human Anima, i.e., Thouȝt, from 8, l.74. Ymaginatif's movement is the same as Will's natural desire for the good ("kynde my creatour to louye," 11., l.326b) but different from Will's concupiscent desire for the good ("coueite," in 8, l.113b). On the one hand, Ymaginatif's prophetic psychology is purely "kynde" (a "kynde knowyng" derived from "craftes" in the "wittes" of the "cors"); on the other, Will, Wit, Thouȝt, Ymaginatif and Kynde develop a "purpos" and answer which intends toward the "grace of God," "cristes loue, þat of Clergie is roote," and the "Sapiencia" of the "heiȝe holy goost" (12, ll.68, 71, 138–9).

If we combine Quirk's finding ("rare psychology") with Bloomfield's suggestion ("medieval theory of prophecy"), then our query concerns a psychology of the "vis imaginativa secundum Avicennam," adapted to a Christian *theology* of prophecy. Between 1150 (the entrance of the *Avicenna Latinus* into Europe) and 1277 (the condemnation of a number of Aristotelian propositions by Stephen Tempier), Avicenna's psychology was hidden in pseudo-Augustine's theology of prophecy. In 1366 (a few years before the composition of the B-text), students *in the Arts curriculum* were permitted to learn the censured parts of the psychology. To understand how, after 1366, the *PP*-poet revived the prophetic psychology of the "vis imaginativa secundum Avicennam" in a more Avicennan form, we differentiate the form of the psychology, adapted by Christian psychologists and theologians, from the form given us by Avicenna.

An Introduction to "Augustinisme Avicennisant"

Between 1150 and 1277, Christian psychologists and theologians concealed Avicenna's psychology of natural prophecy by the "vis imaginativa" within Augustine's psychology of vision. A principle common to both Augustine and Avicenna allowed the disguise: light is truth. Avicenna and Augustine were thought to teach that God created intellectual light when He created the angels. So Avicenna and Augustine were thought to teach that angels communicate the light of truth to men. Avicenna's metaphysics of light (the light of Intelligence and Imagination permeates the universe, from the highest light in the firmament to the lowest light in animals, by means of angels or intelligences) was adapted to Augustine's psychology of human "visio corporalis, visio spiritualis'' (or "imaginaria''), and "visio intellectualis.''

In the well-known study, "Les Sources Gréco-Arabes de l'Augustinisme Avicennisant,''[19] Etienne Gilson coined the term "Augustinisme Avicennisant'' to explain the accommodation.[20] Truth being "l'action illuminatrice et immédiate de Dieu,''[21] God illumines all human knowledge, both in the mind and in the senses. Divine Illumination begins in infinity outside the firmament, descends through each planetary sphere of "soul,'' "intelligence,'' "will'' and "imagination,'' and illumines the sensory imagination of the prophet. According to some Augustinians, such "illumination'' does not descend all the way to the "virtus animalis'' of the prophet; according to other Augustinians, it does.[22] Since, in Passus 11, Kynde does illumine

---

[19] *Archives d'histoire doctrinale et littéraire du moyen age*, 4(1929), 5–149, especially on pp. 5, 7, 56, 62, 100, 101 5.

[20] In his "Pourquoi Saint Thomas A Critiqué Saint Augustine'' (*Archives d'Histoire Doctrinale et Littéraire du Moyen Age*, 1[1926–1927], 46–80), Gilson points to Gundissalinus' compendium *De anima* as one of the principal sources of the Christianization of Avicenna's theories of natural prophecy, and cites de Vaux's agreement with him in the introduction to J.T. Muckle's edition of Gundissalinus' compendium *De anima* ("The Treatise De Anima of Dominicus Gundissalinus,'' *Mediaeval Studies*, 2[1940], 25–6). Roland de Vaux thought that pure "Avicennisme'' existed in its own right in the Latin West before the 1230's (the time of the introduction of Averroes' psychology), as he demonstrates in his introduction to his edition of the *Liber de causis primis et secundis* (*Notes et textes*, 2–3, 22-43). Both Gilson and de Vaux show that "Augustinians'' used Gundissalinus' works to accommodate Avicenna's heterodoxies to the thought of Augustine.

For a brief description of the accommodation, see D.A. Callus, "The Treatise of John Blund on the Soul,'' *Autour d'Aristote: Recueil d'Etudes de Philosophie Ancienne et Médiévale Offert à Monseigneur A. Mansion*, Bibliothèque Philosophique de Louvain, XVI, ed.? (Louvain: Publications Universitaires de Louvain, 1955), pp.478–9, and notes 22–4, and Gilson's *History of Christian Philosophy in the Middle Ages* (New York: Random House, 1955), pp.238–240, 653–654.

[21] Mandonnet, *Siger de Brabant*, p.56.

[22] "Augustinian'' does not refer to the religious order but to a philosophico-theological movement which upheld the Christian authority of Augustine's writing over and against the natural authority of Aristotle's writings, introduced into the Christian Latin West by translations of Arabic-Aristotelian works. The term describes three reactions to the introduction of the Arabic Aristotle. A first group of "Augustinians'' opposed any introduction of the Arabic-Aristotelian psychology into the Christian West (1210–1277), e.g., the Archbishop of Canterbury, John Peckham. Peckham's "Augustinisme'' objected that Thomas Aquinas's introduced "profanas vocum novitates'' (profane new significances to words) which "quidquid docet Augustinus. . . destruat'' (destroy whatever Augustine teaches). A second group of "Augustinians,'' e.g., William of Auvergne or Bonaventure, modified the "Aristotle'' introduced into philosophico-theological psychology by, e.g., Phillip the Chancellor or Jean de la Rochelle or Alexander of Hales or (extremely) Boethius of Dacia and Siger of Brabant. A third group of "Augustinians'' attempted to incorporate Aristotle's metaphysics and psychology into what was taught as the psychology of "Augustine,'' e.g, the same Bonaventure, Alexander of Hales, Jean de la Rochelle, Albertus Magnus or Thomas Aquinas. "Augustinian'' thus describes both a "direction augustinienne'' and a "direction aristotelienne,'' although the direction is

knowledge known by Will's "virtus animalis," i.e., by the rational power in Ymaginatif, a power which Will has in common with brute animals, the *PP*-poet's adaptation of "Augustinisme Avicenissant" emphasizes the "Avicennisme" in "Augustinisme Avicennisant."

If Augustinians emphasize the "Avicennisme" in "Augustinisme Avicennisant," then the "Avicennisme" can be of two different types: one which would emphasize Will's illumination by Haukyn's practical reason (to the denigration of the reason in Ymaginatif) and another which would emphasize Will's illumination by Ymaginatif's reason (as a preparation for Will's ascent through Haukyn's reason to the higher reason of Anima in Passus 15). In the first type of "Avicennisme," Will would literally see through a divine "light" reflected through the two "faces" of his *one* Anima, one face called the "active power" (Haukyn) and the other face the "contemplative power" (the "bisshop" Anima in Passus 15):[23]

> Anima humana, sicut postea scies, est una substantia, habens comparationem ad duo, quorum unum est supra eam et alterum infra eam, sed secundum unumquodque istorum habet virtutem per quam ordinatur habitus qui est inter ipsam et illud. Haec autem virtus activa est illa virtus quam habet anima propter debitum quod debet ei quod est infra eam, scilicet corpus, ad regendum illud; sed virtus contemplativa est illa virtus quam habet anima propter debitum quod debet ei quod est supra eam, ut patiatur ab eo et proficiat per illud et recipiat ex illo; tamquam anima nostra habeat duas facies, faciem scilicet deorsum ad corpus, quam oportet nullatenus recipere aliquam affectionem generis debiti naturae corporis, et aliam faciem sursum, versus principia altissima, quam oportet semper

unclear. For this general meaning of "Augustinian," see Maurice de Wulf (*Le Traité De unitate formae de Giles de Lessines* [Louvain: Institut Supérieur de Philosophie de l'Université, 1901], pp.14-9), P. Mandonnet (*Siger de Brabant et L'Averroisme Latin aux XIIIme Siècle*, Pt.1, pp.55-7), E. Portalié ("Augustinisme: Développement historique de l'," *Dictionnaire de Théologie Catholique*, ed. A. Vacant, E. Mangenot, E. Amann [Paris: Letouzey et Ané, 1908-50], I, pt.2, 2501), and E. Gilson (*History of Christian Philosophy in the Middle Ages* [New York: Random House, 1955], p.707, n.86).

Since "truth" is "l'action illuminatrice et immédiate de Dieu" (Mandonnet, *Siger de Brabant*, p.56), both Augustinians and Aristotelians agreed that knowledge is "light." For both Aristotle and Augustine posit that a "light" or "divine illumination" infuses the "light" of reasoning into the senses and intellect. Both camps wrote or used tracts to explain the "light," e.g., the anonymous *Liber de causis primis et secundis et de fluxu qui consequitur eas*, Gundissalinus' compendium *De anima*, the anonymous Worcester *De potentiis animae et obiectis*, Jean de la Rochelle's *Tractatus de divisione multiplici potentiarum animae* and *Summa de anima*.

[23] *Liber de anima*, I-II-III, Bk.1, ch.5; p.93,l.00-p.94,l.14, and notes 25 and 36 in the "Introduction."

Christians knew Avicenna's doctrine about illumination from the "mirrors" and "two faces of the soul" well (*Liber de anima*, I-II-III, pp.44*-5*; the *Liber de anima*, IV-V, pp.44*-5*, 99-101; Louis Gardet, *La Pensée Religeuse d'Avicenne* [Paris: J. Vrin, 1951], pp.151-152). Gundissalinus' compendium *De anima* refers to the doctrine (Muckle, *Mediaeval Studies*, 86, ll.27-87, l.3; 99, l.12; 102, l.5); the anonymous *Liber de causis primis et secundis* refers to it (De Vaux, *Notes et textes*, pp.39-40, 129, l.19 and note 3).

recipere aliquid ab eo quod est illic et affici ab illo. Ex eo autem quod est infra eam, generantur mores, sed ex eo quod est super eam, generantur sapientiae (As you will deduce later, the human Anima is one substance with a relationship to two. One of the two is above the soul and another is within it; but, from each of the two, the soul receives a power to be set into order in relation to each of the two. This power is the active power when Anima receives the power for duties owed to that which is beneath it, duties of ruling the body. But this [same] power is the contemplative power when Anima receives the power for duties owed to that which is above it, so that Anima submits to it, progresses through it and receives from it. [The relationship between the active power and the contemplative power is] is as if our soul has two faces: one face looking down to the body from which the soul ought not in any way take any affect from any corporeal kind; and another face looking upward toward the highest origins from which the soul ought always to receive something from there and take affects from there. From the face which is beneath the soul are generated good habits; from the face above it are generated wisdoms).[24]

From Passus 9–14 inclusive, Anima's lower face would govern the good habits which Will generates from his body by the light of practical reason, while Will is engaged in trials and errors of practising a sensory *kynde knowyng*. From Passus 15–17, Anima's higher face would lead Will's lower practice to wisdom (15, ll.55–69), i.e., to the so-called "primary light" of "self-evident principles of knowledge" ("principia per se nota"), the *kynde knowyng* innate to Will in Passus 9 but unrealized by Will until Passus 15. The connection between Will's lower illumination by Anima's lower face and higher illumination by Anima's higher face would be Haukyn or "*Actiua vita*" (13, l.224), the hypostasis of Avicenna's "virtus activa."[25] That is, Haukyn would be pivotal to the

---

[24] The "virtus activa" or practical reason produces "mores" or good habits in the body by way of trial and error learned from probable opinion and experiment (*Liber de anima*, IV–V, Bk.5, ch.1; pp.78,l.41–p.80,l.83). The "virtus contemplativa" or contemplative reason produces the certainty of "self-evident truths" ("Principia autem contemplativi sunt ex propositionibus per se notis," *Liber de anima*, IV–V; p.78, ll.40–1).

[25] According to the anonymous Worcester tract, "De potentiis animae et obiectis," the "virtus activa" is the "vita civilis" (Callus, "Powers of the Soul," 159,l.32–160,l.2). The perfection of the concupiscible and irascible appetites, called by the anonymous compiler the "appetitive and aggressive appetites," brings about the prophet's ascent through "voluptuous, civil and contemplative lives" ("possunt distingui [vires motivae] secundum triplicem vitam contemplativam, civilem et voluptuosam").

Gundissalinus' compendium *De anima* calls it a "virtus activa" (Muckle, *Mediaeval Studies*, 84, ll.21–6).

Jean de la Rochelle's *Tractatus* (p.81, ll.401–17) Christianizes Avicenna's "vita activa et contemplatiua" only in the language of Aristotle and only in relation to the Aristotelian division of virtues accompanying the two lives (p.157, ll.263–9).

> Animae rationalis duae sunt vires: una est virtus intelligendi et alia est virtus agendi, sive una est virtus contemplativa et alia est virtus activa (The rational soul has two powers: one is the power of understanding and the other is the power of doing, or, one is the contemplative power and the other is the active power).

achievement of Will's intent both to know kyndely by Passus 15, l.2, and to achieve the higher vision shown by Anima in Passus 15. An Avicennan "virtus activa" would enable Will to ascend from vision through the lower face of his sensory Anima to the higher face of his non-sensory Anima. In 15, l.11, the higher "reson" would reveal the higher Anima, "a sotil þyng" who speaks "wiþouten tonge and teeþ" the mental words which reveal to Will "wherof I cam & of what kynde" (15, ll.11-4) and who elevates the tongue and teeth used by Will's lower Anima in the first vision of the *Vita*. In 15 ll.15-6, 21, the mental words of the higher Anima, "cristes creature" (15, ll.15-16, 21), would introduce Will to a vision of "cristes court," and to the names by which Will uses Anima in his ascent from a vision of Kynde to a vision of charity (15, ll.23-39). The *combined* lower and higher Reson in Haukyn would elevate Will from his sensory Anima to his non-sensory Anima so that lower vision would lead to higher vision by means of the vision of practical patient poverty in Haukyn. Although Thou3t, Ymaginatif, Haukyn and Will's lower Anima would begin Will's ascent toward good in the two faces of Anima, i.e., his lower reason and higher reason, Ymaginatif would have no reason proper to himself.

In the second type of emphasis of the "Avicennisme" in "Augustinisme Avicennisant," Will would literally see through a divine "light" reflected through the lower "face" of Anima and *proper* to Anima's lower face, i.e., through the "vis cogitativa" and "vis imaginativa secundum Avicennam." In accord with Avicenna's dictum that "Anima is, as it were a mirror" ("anima quasi speculum"),[26] Will would use two mirrors in the ascent: one outside of himself and reflected by his lower Anima (the "Mirour" of "middelerþe" in 11, l.9), and the other inside himself and reflected by his higher Anima ("as myself in a Mirour" in 15, l.162), his higher Anima having raised the "Mirours" of kynde wit and Clergie about which Ymaginatif speaks in by 12, l.95. Anima's lower face would provide Will's *body* with two types of sensory reasoning: that of Thou3t and that of Ymaginatif. Thus Will would see in the first inner dream his twofold intent reflected in the "Mirour" of Middle Earth (9, l.9): the intent mirrored by human Thou3t, from 11, ll.7-319, and the intent mirrored by Ymaginatif from 11, ll.320-410. Anima's higher face would provide Will's *soul* with the higher reason ("reson," at 15, l.11). By means of the higher reason, Will would see at the culmination of the higher outer dream in 16, ll.1-17, the perfection of Haukyn's power within himself (the fair showing of charity), the perfection of himself as an Avicennan "Tree of Pacience" whose fruit is charity, and the

---

[26] *Liber de anima, IV-V*; p.146, l.9; repeated in Gundissalinus' compendium (Muckle, *Mediaeval Studies*, 93, ll.39-40).

Christian perfection of himself as *"liberum arbitrium"* by Piers Plowman; and, in the inner dream (16, ll.19–167), Will would see through Anima's higher face, Piers Plowman.

In the second type of emphasis, the two outer and inner visions of the first and third visions of the *Vita* would still be connected by the Christianization of Avicenna's "virtus activa," i.e., *"Actiua vita"* or Haukyn (13, 1.224), i.e., by the mediating vision in Passus 13 and 14. But, in this "Augustinisme Avicennisant," the whole psychology would be erected upon the perfection of a rational light and natural love proper to the "vis imaginativa." Ymaginatif would be essential to Will's ascent, for Ymaginatif would teach Will the corporeal reason and corporeal love upon which the rest of the visions of the B-text build from Passus 13 to 17 inclusive.

If, however, Augustinians emphasize the "Augustinisme" in "Augustinisme Avicennisant," then Jean de la Rochelle's *Summa de anima* would conceal Avicenna's psychology of mirrors and faces within the Augustinian "ratio inferior" and "ratio superior," by way of a Divine First Light ("prima lux") Which illuminates the face of the higher Anima but not the face of the lower Anima:[27]

> Intentio mentis duobis modis dicitur scilicet communiter, ut comprehendat vim rationalem secundum partem sui superiorerem et inferiorem. Nam dicit Augustinus, in ratione est quoddam ad superna et coelestia intendens, respectu cuius dicitur sapientia, et quoddam ad transitoria et caduca respiciens, respectu cuius dicitur prudentia, et dividit se ratio in duo, sursum et deorsum. Dicitur ergo mens communiter ad rationem superiorem et inferiorem.
>
> (Solvuntur obiectiones contra immortalitatem). . . distinguendo faciem virtutis intellectivae duplicem, scl. inferiorem et superiorem, inferiorem quae illuminatur et perficitur per comparationem ad sensibilia, prout sunt

---

[27] I quote J. Rohmer, "Sur le doctrine franciscaine des deux faces de l'âme," *Archives d'histoire doctrinale et littéraire du moyen age*, 2 (1927), 74, who quotes the Domenichelli edition of the *Summa de anima* (Bk.2, ch.9, and Bk.1, ch.43, pp.234–5, 189).

Rohmer's study shows how Jean de la Rochelle's interpretation of the *Liber de anima, I-II-III* (Bk.1, ch.5; p.93,1.00–p.94,1.14) builds upon Gundissalinus' earlier interpretation of the passage ("Sur le doctrine," pp.74–5) but how Jean de la Rochelle's interpretation differs ("Sur le doctrine," p.76). Gundissalinus attributes a "light" proper to the "vis imaginativa."

Jean de la Rochelle's ambivalence about the "two faces of the soul" appears in his *Tractatus*, where he first declares it doubtful (p.103, ll.134–7),

> Hoc, intellige, lector, secundum opinionem Auicenna, qui dicit quod animae sunt quasi due facies: una qua conuertitur ut corpus, ut intellectus actiuus; altera qua conuertitur ad Deum, ut intellectus contemplatiuus; quod magnam habet dubitationem (Understand this, reader, according to the thinking of Avicenna who says that the soul has, as it were two faces: one which turns itself to the body as the active intellect, the other which turns itself to God as the contemplative intellect – which has a great doubt),

and then declares it certain (p.140, 1.111).

imaginationes, vel non, in quantum ad superiorem, secundum quam est nobilis perfectio et potissima; haec enim illuminatur a prima veritate. Quantum ergo ad inferiorem indiget sensu et imaginatione, non quantum ad superiorem. Hinc est etiam in phraeneticis et alienatis quod quamvis impediatur virtus intellectiva quantum ad apprehensionem inferiorem, quia uniri debet formis sensibilibus in imaginatione, propter infectionem virtutis imaginativae et confusionem virtutis intellectivae non potest iuvari; tamen secundum faciem superiorem illuminatur aliquando ab irradiatione quae est illi a luce prima, vel a luminariis mediis scl. angelis. Unde et phraenetici prophetant et multa de sublimibus interdum vident, quamvis prohibiti sint ratiocinari de sensibus istis (In common predication, "intent of the mind" refers to two modes, such that the expression includes the rational power in the mind's higher reason and lower reason. For Augustine says that there are [two] somethings in reason: that which intends to the supernal and celestial and, in that regard, is called wisdom, and that which looks to the transitory and mortal, and, in that regard, is called prudence. So reason divides itself into two, a [reason] from above and a [reason] from below. In common predication, then, "mind" refers to higher and lower reason. (Ojections to immortality are resolved). . . by distinguishing a double face of the intellective power, i.e., the lower intellective face and the higher intellective face. The lower face, related to the sensibles which are images, is illuminated and perfected or is not illuminated nor perfected in relation to the higher face. The higher face is the perfection of nobility and the most powerful perfection, for the higher face [of the soul] is illumined by the First Truth. In relation to the lower face, the higher face requires sense and imagination; but the higher face does not need sense and imagination for itself. Thus it is that, even though the intellective power is impeded in its lower apprehension in persons who are either frenetic or ecstatic, the intellective power ought to be joined to sensible images in the imagination but cannot be aided. For then the imaginative power is infected and the intellective power is confused. But the higher face sometimes illumines the intellective power by means of an irradiation from the First Light or from mediate lights, i.e., the angels. In such a situation, even the frenetic prophesy and then see many sights from on high, in spite of the fact that the condition of their senses keeps them from reasoning).

Jean's "Augustinisme" would emphasize Will's intent and virtues (the Christianization of Avicennan "mores") but attribute Will's "witlees" state in 13, 1.1b, to either a frenzy or ecstasy caused by Ymaginatif. Ymaginatif would have a rationality proper to himself, but would acquire it only from the higher "reson" in Anima, in 15, 1.11. Jean de la Rochelle's "Augustinisme" would ignore Ymaginatif's deliberative functions from 11,1.320–12,1.297 ("imaginative power is infected"), downplay the inner dreams ("the frenetic prophesy"), and emphasize the illumination of Anima in Passus 15.

Jean's "Augustinisme" would conceal Avicenna's psychology of prophecy within the three modes of Augustinian vision ("visio corporalis, visio spiritualis" or "imaginaria," and "visio intellectualis"), by paralleling Augustine's three modes of vision to the perfection of the three appetites which make up the Avicennan will (concupiscible, irascible, rational):[28]

> Per tres differentias sic. Aliud est, inquit [Augustinus], nobis, quo corpora sentimus, quod quinque sensibus facimus; aliud, quo non corpora, sed corporum similitudines inspicimus; aliud, quo nec corpora nec corporum similitudines inspicimus; aliud, quo res, quae non habent imagines et similitudines, sicut Deus, et ipsa mens rationalis, et sicut virtutes, idest prudentia, iustitia, charitas, et quaecumque aliae, quas intelligendo discernimus. Primum pertinet ad cognitivam exteriorem, quae dicitur sensitiva exterior; secunda ad sensitivam interiorem, quemadmodum imaginatio; tertiam ad intellectivam. Et secundum hoc distinguit Augustinus tria genera visionum. Primum corporale, quo per sensus corporis corpora sentiuntur. Secundum spirituale, quo corporum similitudines spiritu mentis cernuntur. Spiritus hic dicit interiorem virtutem sensus, qua rerum similitudines imprimuntur. Tertium intellectuale, quo illae res, quae nec sunt corpus, nec corporum similitudines habent, conspiciuntur (Through the three differences thus. Augustine says, there is one thing in us which we make from the five senses to sense bodies. There is another thing in us by which we look into the likenesses of bodies but not the bodies themselves. There is another thing in us by which we look into neither bodies nor the likenesses of bodies. There is another thing in us by which we look into things which have neither images nor likenesses, e.g., God, the rational mind itself, the virtues such as prudence, justice, and whatever others which we discern by an act of understanding. And according to this, Augustine distinguishes three types of vision. The first is corporeal, by which bodies are sensed by means of the senses in the body. The second is spiritual, by which the likenesses of bodies are espied by means of the spirit of the mind. "Spirit" here refers to the interior power of sense by which the likenesses of bodies are impressed. The third is intellectual, by which those things which are neither a body nor have likenesses of bodies are seen).

Augustine's "corporeal vision" would seem to correspond to Avicenna's psychology of sensory perception. Augustine's "spiritual" or "imaginary vision" ("spiritualis" or "imaginaria") would seem to

---

[28] *Summa de anima*, Bk.2, ch.4 (Domenichelli, pp.225-6), reiterated in the *Tractatus*, p.124, ll.54-77.

Although Alastair Minnis suggests a way to apply Augustine's "tria genera visionum" to the *Vita* ("Langland's Ymaginatif and Late Medieval Theories of Imagination," 92-4), Jean de la Rochelle's *Tractatus* (p.124, ll.65-77) and *Summa de anima* (p.225,l.16-p.226,l.1.) do not take up Avicenna's prophetic psychology, even if accomodated to Augustine's three types of vision. According to Jean's interpretation of Augustine, the first type of vision would be vision through Wit ("Primum pertinet ad virtutem cognitiuam exteriorem, que dicitur sensitiua exterior" [the first type pertains to exterior cognitive power which is called the exterior, sensitive power]), and the second type would be through some ME equivalent to the "spiritualis" or "visio imaginaria" (*Tractatus*, p.124, ll.72-8; *Summa de anima*, p.226, l.9: "in visione autem spirituali, sive imaginaria").

correspond to Avicenna's prophecy by the "vis imaginativa."[29] Augustine's "intellectual vision" would seem to correspond to Avicenna's psychology of "holy intellect" ("sanctus intellectus").[30] But Jean finds no vision corresponding to Avicenna's vision by the "vis activa," and mentions no conferral of Avicenna's "virtus sancta."[31] Although Jean discusses the "vis imaginativa secundum Avicennam" in the context of dreams,[32] he makes no reference to Avicenna's paradigm for the perfection of natural prophecy:

1. perfection of the "vis imaginativa"
2. lower inner dream by the lower mirror and face of Anima,
3. perfection of the concupiscible and irascible appetites,
4. perfection of the "vis activa,"
5. vision through "sanctus intellectus,"
6. higher inner dream by the higher mirror and face of Anima,
7. conferral of the "virtus sancta."[33]

Ignoring both Ymaginatif's reasoning and Will's prophetic ascent through Haukyn to Anima, the "Augustinisme Avicennisant" of Jean de la Rochelle does not account for the prophetic psychology in the B-text.

In the question about Ymaginatif's reasoning, Jean would face a problem, argued not by medical doctors or physiologists but by the psychologists and theologians of "Augustinisme Avicennisant." The problem concerns the accommodation of a *prophetic* reason within Avicenna's "virtus animalis" to Augustinian psychology. As we have seen in the Augustinian psychology in the *Benjamin minor*, the concupiscence in the imagination creates vain thoughts; thus, *animal* sensuality would appear to vitiate the true prophetic knowledge of Thouȝt. The notion is consonant with strict "Augustinisme:" God's light permeates the universe, from the firmament, to the angels, and to the reason in man; but divine light does not extend to the reason in the animal sensory imagination, i.e., to the "virtus animalis" and to the "vis imaginativa," so that the sensory reasoning of the animal soul in men impels them to think and do the good. Strict Augustinizers of Avicenna hold that the effects of the original sin so influence the animal Anima that the "virtus animalis" or "vis imaginativa" is incapable of true reasoning.

---

[29] *Liber de anima, IV–V,* p.18,l.51–p.19,l.61; *Summa de anima,* p.226, l.9.
[30] *Liber de anima, IV–V,* p.151, l.84–p.152,l.90.
[31] *Liber de anima, I–II–III,* p.93,l.00–p.94, l.14; see "Introduction," note 35.
[32] *Tractatus,* p.76, ll.238–42, and p.76, l.251 ("sic accidit in sompniis").
[33] For the steps of ascent, see "Introduction: The Perfection of the Depth Psychology of the 'Vis Imaginativa Secundum Avicennam,' " and note 97 in this chapter.

But less strict Augustinizers of Avicenna claim that the sensory reasoning in the animal soul of man is not possessed by concupiscence and that man *as animal* can reason sensorily without sensuality. According to them, the animal powers in the "vis imaginativa secundum Avicennam" never committed the original sin and are, therefore, not subject to the effects of the original sin. The less strict Augustinizers of Avicenna who hold for a strict "vis imaginativa secundum Avicennam" allow rationality to the sensory imagination, if the "virtus animalis" in humans is governed by the reason of the "vis imaginativa."

Let us define their problem in terms of the first vision in the B-text, in order to clarify it. Both groups of Augustinizers of Avicenna would agree that the "vis cogitativa" (Thouȝt) reasons in (Will's) senses. Both would agree that Thouȝt's reasoning in the senses derives from the higher powers of the soul (Anima's function as *"mens* thouȝt," in 15, l.25, of the "R-group" of mss). If we were to apply their agreement to the B-text, we would conclude that it is Anima's illumination which empowers the reasoning in Will's senses and cooperates with Will's concupiscence from at least 11, ll.7–319. But this interpretation would neither explain the power of Ymaginatif's and Kynde's Reson nor Will's *immediate* illumination by the "myȝt" of Wit in Passus 9 nor the immediate illumination by the "myȝt" of Ymaginatif in 12, ll.7, 10. Most significantly, strict "Augustinisme Avicennisant" would not explain how Kynde and Ymaginatif are not subject to that concupiscence in Will which bends Wit's "myȝt" to Will's "likyng" (11, l.45). Kynde's Reson and Ymaginatif exert such rational power upon Will in the inner dream that we can come to only one conclusion: Ymaginatif's deliberative function reasons *outside and beyond the sensory reasoning power of Will's human Anima*. Since the "bisshop" Anima does not include Ymaginatif in his catalogue of powers in 15, ll.22–39, we can only conclude that the reason in Ymaginatif is not subject to the effects of the original passed down to Anima (the human soul) and Will (the human will).

To continue, Jean's problem is not so much with the physiology of Avicenna's "vis imaginativa" as it is with the prophetic psychology which originates in the faculty. In a few lines, Jean's *Tractatus* takes care of the question about the proper ventricle for the "vis imaginativa secundum Avicennam:"[34] Avicenna's medical works locate the "vis

---

[34] To recall Quirk's point (" 'Vis Imaginativa,' " 83, n.3), the "Vis imaginativa" may be located in the front or middle ventricle of Will's brain. Sometimes, the Latin West held that the "vis imaginativa" could be located in any one of the three ventricles of the brain, depending upon the function that it exercised: whether it recalled "intents" (a function of the third ventricle of memory); whether it represented images (a function of the first ventricle of imagination) or whether it judged (a function of the middle ventricle of sensory

imaginativa'' in the front of the brain ventricle, but his *Liber de anima* locates it in the middle ventricle.[35] Although Jean knows that the names for the ''vis imaginativa'' in the Avicenna's medical tracts are different from the names for the same power in the psychological tracts,[36]

> Secunda quidem virtus est, quam medici cogitatiuam vocant, sed philosophi quandoque ymaginativam, quandoque cogitatiuam vocant (The second power is that which the doctors call thought but which the philosophers sometimes call the imaginative power and sometimes call thought),

he uses the expression ''estimatio imaginativa,''[37] so that the two powers (''cogitativa'' and ''imaginativa'') are collapsed into one power called ''estimatio.'' Jean emphasizes physiology and avoids prophetic psychology.

---

reason). Thus R.W. Chambers can hold that Ymaginatif hypostatizes memory (*Man's Unconquerable Mind*, p.139), but R.W. Frank can hold that Ymaginatif hypostatizes the ''sensus communis'' (*Piers Plowman and the Scheme of Salvation*, p.62 and note).

[35] *Tractatus*, p.110,ll.191–p.111,l.221.

[36] *Ibid.*, p.110, ll.191–3. The section is entitled ''De divisione potentiarum anime secundum medicos, primo secundum Iohannitium, postea secundum Auicenna'' (p.103, ll.3–4).

[37] *Tractatus*, p.110, ll.193–5:
> Si enim ei imperauerit virtus estimativa animalis, vocant eam ymaginativam, si autem ei virtus rationalis imperauerit, vocatur cogitativa (If the animal, estimative power commands it, the [doctors or philosophers] call it the imaginative power; if the rational power commands it, it is called the power of thought).

Fazlur Rahman thinks that Avicenna's ''estimativa'' is different from ''imaginativa'' and ''cogitativa'' (''Ibn Sina,'' *A History of Muslim Philosophy*, I, 493–4):
> The first internal sense is *sensus communis* which is the seat of all the senses. It integrates sense data into percepts. . . The second internal sense is the imaginative faculty in so far as it conserves the perceptual images. The third faculty is again imagination in so far as it acts upon these images by combination and separation. In man this faculty is pervaded by reason so that human imagination can deliberate, and is, therefore, the seat of practical intellect. The fourth. . . internal faculty is called *wahm* which passed into the West as *vis estimativa*: it perceives immaterial notions like usefulness and harmfulness, love and hate in material objects. . . The fifth internal sense conserves in memory those notions which are called by him [Avicenna] ''intentions'' [ma 'ani].

Gundissalinus supports this position (*Liber de anima*, IV–V, pp.5–6, ll.60–88, and note to ll.61–7), naming the second internal sense with the terms ''formalis'' or ''imaginatio.'' The third internal sense is named ''vis imaginativa,'' and the fourth, ''aestimativa.'' In the *Compendium de anima*, however, in comments on the same passage in the *Liber de anima*, IV–V (pp.5–6, ll.60–87), Gundissalinus replaces ''vis imaginativa'' with the Aristotelian ''formalis'' or the Augustinian ''imaginatio'' (Muckle, *Mediaeval Studies*, 73, ll.6–26).

The anonymous *Liber de causis primis et secundis* caused more confusion by confusing Avicenna's terms with Augustinian terms. The text not only uses ''imaginatio'' in place of ''vis imaginativa'' (de Vaux, *Notes et textes*, p.138,l.20–p.139,l.5, and n.1) but introduces into the discussion terminology borrowed from Augustine's *De trinitate*, Bk.10, ch.10: ''imaginativa'' is replaced by ''imaginatio,'' ''imaginaria,'' and even ''phantasia imaginaria.'' Gilson sees in the confusion of terms a Christian attempt find ''intellectual light'' in Avicenna's and Augustine's cognitive theories (''Les Sources Gréco-Arabes'', 77–79, 93, 100).

Fortunately, Books 25 and 27 of Vincent of Beauvais' *Speculum Naturale* preserve an account of all this, and tell us why we fruitlessly attempt to find Ymaginatif's rationality in the works of strict Augustinian psychologists.[38] Chapter Two of Book 25 supports our long-held view from H.S.V. Jones that Ymaginatif, the "spokesman of Reason," is analogous to the "imaginatio" of the Augustinian *De spiritu et anima* and, therefore, to the Augustinian tract, the *Benjamin minor*.[39] Chapter Four upholds the Augustinianism in the first section of A.J. Minnis' explanation of Ymaginatif:[40] Will's processes of "studiosa investigatio"

Fazlur Rahman faults psychologists like Jean de la Rochelle for the confusion and conflation of Avicenna's physiology with his psychology ("Ibn Sina," 493-4). G. Verbeke partially agrees, when he points to the Latin terms used to translate from the Arabic, and to Avicenna's various locations of the ventricles ("Introduction," *Liber de anima*, IV-V, pp.49*-59*, and pp.50*-51* and n.174.)

Rahman is convinced that Avicenna's *Kitab al-Nafs*, an abridgement of the psychology in the *Liber de anima* (translated by Rahman as *Avicenna's Psychology* [Oxford: Geoffrey Cumberledge, 1952]), separated the function of the "vis estimativa" from that of the "vis imaginativa" and that the Latin West collapsed them into one faculty (*Avicenna's Psychology*, p.31, ll.12-22, and note on pp.79-83). Rahman disagrees with H.A. Wolfson's statement that the Arabic commentators themselves conflated the "vis estimativa" and the "vis imaginativa" into one faculty called the "vis imaginativa" ("The Internal Senses in Latin, Arabic, and Hebrew Philosophic Texts," 87, 90). G. Verbeke sees Avicenna's own statements as the source of the confusion ("Introduction," p.51*). For the *Liber de anima* itself conflates the "vis imaginativa" and the "vis estimativa" (*Liber de anima*, IV-V, p.79,l.51-p.80,l.54):

> Principia autem quae imperant virtuti desiderativae ad movendum membra sunt aestimatio imaginativa, et aestimatio activa et cupiditas et ira (The [moral] principles which command the desiderative power to move [corporeal] members are imaginative estimation and active estimation and desire and anger).

Avicenna attributed to both the "vis estimativa" and the "vis imaginativa" the power to compare and divide images; that is, the power to deliberate images.

Thomas Aquinas's treatment of the two powers differs from Jean's and Gundissalinus'. In the psychology of the *Summa theologiae* ("Pars Prima," quest.78, art.4, corpus), he equates the Avicennan "vis estimativa" with the "vis imaginativa" in animals other than man: "quae in aliis animalibus dicitur aestimativa naturalis, in homine dicitur *cogitativa*" (What in other animals is called the power of natural estimation is, in man, called the power of thought). "Cogitativa" is "ratio particularis," located in the middle ventricle of the brain, and is "particularis" in relation to "ratio universalis" of the intellect. In man, the "imaginativa" and "imaginatio" are the same faculty (*Ibid.*, corpus, "Avicenna vero"), so that there are only four powers in the sensory soul of man: common sense, the imagination, the estimative power and the memorative power (*Ibid*, corpus, conclusion). Although in the tract on prophecy in the same *Summa* ("Secunda Secundae," quest.172, art.1, corpus, "Sed quia verius") and in the *Quaestiones Disputatae: De Veritate* (quest.12, art.3) Thomas does allows for a naturally prophetic "vis imaginativa," he does not explain the rationality in the naturally prophetic "vis imaginativa."

[38] (Douai-Graz, 1, 1775-1840, 1917-92). As is to be expected, Book 26, the discussion of dreams and prophecy, disguises the prophetic functions of the "vis imaginativa secundum Avicennam" under Augustinian language, because of the censure of Avicenna's prophetic psychology (Douai-Graz, 1, 1841-1916).

[39] (Douai-Graz, 1, 1776-77), and "Imaginatif in *Piers Plowman*," *JEGP*, 13(1914), 584, 587.

[40] (Douai-Graz, 1, 1777-78), and "Langland's Ymaginatif and Late-medieval Theories of Imagination," 75-6, 79-80.

(our Dame Studie) and "cogitatio" (our Thouȝt) lead to "imaginatio" (allegedly our Ymaginatif), for "imagination begets knowledge" ("Imaginatio [parit] cognitionem") by showing the moral truth derived from study and thought. In the same chapter, however, Vincent speaks about the strict Augustinian prejudice against a rationality in the imagination, a prejudice which would contradict Jones' theory of a rational "imaginatio" based upon the Augustinian psychology of the Victorines. Sensuality ("sensualitas") impedes the efforts of "studium" and "cogitatio," because the senses contain both the instrument of sensuality and the beginnings of "imaginatio:"

> In sensu quidem instrumentum est sensualitatis, & origo imaginationis (In the sense is the instrument of sensuality and also the origin of the imagination).[41]

[41] Augustine, *De trinitate*, as quoted by Phillip the Chancellor, an English theologian of the same period (E 1236), in Dom O. Lottin, "Les mouvements premiers de l'appétit sensitif de Pierre Lombard à Saint Thomas d'Aquin," *Problèmes de morale*, Psychologie et morale aux XIIᵉ et XIIIᵉ siècles (Louvain: Abbaye du Mont César, 1948), II, pt.1, 538, ll.13–24):

> Dicit enim Augustinus quod motus nobis pecoribusque communis est seclusus est a ratione sapientie. . . [Augustinus] in libro 12 de Trinitate. . . segregat sensualitatem a ratione, ponens eam nobis et brutis communem (Augustine says that the movement common to us and the animals is cut off from the reason of wisdom. . . In Bk. 12 of *On the Trinity* he separates sensuality from reason, claiming that sensuality is common to us and the brutes).

Influenced by Aristotle, Phillip the Chancellor nevertheless attributes reasoning power to the sensory imagination (a continuation of the same quotation):

> Ymaginatio a qua per intellectum abstrahentem abstrahuntur species a phantasmatibus est speciei in pha[n]tasmate (The imagination, by which the intellectual likenesses are abstracted through the agent intellect, has the [same] intellectual likeness in the phantasm).

The imagination contains "intellectual likenesses," called "species."

The terms are derived from commentaries on Aristotle's *De anima*, Bk.3, ch.5 (430a, ll.10–7), e.g., Averroes' (*Averrois Cordvbensis Commentarium Magnum in Aristotelis De Anima Libros*, 439, ll.71–82):

> Et fuit necesse attribuere has duas actiones anime in nobis, scilicet recipere intellectum et facere eum,. . . propter hoc quia hee due actiones reducte sunt ad nostram voluntatem, scilicet abstrahere intellecta et intelligere ea. Abstrahere enim nichil est aliud quam facere intentiones ymaginatas intellectas in actu postquam erant in potentia; intelligere autem nichil est quam recipere has intentiones. Cum enim invenimus idem transferri in suo esse de ordine ad ordinem, scilicet intentiones ymaginatas, diximus quod necesse est ut hoc sit a causa agenti et recipienti. Recipiens est materialis, et agens est efficiens (And it was necessary to attribute these two acts to the Anima in us, i.e., to receive intelligence and to make intelligence. . ., for the reason that these two acts are brought into our will, i.e., to abstract things understood and to understand the things understood. To abstract is nothing more than to make the intentions imagined into intentions actually understood, after the intentions were in potency. To understand is nothing more than to receive these intentions. For, when we have discovered the same imagined intentions transferred from one order of actuality to another

Chapters 5–7 explain the confusion of Avicenna's "vis imaginativa" with "sensus communis," "imaginatio," "phantasia," "aestimativa," and "memorativa."[42] Chapter 86 of Book 25 gives the explanation of the "vis imaginativa," according to the "medici:"[43] the "vis imaginativa" in the frontal cavity of the brain, and the "vis cogitativa" in the middle ventricle of the brain. Anatomical locations explain the functions of the interior senses: the front ventricle represents images of things no longer present to the eye; the middle ventricle discerns between true/false and good/bad of images; and the rear ventricle stores the images. In chapter 86, we find sufficient reason to explain Ymaginatif as representation (Jones), as reason (Jones), as memory (R.W. Chambers). So far, Vincent's explanation of the reasoning in the "vis imaginativa" conveniently summarizes all of our conflicting explanations of the meaning and function of Ymaginatif in the B-text of *Piers Plowman*.

In the second chapter of Book 27,[44] Vincent of Beauvais states that strict Augustinians allow no reasoning in the sensory imagination, and quotes Jean de la Rochelle's *Tractatus* as proof:[45]

De confusione et varietate distinctione virium animae (Concerning the confusion and variety of the distinctions of the power of the soul).

order of actuality, we have said that the transfer necessarily follows from a cause which is an agent and a cause which is a receiver. The receiver is the material [intellect], and the agent is the active [intellect].

That is, from the "matter" in the images represented by Thou3t and Ymaginatif in Passus 9–12, the reason in the intellect, i.e., Anima as reason in Passus 15, l.11, would abstract "intellectual likenesses." "Abstract" means that Anima would remove the "likenesses" from the "matter" of images, correctly formed in Will's sensory imagination by Ymaginatif, and make the corporeal "likenesses" into non-corporeal or "intellectual likenesses." The Chancellor's argues that, since the "intellectual likeness" is the same likeness which the intellect abstracts, the imagination must be capable of representing a true likeness. If the sensory imagination derives a true likeness from things sensed, there must be rationality in the imagination. The truth of a concept cannot be derived from the sensibles unless there is reasoning in the sensibles. That is, Ymaginatif discovers true "species" for Will in the "my3t" of Wit. If "nil cognitum nisi prius fuerit in sensu," the "craft" in Will's "cors" to know kyndely and to know with certainty originates in Ymaginatif's ability to find truth-in-images received from Wit. The "craft" does not originate in Will's higher Anima but in Will's "cors." Contrary to the function of "imaginatio" in the *Benjamin minor* (ME *Tretys of the Stodye of Wisdom Pat Men Clepen Beniamyn*), this "imaginatio" represents true likenesses which do not jangle Will's imagination.

[42] (Douai-Graz, 1, 1778–79).

[43] Chapters 4–49 of Book 27 recapitulate almost every contemporary interpretation of Ymaginatif, e.g., the summary given by Joseph Wittig ("Elements," 264): "He (Ymaginatif) has been regarded as a spokesman for reason, as *imago Dei*, as *intellectus agens*, as 'the capacity to profit from experience,' and as the more ordinary *sensus communis*."

[44] (Douai-Graz, 1, 1829).

[45] (Douai-Graz, 1, 1918B).

Vincent and Jean trace the problem to pseudo-Augustine's *De spiritu et anima*:

> In the assignment of the powers of the soul, the *Liber de anima et spiritu* has confused the parts [of the soul] (in assignatione virium animae videtur liber de anima et spiritu partes confundere).

This Augustinian tract confounded the powers of the "vis animalis" with the powers of the "vis rationalis," i.e., the "parts" of Avicenna's animal soul with the "parts" of Avicenna's rational soul. (Like Aristotle, Avicenna distinguishes three "vires" or "animae" or "spiritus" or "souls" in man: the vegetable soul [by which man is comparable to a tree], the animal soul [by which man is comparable to other animals], the rational soul [by which man is comparable to angels]). Although Avicenna allows reasoning to the animal Anima, the strict Augustinians allow no sensory knowledge to the animal Anima. To repeat, strict Augustinians think that brutish knowledge is sensual knowledge.

Therefore and finally, Vincent and Jean state the fundamental objection of the strict "Augustinisme" in the *De spiritu et anima* to Avicenna's "vis imaginativa:"[46]

> Dubitatur etiam de hoc, quod videtur sub virtute rationali comprehendere sensum et imaginationem; unde dicit in eodem libro [*De spiritu et anima*], quod ex rationabilitate omnis sensus anime oritur (One may doubt the seeming unity of sense and imagination under the power of rationality. Hence, [Augustine] says in the same book that every sense in Anima arises out of the power to reason).

Strict Augustinians held that "sensus" were subject to "sensualitas;" sensuality binds man to brute, and, therefore, cannot be rational. Jean's *Tractatus*, however, allowed a rationality proper to and within Avicenna's "vis imaginativa," in as much as it judges the occult goodness and badness in the images of things desired by the concupiscible appetite or repelled by the irascible appetite.[47] Even more

[46] Beginning, "Dubitare potest aliquis de assignatione Augustini" (*Tractatus*, p.127, ll.157–68), with reference to the *De spiritu et anima* (p.127, l.156).
[47] *Speculum Naturale*, ibid.; *Tractatus*, p.127, ll.169–70.
   Although Jean de la Rochelle ascribes the *De spiritu et anima* to Augustine, Vincent of Beauvais ascribes it to Hugh of St. Victor (*Speculum Naturale*, Bk. 25, chs. 1–4 [Douai-Graz, 1, 1775–78]). For the medical significance of these attributions, see L. Norpoth, *Der pseudo-augustinische Traktat: de spiritu et anima* (Cologne: Institüt für Geschichte der Medezin, 1971), pp.47–72. The work has been generally ascribed to Alcher of Clairvaux on the authority of P. Fournier's article "Alcher" (*Dictionnaire d'Histoire et de Géographie Ecclésiastiques* [Paris: Letouzey et Ané,, 1912–); see J.M. Canivez, "Alcher" (*Dictionnaire de Spiritualité Ascétique et Mystique*, ed. M. Viller, F. Cavallera, J. Guibert [Paris: Gabriel Beauchesne, 1937–], I, 294–5; and P. Glorieux, "Pour Revaloriser Migne: Tables Rectificatives," *Mélanges de Science Religeuse*, 9[1952], Suppl., 27. The most recent discussion by Gaetano Raciti ("L'Autore del '*De spiritu et anima*,' " *Rivista di Filosofia Neo-*

specifically, the "vis imaginativa" instinctually judges the concupiscibles or sensuality connoted by Augustine's "appetite" or John Damascene's "appetite."[48] The question to be resolved was this: could the "vis imaginativa," a power in brutes, repress sensuality? In reply, Vincent quotes the opinion of Jean de la Rochelle, the opinion quoted at the beginning of chapter two of this book.[49] As long as Jean de la Rochelle and Gundissalinus' *Compendium de anima* transmit only the medical interpretation of the "vis imaginativa secundum Avicennam,"[50] there would be no rational light proper to Ymaginatif's deliberations. The prophetic psychology would be suppressed.

In the fourth part of the *Tractatus*, "De diuisione potentiarum anime, quibus corpori commiscetur secundum Augustinum," Jean searches through the *De spiritu et anima* to find how the rationality of a "vis imaginativa secundum Avicennam" may be squared with pseudo-

---

Scolastica, 53[1961], 385–401) demonstrates that the *De spiritu et anima* was not the work of any of the authors mentioned above.

48 *Tractatus*, p.77,ll.296–p.77, l.313.

49 See chapter two, note two, and the *Tractatus*, p.79, ll.356–362; p.98, l.993.

50 *Tractatus*, p.79, ll.356–62; p.98, l.993, quoted in Vincent of Beauvais (*Speculum Naturale*, Bk.27, ch.10 [Douai-Graz, 1, 1924AB]); in some texts of the *Compendium de anima* (Muckle, *Mediaeval Studies*, p.73, ll.25–6), the Augustinian "imaginaria" replaces the Avicennan "imaginativa:"

> in quantum vero illi imperat virtus animalis vocatur imaginativa [imaginaria] (when commanded by the animal power, it is called the imaginative [imaginary] power).

Both Jean de la Rochelle and Vincent of Beauvais refer to the chapter, "De virtutibus animalibus comprehendentibus," in Avicenna's medical work, translated by Gerard of Cremona as *Avicenna Arabum Medicorum Principis Canon Medicinae*, Bk.1, Fen.1, Doctrina 6, ch.5 [Venice: Apud Iuntas, 1595], 1, 75¹, ll.55–63):

> Et secundum quidem est virtus, quam medici vocant cogitatiuam sed certificatores quandoque imaginativam, quandoque cogitatiuam. Si enim imperauerit ei uirtus existimatiua animalis, quam postea nominabimus, & ipsam ad suam peruenerit comparationem, vocant eam imaginatiuam. Et si virtus rationalis ei imperauerit, & reduxerit eam ad illud, quod ei prodest, vocatur virtus cogitatiua (And the second [of the interior powers] is a power which the medical doctors call thought but which the philosophers sometimes call the imaginative power and sometimes call thought. For, if the estimative power of the animal soul (which we shall name presently) commands the second power and brings the second power to compare [and divide images] by estimation, the philosophers call it the imaginative power. And if the rational power commands the second power and brings it back to purposes useful to the rational power, it is called the power of thought).

The "medici" and Avicenna's *Canon medicinae* combine the "vis cogitativa" and "vis imaginativa" and "vis estimativa" into one faculty called the "vis cogitativa," when they discuss physiology. When they discuss psychology, however, the philosophers ("certificatores") and Avicenna's *Liber de anima* distinguish the "vis cogitativa" from the "vis imaginativa." Avicenna's *Canon medicinae* discusses the physiology of these faculties; Avicenna's *Liber de anima* and *Philosophia prima* address the non-sensory and prophetic powers of the "vis imaginativa" (Ymaginatif) or the "vis cogitativa" (Thou3t) or the "appetitus concupiscibilis" and "irascibilis" (Will).

Augustine's ideas about rationality in the sensory imagination, explained in the first part, "De diuisione potentiarum anime secundum philosophos, specialiter Auicennam."[51] Avicenna's "vis imaginativa" becomes only the "imaginatio" (the interior sense which stores images and does not reason-in-images):[52]

> Anima, sicut dicit Augustinus in libro *De spiritu et anima*. . . habet vires, quibus corpori commiscetur, id est unitur. Vires anime. . .sunt tres: prima est naturalis, secunda est vitalis, tertia animalis. . . Vis animalis est in cerebro. . . Tres namque sunt ventriculi cerebri, unus anterior, a quo omnis sensus, unus exterior, a quo omnis motus, tertius inter utrumque medius, id est rationalis. . . In prima parte cerebri vis animalis vocatur fantastica, id est ymaginativa, quia in ea rerum ymagines et similitudines imprimuntur (The soul, as Augustine says in his *De spiritu et anima* [chs.20–22] has three powers by which it is mingled or united with the body. The powers of the soul are three: the first is natural, the second is vital, the third is animal. The animal power is in the brain. There are three ventricles in the brain, one in front (from which comes all sense), the second in the back (from which comes all motion), and the third midway between the first two, that is, the rational. In the first part of the brain the animal power is called the fantastical, that is, the imaginative, because the images and likenesses of objects are impressed in it).

A subtle light diffuses from the middle ventricle of the brain to the five exterior senses,[53] but the "vis imaginativa" only represents images. Pseudo-Augustine's "Augustinisme" does not permit reasoning in the "virtus animalis."

Therefore, when Vincent of Beauvais proceeds to his discussion of prophecy in Bk.26, chs.52–111,[54] the discussion adapts Aristotle's alleged psychology of dreams to Jean de la Rochelle's "Augustinisme Avicennisant," with minimal reference to Avicenna's psychology. Chapter 52 discusses prophecy in the context of Aristotle's alleged seven questions in "De somnio" (Aristotle's one tract separated into two tracts, *De somniis* and *De divinatione per somnium*, with the "questions" stated at the end of ch.2 of *De divinatione per somnium* [464b, ll.19–22]). Vincent attributes to Avicenna's "vis imaginativa" the power to interpret a prophetic dream, as Aristotle defines a prophetic dream:[55]

> Qvarta quaestio Arist. est, vtrum futura contingat in somnio praevidere (Aristotle's fourth question is whether it happens that the future is foreseen in dreams).[56]

---

51 *Tractatus*, pp.70,ll.64–5, 76, 1.242.
52 *Ibid.*, p.122,l.5–p.123,l.42 passim.
53 *Ibid.*, p.123, ll.27–35.
54 (Douai-Graz, 1, 1871B–1916E).
55 Bk.26, ch.52 (Douai-Graz, 1, 1871B).
56 Bk.26, ch.52 (Douai-Graz, 1, 1871CD), quoting directly from the *Liber de anima, IV–V*, Bk.4, ch.2; p.32; ll.39–46. In such dreams as occur just before daybreak, the "vis

Ymaginatif would have, therefore, the "scientia somnialis quae habetur per proprietates imaginum apparentium" (the science of dreams, possessed by the properties of the images which appear).[57] Then Vincent quotes Jean de la Rochelle's *Summa de anima*, in order to reconcile the psychology of dreams in the *De spiritu et anima* with Avicenna's psychology of sensory vision by angels:[58]

> Notanda etiam est differentia quantum ad causam visionum in somniis. Causa enim visionum duplex est, intrinseca et extrinseca. Intrinseca vero duplex est; curiositas animae, et appetitus corporis. Unde Augustinus: Sunt multa visa usitata, quae vel a spiritu nostro multipliciter existunt, vel ex corpore quodam modo surgunt. Ex spiritu secundum studia, quae quisque exercuit et solitas artes, similitudines apparent. . .. Nam, sicut dicit Augustinus: Humanum spiritum aliquando bonus assumit spiritus, aliquando malus, nec facile discerni potest a quo spiritu assumatur quantum ad visionem, his quia bonus instruit, malus fallit. Cum enim bono spiritu assumitur anima, falli non potest, quia sancti angeli miris modis visa sua quadam facili et praepotenti mutatione vel mixtione, nostra faciunt, et visionem suam quodam ineffabili modo in spiritu nostro informant; et hoc est in ipsa virtute imaginationis. . . Et intellige, quod illud assumere, nihil aliud est quam in virtute imaginaria similitudines rerum imprimere, sive praesentare, et per has ad cognitionem occultorum levare. . . Sufficiant ergo quae dicta sunt de visionibus somniorum, ut plenius manifestentur operationes virtutis imaginationis, et virtutis imaginativae (We ought to observe the differences in the cause of visions in dreams. There is a twofold cause of visions, intrinsic and extrinsic. The intrinsic cause is itself twofold: the curiosity of the soul and the appetite of the body. Hence, Augustine [says] that we see many things which we are accustomed to, for either the accustomed things have a many-faceted being in our own spirit or they arise from our body in some fashion. The liknesses [of dreams] appear from our own spirit, exercised in study and in habitual practices. Hence, Augustine says that sometimes a good spirit and sometimes a bad spirit takes over the human spirit, and that one cannot easily discern which spirit takes over the vision. To this person, the spirit is good, because the spirit instructs; to that person, the spirit is bad, because the spirit deceives. When Anima is taken over by a good spirit, Anima cannot be deceived, because the holy angels make our sights over into their sights by a kind of easy and forceful transformation or blending, in a marvellous fashion. Then [the holy angels] inform us in our own spirit with their vision in a kind of inarticulable manner. And this is [done] in the power of the imagination itself. Please understand that for them to take over the imagination is nothing other than their impressing or re-

cogitativa" does not impede the prophetic power of the "vis imaginativa." Then the "servitium imaginativae quo servit animae est quale melius esse potest" (the imaginative power serves Anima as best as it can).
[57] Bk.26, ch.52 (Douai-Graz, 1, 1871E).
[58] (Douai-Graz, 1, 1877BC), and the *Summa de anima*, ch.25 (Domenichelli, pp.266–7), where Jean compares Avicenna's prophetic dreams with pseudo-Augustine's prophetic dreams, and glosses quotations taken from the *De spiritu et anima*, chs.25 and 27 (*PL*, 40, 798–9).

presenting the likenesses of things in the imaginative power so as to elevate us to a knowledge of the occult through the likenesses. Let these words about the visions in dreams suffice, in order that the functions of the power of imagination and the imaginative power may be more fully explained).

According to this "Augustinisme Avicennisant," Ymaginatif would be the good "angel" in Will's "imaginative power," who, having discerned the occult good and bad in Will's spirit, answers to Will's curiosity and sensuality ("appetite of the body").[59]

If we accept Vincent of Beauvais' account of the problems related to the transmission of the "vis imaginativa secundum Avicennam," we see that, after 1366, the *PP*-poet kept some of Jean de la Rochelle's "Augustinisme" (e.g., Will's curiosity and sensuality). But the poet restored the "Avicennisme" hidden by Jean de la Rochelle (e.g., the prophetic rationality of Ymaginatif, the inner dreams, the images becoming speakers, the prominence of Kynde, the unity of Will's "my3t" with Kynde's "my3t").

Our long-held opinion about Ymaginatif is born out. He is the "spokesman of Reason." But our long-held source for Ymaginatif's deliberative powers ("Augustinisme" in either the *Benjamin minor* or the *De spiritu et anima*) is doubtful. Ymaginatif's reasoning powers stem from a prophetic psychology. The "Augustinisme Avicennisant" in the B-text is more "Avicennisme" than "Augustinisme."

"Augustinisme Avicennisant" in England and in Worcester

To understand why Ymaginatif's deliberative functions and two inner dreams are unique to the B-text, we must now understand the invention of "Augustinisme Avicenissant" around the 1230's in England, especially in the environs of Worcester and the Midlands of England. Although we are not sure that *MS Q 81* was in Worcester in the fourteenth-century,[60] the ms preserves a thirteenth-century copy of the Gundissalinus translation of Avicenna's *Liber de anima* (fols.28–41).[61] On

---

[59] Ymaginatif would possess the "discernment" of occult "spirits," prized by the medieval mystics. For the mystical applications of the "vis imaginativa secundum Avicennam," see Louis Gardet (*La Connaissance Mystique chez Ibn Sina et Ses Présupposés Philosphiques* [Cairo: Institut Francais d'Archéologie Orientale du Caire, 1952], pp.43–9; and his *La Pensée Religeuse d'Avicenne*, pp.150–96).
[60] N.R. Ker, *Medieval Libraries of Great Britain: A List of Surviving Books*, 2 ed. (London: Offices of the Royal Historical Society, 1964), p.214. See "Introduction," note 26.
[61] Described in the *Catalogue of Manuscripts Preserved in the Chapter Library of Worcester Cathedral*, by J.K. Floyer and S.G. Hamilton (Oxford: James Parker & Co., 1906),

fol.56^{r1} of *Worcester MS Q 81*, the nine remaining lines of the tract (whose Incipit is "Principium principiorum est Deus gloriosus et excelsus") suggest to us that the environs of Worcester was a place where the "vis imaginativa secundum Avicennam" and "Augustinisme Avicennisant" were so well known that the rest of the tract could be omitted.[62] Chapter 7 of the excised tract assumes that the reader knows the censured Metaphysics of Avicenna's psychology of prophecy by the "vis imaginativa" or "virtus animalis."[63] At the beginning of chapter 7, the anonymous author simply declares that he does not teach Avicenna's

pp.150–152, and, more recently by M.T. d'Alverny, "Bibliotheca Capituli Q.81: Codex Wigornensis: Avicenna Latinus," *Archives d'Histoire Doctrinale et Littéraire de Moyen Age*, 32(1965), 297–302.

[62] Only these lines remain (fol.56):

> Principium principiorum est deus gloriosus et excelsus cujus entitas est ineffabilis et unitas indivisibilis. . . secundum quam et in quam est omne esse et omnis unitas habens fixionem.

See the description in M.T. d'Alverny, "Bibliotheca Capituli Q.81: Codex Wigornensis: Avicenna Latinus," 298, under "Liber de causis primis et secundis." After an interval of approximately three spaces, the scribe or author inserts an explanatory comment:

> Habitudines earum et quae aequivalent in illis rationes essentiales re propter similaritatem (Their relationships and what the equivalent essential reasoning is in them "in re" because of their similarity).

The comment introduces the next tract, entitled "Dionisius in libro de Diuinis Nominibus," excised at the end of folio 56^r. The tract was used to link Avicenna's theories to the recognized authority of pseudo-Dionysius (see Jean de la Rochelle's *Tractatus*, p.92, ll.762-4, and note a; and Etienne Gilson, "Les sources Gréco-Arabes de l'Augustinisme Avicennisant," 46-8, 71-7, 80-111).

"Principium principiorum" is one of the important witnesses to "Augustinisme Avicennisant." Fr. Roland de Vaux's edition of it as the *Liber de causis primis et secundis* (*Notes et textes*, pp. 88–140), supplements the sixteenth-century edition of it, published as the *Liber Avicenne in primis et secundis substantiis et de fluxu entis*, (fol.64^{v1}–67^{v2} of the Venice, 1508 edition of Avicenna's works, entitled *Avicenne perhypatetici philosophi ac medicorum facile primi opera*. . . [repr. Minerva, 1961]). Although close enough to pseudo-Aristotle's *Liber de causis* to quote it and be confused with it, the *Liber de causis primis et secundis*, like the *Liber de causis* seems to be anonymous, though sometimes attributed to Gundissalinus. The Augustinian Canon who edited it in the sixteenth century, Caecilius Fabrianensis, thought it to be the work of Avicenna himself, as is evident from his title.

The significance of the "Principium principiorum" is that chapter seven of the tract refutes Avicenna's "unity of intelligences" by disjoining the human Anima from the celestial Anima (*Notes et textes*, 116, ll.13-3, and note 2) and that chapter nine accomodates Avicenna to Augustine by a common "light of intelligence" ("intelligentia. . .est lumini primo similius," *Ibid.*, 124, ll.1-2). The censured metaphysics of Avicenna are converted into the mystical hierarchies of knowledge in pseudo-Dionysius (*Notes et textes*, p.116, ll.13-9, and note 2). According to R. de Vaux (*Notes et textes*, 141-6), Ch.10 of the anonymous *Liber de causis primis et secundis* contains the same Avicennan materials as Chapter 10 of Gundissalinus' compendium *De anima*, also written to reconcile Avicenna with Augustine (*Notes et textes*, 147–78). Although there are questions about the authorship of the compendium (de Vaux, *Notes et textes*, 66, n.6, and 141-6; and M. Alonso Alonso, *Temas Filosoficos Medievales* (Ibn Dawud Y Gundisalvo) [Madrid: Universidad Pontificia Comillas, 1959], pp.17–60), this work contains a brief of all the Avicennan prophetic theory so far discussed and to be discussed.

[63] See the *Liber de causis primis et secundis et de fluxu entis* (*Notes et textes*, 116, ll.13-9, and note 2) for the verbal parallels to this passage in Avicenna's *Philosophia prima*.

psychology of the unity of intellects but teaches pseudo-Dionysius' mystical psychology of the unity of intellect.[64] Therefore, his concept of a prophetic "virtus animalis," the power which enables Ymaginatif, is as orthodox as that of Dionysius the Areopagite. In chapter 10, the author shows how divine illumination permeates sensory reason, rational reason and intellectual reason, according to theory of immediate divine illumination expounded by Augustine in the *Soliloquies*.[65] Converting Augustine's "vis cogitativa" into Avicenna's "vis cogitativa" *and* "imaginativa,"[66] the anonymous author concludes the tract, claiming that the two sources of sensory reasoning in Avicenna's psychology (the "vis cogitativa" and the "vis imaginativa") are compatible with Augustine's doctrine of sensory vision and prophecy:[67]

> Si autem convertatur [vis imaginaria] ad eam [vis imaginativa] per voluntatem, sequitur visio intrinseca, et propter hoc credimus cogitationis radices esse duas, sed non simul (If, however, the power of the imagination is converted to the imaginative power by will, interior vision follows. On account of this, we believe that there are two roots of thought, although the roots are separate).

This tract would attribute a rationality proper to Ymaginatif, would describe how Ymaginatif opposes Thou3t, and describe Avicenna's psychology in the terms of pseudo-Dionysius' Metaphsics and Augustinian psychology. The evidence in *Worcester MS Q 81* points to a prophetic psychology more Avicennan than Augustinian in the environs of Worcester, if the manuscript was in the Worcester Cathedral Library in the fourteenth century.

More important to the English provenance of Ymaginatif in the B-text is the evidence provided by an anonymous tract in *Worcester MS F 57*. Titled "De potentiis anime et obiectis," the anonymous tract has been edited by Fr. Daniel Callus who found two other copies of it in Balliol College, Oxford and in Lincoln Cathedral.[68] Not only was this tract in

---

64 *Ibid.*, 117, ll.4–12.
65 *Ibid.*, 128, ll.12–3; 132, ll.10–20, and note 1.
66 *Ibid.*, 138, ll.20–3.
67 *Ibid.*, 139, ll.2–5.
68 See "Introduction," notes 13 and 14. According to Fr. Callus ("Powers of the Soul," 131), Jean de la Rochelle was "the first to give a systematic classification of the powers of the soul," and used the anonymous tract, possibly the copy in *Worcester MS F 57*, to reconcile Avicenna's theories of prophecy with those of the followers of St. Augustine ("Powers of the Soul," 131–132, 140–145). "Written. . . in a thirteenth-century English hand," the tract is "survival of the medieval Benedictine Priory" ("Powers of the Soul," 136; Ker, *Medieval Libraries*, p.211). Fr. Callus gives a detailed description of the two other copies in Lincoln Cathedral and in Balliol College on pp.132–6. In his article, "A propos de Jean de la Rochelle" (*Problèmes d'Histoire Littéraire de 1160 à 1300*, Psychologie et morale aux XIIe et XIIIe siècles, VI, 190 [Gembloux: J. Duculot, 1960]), Dom Odon Lottin quotes *Worcester MS F 57*.

the Worcester Cathedral Library in the fourteenth century; but, according to Fr. Callus, it was the earliest tract to reconcile Avicenna's psychology with Augustine's psychology. For Jean de la Rochelle used the anonymous tract, to compose his authoritative *Tractatus de divisione multiplici potentiarum animae* (A Discussion of the many divisions of the powers of the soul) and his *Summa de anima*, both early works of "Augustinisme Avicennisant" dating from the 1230's. Fr. Callus' discovery means that *Christian* prophecy by the "vis imaginativa secundum Avicennam" originated in the environs of Worcester, or Oxford or Lincoln, and that Jean de la Rochelle used the tract to disseminate Avicenna's psychology in France.

Avicenna's prophetic psychology of the "vis imaginativa" came to the Christian and Latin West by way of Toledo; but the "Augustinisme Avicennisant," peculiar to Will's prophetic ascent in the B-text of *Piers Plowman*, originated in England. From *Worcester MS Q 81* (possibly) and *F 57*, we surmise how the "vis imaginativa secundum Avicennam" was baptized into the concepts and terms of St. Augustine's "imaginatio," how an English "Augustinisme Avicennisant" originated, and how the *PP*-poet revived the deliberative and prophetic psychology of the "vis imaginativa secundum Avicennam" in the B-text, after 1366. Between 1150 and 1250, four other Latin texts converted Avicenna's psychology of natural prophecy to "Augustinisme:"[69]

1. Gundissalinus' translation of Al-Ghazali's *Maqasid al-Falasifah* (entitled in the printing of Avicenna's *Opera* [Venice, 1508], *Logica et Philosophia Algazelis Arabis*, and contained in *MS Q 81* [fols. 94–6, 99–104] of the Worcester Cathedral Library);
2. a *Compendium de anima*, composed by the Archdeacon himself to reconcile Avicenna's theories with Christian thinking;[70]
3. the anonymous *Liber Avicenne, in primis et secundis substantiis et de fluxu entis*, truncated in *Worcester MS Q 81*, fol.56;
4. the anonymous tract in Worcester *MS F 57* (fols. 174^{r1}–177^{v1}).

If *Worcester MS Q 81* was at Worcester in the fourteenth century, the *PP*-poet had at his disposal sufficient tracts to convert the "vis imaginativa secundum Avicennam" into the Christian Ymaginatif of the B-text. Since the anonymous tract in *Worcester MS F 57* was at Worcester in the fourteenth century,[71] at least one copy of the tract links "Augustinisme

---

[69] For the influence of first three of these texts up to the beginnings of the fourteenth century in England, see A. Badawi, "L'influence de la psychologie d'Ibn Sina sur le moyen age Latin" (*Histoire de la Philosophie en Islam* [Paris: J. Vrin, 1972], 2, 692–695).

[70] To repeat, *Worcester MS Q 81* does not contain the compendium, but does contain the Incipit, "Principium principiorum est deus gloriosus et excelsus," chapter 10 of which contains the same materials as ch.10 of the compendium.

[71] Ker, *Medieval Libraries*, p.211.

Avicennisant" to the environs of the Malvern Hills,[72] and the other two copies of the tract link the invention of "Augustinisme Avicennisant" to thirteenth-century England. If the *PP*-poet conceived the B-text of *Piers Plowman* near the Malvern Hills after 1366,[73] then he had nearby, in at least one of the two Worcester mss, the means to conceive Ymaginatif's deliberative functions and prophetic powers, and to convert this Avicennan hypostasis to Christian prophecy.

The English manuscripts reach to the heart of our concern with the Reson in Ymaginatif and to the heart of the medieval concern with the reason in the "vis imaginativa secundum Avicennam." Our critical problems with Ymaginatif's Reson and prophecy are the same problems that the Latin West had with Ymaginatif's Reson and prophecy. How is the sensory imagination rational? Why is the sensory imagination prophetic? The "Augustinisme Avicennisant" in manuscripts in England answer the two questions that Quirk and Bloomfield raise: why the "vis imaginativa secundum Avicennam" entered the Latin West hidden in the concepts and terms of St. Augustine's psychology, and how the "vis imaginativa secundum Avicennam" became a force in the Christian psychology of prophecy. An answer to the first question, supplied by the anonymous tract in *Worcester MS F 57*, leads to an answer to the second, also supplied by the same tract.

How is the imagination rational? The "Augustinisme Avicennisant" in the anonymous "De potentiis animae et obiectis" answers, by describing how Avicenna's psychology of Ymaginatif is an answer to Will's Augustinian sensuality:[74]

---

[72] Although the two other copies of the tract at Lincoln Cathedral and Balliol College, Oxford, contain the same text up to "Quod potest videri in sermone Domini in monte" ("Powers of the Soul," 165, 1.9–10), only the Worcester copy of the tract has a continuation significant to the second inner dream in the B-text of *Piers Plowman*. The continuation contains and describes the Latin epithets describing the three props which Piers Plowman uses to prop up the Tree of Trinite in 16, ll.30, 36, 50–2: "potentia, scientia, voluntas" ("Powers of the Soul," 170, 1.18). These are the *one* grace ("gratia") by which the three powers in Anima ("anima rationalis") imitate the Trinity in God ("Powers of the Soul," 170, ll.17–9):

> Tres enim sunt secundum que imitatur summam trinitatem anima rationalis, scilicet potentia, scientia voluntas (For there are three [powers] according to which the rational Anima imitates the highest Trinity: power, science and will).

See "Introduction," notes 26 and 32.

[73] Prologue, 1.5; 7, 1.147; Walter W. Skeat, *The Vision of William Concerning Piers the Plowman in Three Parallel Texts*, 2, xxxi–iii.

[74] Callus, "The Powers of the Soul," 159, ll.25–31. The anonymous compiler adapts Avicenna's mirrors, faces and prophecy by dreams to Christian psychology. He says that within the senses, there is a "speculatio" ("Ibid.," 158, 1.15–6). The "speculatio" is a "mirror" which *moves* the will by transforming images in prophetic sleep. The "mirror" which moves the will is within the images of sensation ("una [speculatio] est de ipsis formis in se," ["Ibid.," 158, 1.19). In lower vision, the mirror moves the will by a "gift of

Est iterum motiva inferiori respondens mota, et hec dicitur sensualitas, movens vero est inferior pars rationis. Et hec sensualitas dupliciter se potest habere: nam potest accipi in homine secundum id in quo communicat cum brutis, vel secundum ordinem quem nata est habere ad rationales vires. . . Nam in una dicuntur primi motus qui non sunt peccata, in alia eadem altero modo se habente sunt primi motus qui sunt peccata (There is also the [Avicennan power of] the moved motivator, corresponding to [Augustine's] lower [reason], called sensuality. But the [Avicennan] moving [power] is part of [Augustine's] lower reason. So sensuality can be regarded in either of two ways: as that part in man which has something in common with animals or that part in man which has been instilled to relate to the rational powers of man. . . In the first sensuality are said to be the first [Avicennan] motions which are not sins. In the second sensuality, that which has relationships to reason, are the first movements which are sins).

When Will's sensuality is common to himself and all other beasts such that movement ("myȝt") of his sensuality is not subject to sin, Ymginatif's and Will's functions are those of "moved mover."[75] The "mover" is the power of the Augustine's "ratio inferior" in Will; the "moved" is the power of Avicenna's "virtus animalis," inspired by a divine power: Ymaginatif, moved by Kynde, moves Will. The anonymous author understands the "moved mover" to be the "formal

prophecy or inspiration of vision in a dream" ("Ibid.," 158, ll.34-5, 38); and the lower mirror is a *good* power in sensuality.

The author of the *Liber de causis primis et secundis* only alludes to the mirrors with phrases from Avicenna's *Liber de anima, I-II-III*, Bk.1, ch.5 (p.94, ll.9, 11), "faciem scilicet deorsum ad corpus. . ., et aliam faciem sursum, versum principia altissima" (*Notes et textes*, de Vaux, 129, note 3).

Jean de la Rochelle also discusses this "virtus motiva" but attaches to it no theory of prophecy or rapture or even Avicenna's name (*Tractatus*, p.98,ll.989–p.101,l.077), until he declares the Avicennan "mirrors" a great doubt, we recall (*Tractatus*, p.102,l.126–p.103,l.160).

Since Jean de la Rochelle (sometimes confused with Odon Rigaud) and Phillip the Chancellor and the *Summa Duacensis* all depended upon the anonymous tract, Fr. Callus, Dom Odin Lottin and Pierre Michaud-Quantin tell us about an English mainstream of Christian psychology, parallel to the psychology in the B-text (D.A. Callus, "The Powers of the Soul," 138-9, 143-5; Dom Odon Lottin, "A propos de Jean de la Rochelle," 181-223; and, in the same volume, "L'influence littéraire du chancelier Philippe," 150, 159, 168, 182, 190-1, 200-1, 204, 206; Pierre Michaud-Quantin, *Tractatus*, pp.12, 15, 21). From the anonymous tract, we derive an intellectual geneology of "Augustinisme Avicennisant" very different from the intellectual tradition described by by William Courtenay (*Schools and Scholars*, pp.175-92, 276-303, 307-11, 321-4). The psychology of the B-text of *PP* originates in England, not in Paris.

[75] For the notions of "mota motiva" and "movens," see *Liber de anima, I-II-III*, p.82,l.42–p.83,l.53. The "vis apprehendens" (rational power) and "vis motiva" (appetitive power) have both physiological functions ("vis movens efficiens motum") and intellectual-volitional functions ("vis movens imperans motum"). The former moves muscles in the body (e.g., Will "aroos" up to greet Ymaginatif, in 11, l.440a, and, in 13, l.2b, "walks" in the manner of a mendicant); the latter moves the mind and the will (e.g., Will mentally "aroos" and wills to adapt the mendicant life).

power," i.e., the power to make images in the imagination. That is, Ymaginatif's movements and images would oppose the second sensuality in Will, that sensuality which relates to the Augustinian lower reason. No effects of sinful sensuality interfere with Ymaginatif's formation of images.[76]

Our accustomed axiom, "by means of acts powers of knowledge are necessarily known" ("per actus oportet cognoscere potentias"),[77] explains how the "moved mover" first transforms into Avicenna's "vis imaginativa" and then into our rational Ymaginatif. In the act of transforming images of waking into dream images, the same power is named the "vis imaginativa:"[78]

> Dicitur [potentia] iterum imaginativa secundum transformationes que fiunt in sompno, et fit reditio iterum super sensus prout apparet quod videat (The power is now called the imaginative power according to the transformations which occur in sleep. For now there is a return over the senses so that what is seen actually appears).

Other acts of the same power may be called the power of prophecy, the power of lower vision, or the power of synderesis (natural reason).[79] Although the anonymous compiler never uses the expression "vis imaginativa secundum Avicennam," he explains Augustine's "ratio inferior" and "visio corporealis" in concepts borrowed from Avicenna's "vis imaginativa."[80]

Why is the imagination prophetic? The same anonymous tract answers the second question, and again so Augustinizes Avicenna's psychology of sensory prophecy that we would not recognize it, were we not aware of the Augustinian adaptation of Avicenna's "mirrors" and "faces" of Anima and of prophecy by holy intellect:[81]

> Sed super formas quae sunt in anima rationali, non sine ministerio sensus nec tamen per phantasmata sensibilia, est alius modus intelligendi. In hiis

---

[76] Avicenna's "vis imaginativa" introduced into Christian psychology the notion that there is innocence in the reasoning of the animal and sensory imagination, uncorrupted by the effects of original sin (L. Gardet, *La pensée religeuse*, p.172, and note 20 in this chapter).

[77] "Powers of the Soul," 154, ll.6–7.

[78] "Ibid.," 154, ll.19–22. This passage, quoted both by Jean de la Rochelle and by Vincent of Beauvais, proves that the anonymous author well knew Avicenna's psychology of the "vis imaginativa" (see "Introduction," note 14).

[79] "Ibid.," 158, ll.33–5, and 159, ll.8–10. "Synderesis" signifies "natural conscience," the last gift of innocence remaning in Adam's progeny after the Fall.

[80] In the early thinking in his *De veritate* (quest.13, art.1, corpus), Thomas Aquinas describes the acts of the power in terms of a prophetic ecstasy in the senses. Vincent of Beauvais repeats this opinion verbatim without reference to the "vis imaginativa" or "vis imaginativa secundum Avicennam" (*Speculum Naturale*, Bk.26, ch.101 [Douai-Graz, 1, 1907D]). Christian commentary employs the psychology of Avicenna but carefully avoids the terms of the *prophetic* psychology of Avicenna.

[81] "Powers of the Soul," 158,l.13–159,l.2.

enim non potest esse abstractio, sed in hiis potest esse duplex speculatio:
(i.) aut speculatio fit de scientiis quantum ad scibilia, vel virtutum
quantum ad motiva diversa differentium virtutum; (ii.) aut fit speculatio
de hiis per modum per quem haberi debent.

Reliqua vero pars, que est quantum ad cognitionem veri ex parte
superiori sive per illuminationem superiorem, aut est omnino per
superiorem illuminationem, aut in parte per inferiorem. . . Si vero fuerit
in parte per inferiorem, iterum aut est per gratiam gratum facientem, aut
per gratiam gratis datam tantum. Si per gratiam gratis datam tantum, tunc
est donum prophetie aut inspiratio visionis in somnio; utraque enim est
per gratiam gratias datam tantum, non gratum facientem. Sed in hoc
differunt ab invicem, quod una plus se habet ad superiorem, sicut
prophetia, et dicitur propter hoc cognitio in speculo eternitatis aut visio;
altera vero plus se tenet cum inferiori, scilicet visio divina in somnio; et
manifestum est utramque quodammodo per inferiorem esse. Nam in
utraque fit representatio sub formis corporalibus (But there is another way
of understanding the images in the rational soul, i.e., images present with
the help of senses but present not by means of images from the sensibles.
There cannot be an abstraction in these images, but there can be a twofold
mirroring in them: 1. either the mirroring which comes from the sciences
extended to the knowables, or the [mirroring] of the powers extended to
the diverse movement of differing powers; 2. or the mirroring of images
according to the mode whereby they ought to be thought of.

As for the remaining part which pertains to the knowledge of the true on
its higher aspect by higher illumination – either that part is completely by
superior illumination or somewhat by inferior illumination. . . If some-
what by inferior illumination, it is by either sanctifying grace or by
charism. If by charism, then it is a gift of prophecy or the inspiration of a
vision in a dream. For, in any case, it is by charism, not by sanctifying
grace. But [higher vision] differs from [lower vision] in this: the former is
more related to higher illumination, i.e., prophecy; and is called for that
reason "knowledge in the mirror of eternity" or vision. The other is
contained within inferior vision, the divine vision in a dream. Obviously,
both types of vision are, in a sense, types of lower vision. In each,
representations are effected through corporeal imagery).

In the first paragraph, the compiler replaces Avicenna's terms, "mirror"
and "face," with the terms of "Augustinisme Avicennisant:"
"speculatio" (mirroring) and "illuminatio" (illumination).[82] In the next
paragraph, the compiler Augustinizes Avicenna's natural prophecy into
a charism, a grace or "gratia gratis data" (grace freely given). Then, the
anonymous compiler converts Avicenna's "two faces of the soul" into
Augustine's "ratio superior" and "ratio inferior," the so-called higher
reason of the mind considered as Adam's speculative knowledge, and
the so-called lower reason of the same mind considered as Eve's
practical or active knowledge.[83] Both types of vision involve rational

82 "Ibid.," 158, ll.15–7, 22–4.
83 "Ratio superior" (compared to Adam's reason) and "ratio inferior" (compared to

functions ("cognitio"). The prophet's knowledge is both natural ("visio divina in somnio") and supernatural ("in speculo eternitatis aut visio"). Revelation is expressed in sensory images ("in utraque fit representatio sub formis corporalibus"). The anonymous compiler well accounts for the conversion of Ymaginatif's prophetic powers to Christian theology and for Will's ascent from his animal Anima in Passus 9 to the "bisshop" Anima in Passus 15.

For the fact that the anonymous Worcester tract is the earliest tract to disguise Ymaginatif's rationality and naturally prophetic powers in the language of Augustine,[84] it would seem plausible that the *PP*-poet revived the deliberative and prophetic psychology of the "vis imaginativa secundum Avicennam" in the B-text, after 1366, along the lines suggested by the anonymous Worcester tract and with an emphasis on "Avicennisme." If so, then the physiology and psychology of a naturally prophetic "vis imaginativa secundum Avicennam" was and is rare. For the *PP*-poet revived Avicenna's *theology* of a *naturally* prophetic "vis imaginativa secundum Avicennam" and applied it to the solution of theological questions raised in the B-text, in order to bring *natural* reasoning to bear on the solution of theological questions, confused by theological sophistry.

An Introduction to Natural Prophecy

Since Kynde's angel, Ymaginatif, blurs distinctions between Will's natural and supernatural knowledge, we know that Bloomfield's definition of the problem of Ymaginatif restates the objection raised by the Christian theologians: that the sensory powers of the "vis imaginativa" are "elevated. . . through the medieval theory of prophecy."[85] Ymaginatif tranforms Will's sensory knowledge into

Eve's reason) are Augustine's expressions (*De Trinitate*, Bk.12, chs.7, 14 [*PL*, 42, 1005, 1009]).

[84] The anonymous tract converts Avicenna's notion of "motiva" (the impulse toward good and away from evil [p.159, l.32]) into the Christian virtues, e.g., the cardinal virtues ("prudentia, iustitia, temperantia, fortitudo" [p.161, ll.2–5]), the theological virtues ("fides, caritas, spes" [p.162, ll.1–2]), the gifts ("dona" [p.162, l.5ff.]), the beatitudes of poverty and patience ("paupertas" and "sustinentia" [p.162, ll.6–7]), and the fruits ("caritas" for the concupiscible appetite and "patientia" for the irascible appetite [p.165,ll.20–5]). Avicenna's concupiscible ("appetitiva") and irascible ("aggressiva") appetites are converted to the search for the highest ("superiora") and middle ("media") and lowest ("inferiora") good, according to the three "lives" accompanying such intent ("secumdum triplicem vitam contemplativam, civilem et voluptuosam" [p.159,l.32–160, ll.2]).

[85] *Fourteenth-Century Apocalypse*, p.173. Although Bloomfield mentions Moses Maimonides' *Doctor Perplexorum* as another possible source for the naturally prophetic powers of

supernatural revelation by means of outer and inner dreams. The inner dreams especially blur distinctions between the natural and the supernatural, on account of the elevation of Will's sensory imagination to the Paradise of Adam from which Ymaginatif speaks (11, 1.417, in the "F-group" of mss). Raised from "middelerþe" to the firmament of Kynde Himself, Will's imagination is elevated to the geographically supernatural, i.e., "above" ("super") "nature" ("natura").[86] The konnynge Will learns from Kynde is, therefore, both natural and supernatural because Kynde has both natural ("virtus animalis") and divine (celestial "Virtus Animalis") attributes.

Ymaginatif speaks from the supernaturality of Adam's paradise when Adam was in the state of original justice or, in the Christianized notion of Aristotle, in "puris naturalibus" ("in the state of pure Nature" possessed by Adam). In Paradise, there was no distinction between natural knowledge and supernatural knowledge or between sensory knowledge and spiritual knowledge. Adam – and Will in the inner dream – were in Paradise, illuminated by Ymaginatif and Kynde (11, ll.417–20). The elevation of the imagination is geographically and historically supernatural, or at least preternatural. Though Will is well elevated above the sublunary world, Ymaginatif prophesies sensorily within Will's imagination. This is to say that the "vis imaginativa secundum Avicennam" prophesies naturally, when Will sees images *through and in his own individual mind*. When, however, Avicenna's "vis imaginativa" elevates Will to see *through and in the angelic or divine mind*, Will knows supernaturally, in Avicenna's sense of "supernatural." Will sees and knows literally "above" himself and "outside" of himself.

---

the "vis imaginativa" (*Ibid.*), A.J. Reines has recently demonstrated that Maimonides holds for the supernatural origins of the prophecy by the "vis imaginativa" (*Maimonides and Abrabanel on Prophecy* [Cincinnati: Hebrew Union College Press, 1970], pp.85–94).

  Bloomfield's suggestion of the Arabic-Latin provenance of Ymaginatif is supported by Louis Gardet's definitive "Quelques aspects de la pensée avicenienne dans ses rapports avec l'orthodoxie musulmane," *Revue Thomiste*, 45(1939), 708–20. Gardet traces sources for the naturally prophetic powers of the "vis imaginativa" to Latin translations from the Arabic texts of Alfarabi and Ibn Sina (Avicenna). By "natural" is meant that ("Quelques aspects," 716):

  Aucun facteur surnaturel au sens strict du mot même modalment surnaturel, n'entre en jeu. Et rien dans la connaissance prophétique ne dépasse de soi les facultés de l'âme humaine.

In *La pensée religeuse* (pp.112, 120–24, and 124, n.1), Gardet finds that Latin translations of Avicenna's *Al-Shifa* transmitted to the Christian West the idea of a naturally prophetic "vis imaginativa." In 1940, Bruno Decker studied the influence of the Latin translations of *Al-Shifa* upon individual scholastics (*Die Entwicklung der Lehre von der prophetischen Offenbarung von Wilhelm von Auxerre bis zum Thomas von Aquin*, Breslauer Studien zur Historische Theologie, VII [Breslau: Müller and Seiffert, 1940], pp.13–28, 39–47, 47–217).

[86] For the "arbitrary" distinction between natural and supernatural, made by Christian theologians, see Fazlur Rahman, "Ibn Sina," 499–500.

Expounding a psychology of prophecy "in puris naturalibus," Avicenna does not differentiate the natural from the supernatural. So Ymaginatif's sensory prophecy takes a peculiarly Avicennan twist in Will's inner dream, because of Avicenna's interpretation of Aristotle's "agent intellect:" the non-sensory and Divine Anima's power to abstract ("agent") concepts from the matter ("matere") of the sensory information Will receives from his body.[87] Avicenna does not differentiate the natural from the supernatural, because Avicenna does not differentiate prophetic vision through an individual mind from vision through an angelic or divine mind. All prophetic vision is one, because the prophet sees through the "my3t" of one "agent intellect" in a Divine Anima, we recall.

Thirteenth-century theologians would strongly object to the Avicennan twist: the "unity of intellects," we recall. We also balk. In such a psychology, the Divine Anima would abstract Will from the fourteenth-century state of human kynde into a state of human kynde "in puris naturalibus," at least from 11, 1.7, and possibly from 8, 1.68. The Divine Anima (Kynde as "Virtus Animalis") would ravish Will to Adam's Paradise (11, ll.6–7); Will would see through Kynde's Providence (11, 1.321b) and use Kynde's Reson (11, 1.335); he would reenact Adam's sin by rebuking Kynde's Reson (11, ll.374–5); he would be told that he *was* in Adam's Paradise (11, 1.417, in the "F-group" of mss); Ymaginatif would inform him with the Clergie of Kynde (11,1.414–12,1.297). Line 1 of Passus 13 would intend Will to awake "witlees" and intend us to come to the surprising conclusion that medieval theologians reached. Ymaginatif reveals natural-supernatural truth in an inner dream where Will, elevated to Adam's Paradise, possesses Adam's wit in unity with Ymaginatif and Kynde. While Will is in this world of "invisibles" (we recall[88]),

Cito aderit comparatio quae est necessaria inter absentiam et animam et inter virtutem imaginativam, et videbitur subito visum (Quickly will be

---

[87] That is, Avicenna's interpretation of Aristotle's *De anima*, Bk.3, ch.5; 430a, ll.10–4, Et quia, quemadmodum in Natura, est aliquid in unoquoque genere quod est materia (et est illud quod est illa omnia in potentia), et aliud quod est causa et agens (et hoc est illud propter quod agit quidlibet, sicut dispositio artificii apud materiam), necesse est ut in anima existant hee differentie (And since in Nature, there is something in each class which is matter (and that is that which is everything in potency) and something else which is the cause and agent (and this is that on account of which anything acts, like an arrangement of the artifice [imposed] upon the matter), necessarily these [two] differences exist in Anima),
in the *Liber de anima, IV–V,* Bk.5, ch.6; pp.150, 1.59, 151,1.84 ("intelligentia agens," "intellectus materialis").

[88] *Liber de anima, IV–V,* p.28, ll.76–8.

present the comparison, necessary among the world of invisibles and Anima and the imaginative power. And the seen will be seen suddenly),

Ymaginatif suddenly appears as "oon" (11, 1.320), then gives vivid names to Will's images of the "invisibles" (11,1.417–12,1.297) and then disappears just as suddenly (12, 1.297).

To understand why inner dreams are essential to the development of Will's naturally prophetic psychology, we look again at the well-known passage from Avicenna's *Liber de anima, IV–V,* Bk.4, ch.2. In chapter one, the passage explained the naturally prophetic functions of Ymaginatif. Here the passage explains the unity of Will with the Reson of Kynde through Ymaginatif:[89]

> Contingit autem aliquibus hominibus quod haec virtus imaginativa sit creata in illis fortissima et praevalens. . . Isti habent in vigilia quod alii in somnis, sicut postea dicemus: haec enim est dispositio dormientis dum apprehendit visiones, ut certificentur ei. . . Saepe enim inter utrumque istorum [idest vigiliae et somni] contingit eos in ultimo absentari a sensibilibus et accidit eis quasi dormitatio;. . . multotiens apparet similitudo et videtur eis. . . quod sit locutio imaginis veluti verba audita quae tenent et legunt. Et haec est propria prophetia virtutis imaginativae (In some men the imaginative power has been made very powerful and predominant. . . Such men have in waking what others have in sleep, as we shall discuss a little later: the mental state of a sleeper who, while seeing visions, has certitude. . . Sometimes between states [of waking and sleeping] they are taken out of their senses to experience a quasi-sleep;. . . many times the appearing image is seen by them as an image which speaks, as it were, in spoken words which they hold and read. And this is the essence of the prophecy of the imaginative power).

Between waking (8, 1.66, and 13, 1.1) and outer sleeping (8,1.67–11,1.5; 11,1.406–12,1.297), Will is abstracted from his senses, and experiences a quasi sleep (11, ll.7–406). We recall that Anima creates Will's quasi-sleep or inner dream, in order that Will see his intent *stably,* i.e., compare his intent among the "world of invisibles, Anima and Ymaginatif."

To understand why Will's human Anima *and the Divine Anima* both cause the inner dreams, we reread the words, "sometimes between states [of waking and sleeping]. . . the essence of the prophecy of the imaginative power." These words are to be interpreted in light of Avicenna's *Metaphysics,* we recall: in an inner dream, the motion ("my3t") of the human animal Anima and the Divine Animal Anima are united into one Anima. We now understand that the celestial "Virtus Animalis" or Animal Anima (Kynde) ravishes Will into the inner dream. At 11, 1.7, not only Will's Anima's desire ravishes Will into the land where Will's desire ("longynge") and natural love ("loue") for Fortune

---

89   *Ibid.,* p.18,1.46–p.19,1.62, passim.

move Will. But also Kynde's Anima's Desire ravishes or absracts Will from his senses.

For, up to 11, l.319, Will has used the power of Thouȝt, the minister of the human Anima, to reason out the means to kynde knowyng by the "myȝt" of Wit. So, from 11, ll.7–319, Will has seen through only one side of the "Mirour" of Middle Earth, the side represented by Anima's Thouȝt and his own "coueitise;" and Will reasons to a Divinity Whom he names "Fortune." Then, at 11, l.320, the angel of Divine Anima, Ymaginatif, enters the inner dream to show the other side of the "Mirour" and directs Will's sight at a Divinity Whom Will names "Kynde:"[90]

> Si vero sensus impedierit eam [comparationem inter absentiam et inter animam et inter virtutem interiorem imaginativam] aut intellectus impedierit. . ., non vacabit aliis, sicut speculum cum occupatum fuerit ex una parte, multae formarum quae solebant describi in speculo illo, peribit comparatio quae erat inter illa et non describentur; et idem est hanc occupationem fieri sensu an retentione intellectus. Cum vero aliquid eorum removebitur, cito aderit comparatio quae est necessaria inter absentiam et animam et inter virtutem imaginativam, et videbitur subito visum (If the sense hinders it [the comparison among the world of invisibles and Anima and the imaginative power] or the intellect hinders it, the comparison will not be free from other concerns, just as a mirror, filled on one side [with] the multitude of images usually inscribed in the mirror. Then the comparison [of images] which was to among them will not be and the images will not be inscribed [in the mirror]. It is the same when the sense or intellect occupies [one side of the mirror]. When, however, something will be removed, quick will be the comparison necessary among the world of invisibles and Anima and the imaginative power. The seen will be seen suddenly).

Both Anima's create the inner dream in order that Will use both sides of the lower mirror of Anima to see his intent *stably*.

On one side of the lower mirror (11, ll.13–5), Ymaginatif transforms Will's latent "coueitise" into three bodies and speakers, e.g., "*Concupiscencia carnis*," "Coueitise of eiȝes" and "Pride of parfit lyuynge" (11, ll.14–5), so that Will's covetous intent schemes for salvation by Fortune (11, ll.53–83, and 117–39), until Ymginatif transforms Will's latent and contradictory "lewte" and "heþen" into the speakers Lewte and Trajan who speak to Will's natural desire for salvation by Kynde (11, ll.85–106, 140–53). At 11, l.319, where Will thoughts are confused by two contradictory intents and the second part of inner dream begins (11, ll.320–405), Ymaginatif transforms the concepts of Will's previous outer dream, "kynde" and "reson," into Divine Speakers of Will's

---

[90] *Liber de anima, IV–V*, p.27,l.70–p.28,l.78.

concern about kynde knowyng, e.g., Kynde or Reson. From 11, l.320, Will sees through another side of the lower mirror of Anima. As soon as Ymaginatif's physiological function, shame, affects Will (11, l.405b), so that Will awakes from the inner dream into the continuing outer dream, Will states the act by which he distinguished his "my3t" from Kynde's "my3t" (11, l.437):

'Why ye wisse me þus was for I rebuked Reson.'

Will is shamed for having thought *naturally* illogical thoughts and having committed *naturally* immoral mental acts. Awakening from the outer dream into the waking of Passus 13, l.1, Will summarizes both what he saw in the inner dream ("kynde and his konnynge") and what Ymaginatif concluded from all of the previous outer and inner vision, the revelation "scarcely will the just man be saved" (12, l.281; 13, ll.4–20): that Trajan's natural desire and natural works saved him. The sensory data of Will's sensory experience in the inner dream, "kynde and his konnynge," becomes the matter for the revelation "*vix saluabitur [iustus]*." Although Ymaginatif's sensory activities in Will's imagination prophesy in Will's senses and reveal in Will's senses, Kynde as the Divine Anima or "Virtus Animalis" causes the inner dream and ravishes Will to the world of invisibles. If the medium of inner dreams is essential to natural prophecy, then an Avicennan Anima causes the dreams so that an Avicennan Ymaginatif gives Will the revelation and the words for the revelation.

This interpretation of Ymaginatif's power to elevate the sensory imagination and reveal in it is as heterodox to the modern interpreter of Ymaginatif as it is to the medieval theologian. Even so, the heterodoxy explains why outer and inner dreams are essential to the psychology of a prophetic Ymaginatif. When an Avicennan prophet dreams vivid inner and outer dreams, the human-and-divine-"Virtus Animalis" raises the prophet's imagination to the world of invisibles so that the prophet can see his intent in relation to the Intent of Nature; and, in the inner vision, the "vis imaginativa secundum Avicennam" transforms the data of human sensory experience into the matter of revelation, because the prophet's imagination is literally united to the divine Imagination, Will, Soul and Motion by a messenger or angel of the divine Imagination, Will, Soul and Motion. When Will dreams vivid inner and outer dreams, the human Thou3t of a human Anima and animal Ymaginatif of an animal Anima weld Will's natural and supernatural truths together in vivid inner and outer dreams, because Will literally sees his intent through both the Thou3t and Ymaginatif of a human and Divine Anima. From Passus 8 to 11, l.320, Will sees through the Thou3t of his own human kynde; from 11, 1.320 to the end of Passus 12, Will literally sees through the Ymaginatif of his own human kynde united with the Ymaginatif of Kynde Himself.

An Introduction to Prophetic Preaching

The B-text applies the rare psychology in order to represent how Will (and the readers) develop an "insight" into intricate theological questions which the B-text added to the A-text:[91]

> This insight. . . is termed by Ibn Sina the active intellect and is identified with the angel of revelation. . . The prophet *qua* prophet is identical with the active intellect. . . But although the intellectual-spiritual insight is the highest gift the prophet possesses, he cannot act creatively in history merely on the strength of that insight. . . Requisite qualities are that the prophet must possess a very strong and vivid imagination,. . . and that he be capable of launching a socio-political system. . . By the quality of an exceptionally strong imagination, the prophet's mind transforms the purely intellectual truths and concepts into lifelike images and symbols so potent that one who hears or reads them not only comes to believe in them but is impelled to action. . . This symbolization and suggestiveness, when it works upon the spirit and intellect of the prophet, results in so strong and vivid images that what the prophet's spirit thinks and conceives, he actually comes to see and hear. This is why he 'sees' the Angel and 'hears' his voice.[92]

Visionary dreams transform the prophet's innate but abstract moral insight into vivid images. That is, in inner vision, Ymaginatif transforms Will's innate but abstract moral insight, termed "kynde knowyng" by a "craft" in his "cors," into the vivid images of Kynde's Wit and Reason. For the "vis imaginativa secundum Avicennam" forms words which the prophet can see and hear, as if written in a book, we recall. Such words

---

[91] Fazlur Rahman, "Ibn Sina" 499–500; in the *Liber de anima, IV–V*, Bk.4, ch.6 (p.151, 1.79; p.153, 1.12), the "insight" is termed "subtilitas" (ME "konnynge") or "ingenium" (ME "kynde").

In the *Kitab al-Najat* (*Avicenna's Psychology*, p.30, ll.29–30; pp.35–36), the "insight" or "intuition" is the prophet's capacity to "acquire knowledge within himself;. . . indeed, it seems as if he knows everything from within himself," we recall. In the *Liber de anima, IV–V* (p.151, ll.82–3), Avicenna calls the insight "holy intellect" ("sanctus intellectus"): "whatever the prophet knows he knows through himself" ("quicquid est, per se scit"). In short, the prophet's "holy intellect" is the *matter* out of which the Divine "Agent" Intellect abstracts the sermon which the prophet is to preach.

[92] Christians approve the "sight" of the Angel and the "sound" of his voice, we recall.

For "active intellect," see note 87 in this chapter, and Avicenna's discussion of it in Fazlur Rahman's *Avicenna's Psychology*, pp. 35–8, 93–5 (a translation of Avicenna's *Kitab al-Najat*), there being no English translation of Avicenna's *Liber de anima* (*Kitab al-Nafs*) available.

and such a book, if heeded, would lead all men to resolve intricate theological questions so as to observe the Law, we add. Ymaginatif begins to impose such vivid words upon Will's vivid images that Will not only gains insight into the Law but, in Passus 13 and 14, is launched on a mission to preach the Law, i.e., to preach-by-practice the "socio-political system" represented in Passus 13 and 14. Will's images are lifelike and the symbols potent, because Ymaginatif helps Will to develop a poetic appropriate to the preaching of the "Promise of the Law."[93]

Therefore, when Will " 'sees' the Angel and 'hears' his voice,' " Ymaginatif begins to make sense of Will's confused Clergie, i.e., to uncover truth in the theological jargon which Will receives from Wit, Thouȝt, Dame Studie, Clergie, and Scripture. His showing from 11, ll.320–410, and telling from 11,ll.414–12,l.297, transform Will's confused theological thoughts into the insight and vivid words of a coming sermon, the "makynges" of which Will defends in 12, l.22b, on the grounds that he has discovered the beginnings of " 'dowel and dobet and dobest at þe laste' " (12, ll.25–6). Although Ymaginatif wants Will to *do* (12, l.17) and not to write "makynges" (12, l.16), Will says, " 'I make' " (12, l.22b) for the reason that his work ("werk," in 12, l.27a) is both to discover and to articulate what " 'dowel and dobet and dobest at þe laste' " is. Contrary to Ymaginatif's claim, " 'þer are bokes y[n]owe to telle men what dowel is. . .,' " and " 'prechours. . . of many a peire freres' " who " 'preuen what it is' " (12, ll.17–9), the two friars who began the vision could not give Will the kynde knowyng to "conceive" such a Dowel (8, l.57). Moreover, the friar confessor in the inner vision deceived Will (11, ll.63–4); and Scripture's "bokes" were refuted by Trajan (11, ll.139–40). Will, therefore, responds that no " 'wight' " has been able to tell him what Dowel " 'at þe last' " is (12, l.25).

At 12, l.16, Will's "makynges" are, as it were, the sketch of such a sermon; at Passus 15, ll.605–13, Will's insights, developed from practice in Passus 13 and 14 and illumined by the vision of charity in Passus 15, are preached by Anima the "bisshop" to Will's countrymen and to all mankind; at Passus 16, ll.90–1 the Holy Spirit *speaks* the historical beginnings of the sermon (the Incarnation) in the angel "Gabrielis mouþe;" at Passus 18, ll.111–2, 262, Will sees and hears the Spirit speak the conclusion of the sermon (the Redemption) to Lucifer; in Passus 19

---

[93] *Liber de philosophia prima sive scientia divina, V–X,* tractatus 10, ch.1; p.522, l.1 (for the "Promise" in the Law); p.523, ll.23–30 (for the Angel "seen and heard"); p.523, ll.30–33, and p.527, ll.4–14 (for the development of the insight from the one "motion" or "myȝt" in common and for the miracles performed as a consequence of such insight); p.528, ll.27–35 (the *theological* questions to be answered by powers of *natural* knowledge); p.529, ll.49–60 (the granting of "poetic devices" for the prophet's articulation of such insight).

and 20, the words of the sermon are applied to Conscience's practice of the New Law (evangelical poverty). Despite Ymaginatif's criticism of the ''makynges,'' Will's kynde knowyng insists on the articulation of such a God-given knowyng: the articulation of the syllogistic implanted by God in Will's human kynde and in every human kynde. If Will acquires such insight by the syllogistic and can articulate with mental words or kynde concepts, then perhaps the written words of the B-text may inspire Will's readers to discover the same syllogistic and kynde concepts from within themselves. Will's ''makynges'' would show others his mental trek into the Law, i.e., the Law of Dowel.

We recall Avicenna's dictum: Will has the ''quicquid est'' (whatever is) within himself to know and to will and to speak. But we perceive Will's problem: Will cannot find the words to articulate the insight, if the insight is buried in the confusing language of theology. Up to and into the inner dream, Will has mentally worked to come to the kynde knowyng which would allow him to achieve Avicenna's ''active intellect'' (the highest but most abstract function of knowledge with Whom all other intellects are ''one:'' the Divine Intellect located literally in the Firmament), and has worked to come to know Ymaginatif as Avicenna's ''angel of revelation.'' Will's work achieves the insight, and Ymaginatif provides the vivid images and words for Will's insight. Thus Will's ''makynges'' are to become a sermon to be preached so that his hearers or readers will be impelled to reform the concupiscence in their lives and their state. Ymaginatif's answer serves the beginnings of Will's higher ''purpos:'' Will's use of the insight to find the right words to preach the Law to his countrymen. But Ymaginatif's emphasis on action rather than writing is itself to be perfected by 15, ll.605–13, where Anima gives Will the words of a sermon to be preached to Greek Catholics, Jews and Saracens, who, having heard them, may practise the Law without theological squabbling.

Will's insight develops from the numerous explanations of kynde knowyng of the degrees of ''Do-,'' given to him in the first vision of the *Vita* and spoken by the various ''I's'' throughout the B-text. In the process, Will's memory becomes, in Avicenna's words, a ''treasury'' of images,[94] indeed, a more much articulate ''treasury'' than the ''tresore'' of Truth that holy chirche babbles about (1, ll.85–207). A ''craft'' in Will's ''cors,'' rather than in her theological clichés, articulates his treasury of thoughts and words. Although, in Passus 1 Will cannot conceive from holi chirche the ''tresore'' for lack of a ''craft in my cors'' (1, ll.138–9), Ymaginatif corrects Will's dull wits (1, l.140) by means of of an extraordinary psychology. For Ymaginatif transforms Will's innate

---

[94] *Liber de anima, IV–V*, p.20,l.76; p.147,l.21; p.150,l.68.

concepts into speakers who give Will the words and even a "book" which he holds.

The B-text added this heterodox psychology to the A-text, in order that Will's mental acts both develop and preach a simple Law encapsulated in Piers Plowman's Clergie, " 'Dilige deum' " (13, l.127a), clarified by Anima, " 'Dilige deum & proximum' " (15, l.584), as revealed by Scripture, just before Will's theological rebellion (10, ll.360–2),[95]

> 'He sholde louye and lene and þe lawe fulfille.
> That is, loue þi lord god leuest abouen alle,
> And after alle cristene creatures, in commune ech man ooþer,'

and first enunciated by holi chirche (1, ll.142–3):

> 'It is a kynde knowyng þat kenneþ in þyn herte
> For to louen þi lord leuyere þan þiselue.'

Will's mental acts reduce the maze of theological jargon to the preaching and practice of Piers Plowman's simple Clergie, " 'Dilige deum.' "

The Elevation of Ymaginatif's Sensory Prophecy

We conjecture that the B-text has something to do with preaching. Avicenna's psychology of the "Active Intellect" shows us how the elevation of the "vis imaginativa secundum Avicennam" is related to preaching. In short, the rest of the visions in the B-text of the *Vita* perfect Ymaginatif's prophetic work in Will, in order that Will preach the practice of the Law (" 'Dilige deum' ") he has discovered in himself. According to the *Liber de anima*, IV–V, natural prophecy by the "vis imaginativa," is perfected by practice of the "virtus activa" (our Haukyn) which, in turn, is perfected by higher vision of the "virtus contemplativa" (our "bisshop" Anima in Passus 15) which, in turn, is perfected by practice of the "virtus sancta" (Will's reception of a "tresore" in his wits to guide him infallibly in 19, ll.215–8).[96] In the *Vita*

---

[95] From Avicenna's psychology of "heart, soul, mind," Jean de la Rochelle and Alexander of Hales develop the psychology of the Law of charity, stated in *Deut.*6:5, "Diliges Dominum Deum tuum ex toto corde tuo et ex tota anima tua et ex tota fortitudine tua" (You shall Love the Lord your God with your whole heart, your whole mind, your whole strength), from distinction 27 of Peter Lombard's *III Sententiae*. Will's self-taught Clergie, modelled upon Piers Plowman's "Dilige deum," would develop the Avicennan psychology of "heart, soul, mind," from within the Mosaic Law, in order to attain the perfect Law of Charity.

[96] For the Arabic equivalents of the Latin terms "activa" and "sancta," and the meanings of the terms, see "Introduction," notes 27 and 34. Amélie-M. Goichon's *Lexique de la langue philosophique d'Ibn Sina (Avicenne)*, p.337, paragr.26, defines the "virtus

of the B-text, Will perfects natural prophecy by the "vis imaginativa secundum Avicennam" in seven steps of ascent, we recall:[97]

1. vision by the "vis cogitativa" and "vis imaginativa" (Passus 8–12),
2. a lower inner dream by the lower mirror and face of Anima (11, ll.6–406),
3. a perfection of the concupiscible and irascible appetites (Passus 13 and 14),
4. perfection of the "vis imaginativa" by vision through the "vis activa" (13,l.221–14, l.334a),
5. ascent from the "vis activa" to the "virtus contemplativa" and vision through "sanctus intellectus" (15,l.162–17,l.356),
6. a higher inner dream by the higher mirror and face of Anima (16, ll.19–167),
7. conferral of the "virtus sancta" (19, ll.215–8).

After the Avicennan natural prophet has been moved by the imaginative power, he perfects his concupiscible and irascible appetites by the practice of poverty (the concupiscible appetite for good) and patience (the irascible appetite for the arduous good), so that his practice produces "joy" ("gaudium") and "sorrow" ("tristitia"), prophesied by the "vis imaginativa."[98] While perfecting the two lower appetites, the prophet acquires the power to make sure judgements about good and evil in concrete cases;[99] then he confirms his judgments by

contemplativa" as the Arabic "Quwwa nazariya:. . . une faculté à laquelle il appartient de recevoir l'empreinte des formes universelles abstraites de la matière."

[97] Gardet refers to five of the perfections (*La pensée religeuse*, pp.114–125), but lists only three: "clarté et lucidité de l'intelligence, perfection de la vertu imaginative, pouvoir de se faire de la matière extérieure" (p.121), listed also by S. van Riet and G. Verbeke (*Liber de anima, IV–V* (p.153, n.17). Van Riet and Verbeke add the perfection of the "facultés motrices" (i.e., the concupiscible and irascible appetites) as part of the prophet's power over matter (*Liber de anima, IV–V,* p.66, ll.59–64, and note to ll.60–4) and separate the state of "sanctus intellectus" from the acts of the "virtus sancta." I have added the two inner dreams, because they are peculiar to the psychology.

Again, we see why this psychology is not Thomistic. Thomas Aquinas objects to the prophet's capacity to transform matter (*De veritate*, quaest.12, art.3, obj.9), as Gardet and the editors of the *Liber de anima, IV–V* elucidate (*La Pensée Religeuse*, p.124, n.1; *Liber de anima, IV–V,* p.65, ll.39–41).

[98] *Liber de anima, IV–V,* Bk.4, ch.4; p.56,l.6–p.57,l.9 (the two appetites); p.66, ll.59–64 (perfection of the two appetites perfects prophecy by the "vis imaginativa"); p.58,l.26–p.59,l.36 (joy and sorrow prophesied).

The Christianization of the two appetites into patience and poverty appears in Jean de la Rochelle's *Summa de anima* (Domenichelli, pp. 192, 277), his *Tractatus* (pp.124, ll.76–8, 142, ll.182–183; 143, ll.214–215), and in the anonymous Worcester tract (Callus, "The Powers of the Soul," 163, ll 6–7, 164, ll.11–15).

[99] *Liber de anima, IV–V,* Bk.5, ch.1; p.78, l.37:

Haec autem virtus activa est de bono et malo in particularibus (This active power concerns itself with good and evil in concrete circumstances).

performing miracles.[100] Accordingly, Will would realize joy, if Haukyn's "virtus activa" were naturally perfect. For Will would acquire from Haukyn not only the power to judge good and evil in concrete cases but also the power over matter, i.e., the miraculous power to feed and heal other men (13, ll.240–70):[101]

> Immo cum anima fuerit constans, nobilis, similis principiis, oboediet ei materia quae est in mundo et patietur ab ea, et invenietur in materia quicquid formabitur in illa. Quod fit propter hoc quod anima humana, sicut postea ostendemus, non est impressa in materia sua, sed est providens ei (Indeed when Anima has been constant, noble and like to its Origins, then the matter in the world will obey Anima and submit to Anima. Whatever will be imagined in Anima will be discovered in matter. Such is done because the human Anima is not impressed in its matter but is provident for matter, as we shall show presently).

But, to Will's sorrow, Haukyn lacks the power to "provide," because Haukyn lacks the charity to perfect his practice of patient poverty and to rid himself of concupiscence. Will's perfection of Ymaginatif by ascent through Haukyn here means not only that Ymaginatif is Jones' "spokesman of Reason," but that Ymaginatif also prophesies Will's "sorrow" in Passus 13 and 14, until charity transforms Will's higher

---

[100] See "Introduction," note 28. Avicenna would explain Haukyn's prophetic power over matter both as an evil (*Liber de anima, IV-V*, p.65, note to ll.37–8) and as a good (*Liber de anima, IV-V*, p.65, ll.38-42, 48-53, 59-64). Accordingly, Haukyn would have the *potential* to produce food for the commune (13, ll.235–43) and to heal disease (13, ll.247-53); but Haukyn's power fails (13, ll.255-70) for the reason that he consults and uses witches (13, ll.337–41).

[101] *Ibid.*, p.65, ll.38–42 (quoted), and p.66, l.49:
> Contingat permutari sibi elementa (It happens that the elements change for him).

When the "virtus activa" is ruled by the "virtus contemplativa," then matter obeys the *will* of an Avicennan prophet (*Ibid.*, p.66, ll.55–6):
> materia oboedit ei naturaliter et fit ex ea secundum quod videtur eius voluntati (matter obeys him naturally and shapes itself according to his will).

Like Piers Plowman in both the *Vita* and the *Visio* (in Passus 16, ll.104–18, Piers Plowman cures the ill, and, in 6, ll.173–80, weakens the depraved), Haukyn as "virtus activa" could
> Sanet infirmos et debilitet pravos (cure the ill and weaken the depraved),

as Avicenna claims (*Liber de anima, IV-V*, p.65,l.48–p.66,l.49). But Haukyn's lack of charity actually produces the food failure of 1370 (13, ll.265–70). Like Truth's pardon "*a pena & a culpa*" given to Piers Plowman (7, l.3), the papal indulgence "*a poena*" could cure disease by means of Haukyn's power (13, ll.247–9):
> 'Hadde ich a clerc þat couþe write I wolde caste hym (i.e., for the Pope) a bille
> That he (the Pope) sente me vnder his seel a salue for þe pestilence,
> And þat his blessynge and his bulles bocches myȝte destruye:
> *In nomine meo demonia e[j]icient & super egros manus imponent & bene habebunt'*
> (In my name they will cast out devils and put hands upon the ill, and the ill will be well).

Haukyn potentially has the powers of Piers Plowman and Jesus, (16, ll.104–18), so much so that people would say of Haukyn what they will say of Piers and Jesus: that the miracles are done through the power of "wichecraft" and the "demon" (16, l.120).

Anima "like to its Origins," i.e., into the likeness of "cristes creature," (15, ll.15-43) so that Will realizes "joy," i.e., an ability to perfect Haukyn's power and to provide for his Anima and the Anima's of other men.

The fifth step to the perfection of natural prophecy brings joy to the prophet, when he envisions the Law to be preached, through his own Anima as a "mirror:"[102]

> Aptitudo aliquando in aliquibus hominibus ita praevalet quod ad coniungendum se intelligentiae non indiget multis, nec exercitio, nec disciplina. . .; immo quia, quicquid est per se scit: qui gradus est altior omnibus gradibus aptitudinis. Haec autem dispositio intellectus materialis debet vocari sanctus intellectus (The aptitude sometimes is so strong in some persons that it does not require much to be conjoined to the Intelligence, neither practice nor formal education. . . for the reason that whatever is they learn through themselves. This state of material intellect ought to be called the state of holy intellect).

For the fact that Will has learned everything from within himself ("quicquid est, per se scit"), Will is said to have reached what Avicenna calls "intellectus materialis" or "intellectus sanctus." The former expression means that the higher Anima "abstracts" higher self-knowledge and practice out of the "matter" of the lower Anima (the lower self-knowledge and practice), so as to actualize the power in the "virtus activa." Will's exclamation to Anima (16, ll.1-2),

> 'Now faire falle yow', quod I þo, for youre faire shewyng!
> For Haukyns loue þe Actif man euere I shal yow louye,'

means that Will now actualizes Haukyn's power because of Anima's showing of Charity. Charity allows Will to perform Avicennan miracles of feeding, healing and converting men to the Law. The latter expression, "intellectus sanctus," means that Will, in 15, ll.162-212, is being prepared for a second inner vision through Piers Plowman, in order that he receive the "virtus sancta" in 19, ll.215-7.

At this fifth step, the prophet's practical judgment becomes "contemplative" or universal judgment. In Avicennan terms, this is to say that the lower face and mirror of Anima become the "matter" from which the higher face and mirror of Anima either "abstracts" ideas or is "illumined" from on High.[103] In Augustinian terms, this is to say that Will learns from Anima a universal charity and, more significantly, that

---

[102] *Liber de anima, IV–V*, Bk.5, ch.6; p.151, ll.80-6, passim. To be joined to the Intelligence is an act of the higher face of Anima. To see in a mirror is a Christianization of Avicenna's higher psychology, to be taken up shortly.
[103] For "abstracts," see note 41 in this chapter; for "illumined," see note 22.

"cristes creatures" may very well be Anima's who are Jewish and Greek and Saracen (15, ll.390-6, 502-3, 605-6). Anima's explanation of Charity so illumines Will that he learns from Anima how to use Haukyn's power to confirm the truth of his preaching. If Will's practical preaching to all men be "clene," then his hearers are amended " 'moore þoruȝ miracles' " of Will " 'þan þoruȝ much prechyng' " (15, l.449), and so more convinced that Christ was a prophet by His miracles of feeding and healing (15, ll.588-98). The charity in Will's prayers would heal men and bring peace to all men (15, ll.426-8a):

> 'And folkes sholden [fynde], þat ben in diuerse siknesse,
> The bettre for hir (the preachers') biddynges in body and in soule.
> Hir preires and hir penaunces to pees sholde brynge
> Alle þat ben at debaat and bedemen were trewe:
> *Petite & accipietis &'*
> (Ask and you shall receive).

Avicenna's "Active Intellect," i.e., Will's intellect in unity with the "bisshop's" intellect and Christ's Intellect, would not only give Will the words of the sermon about the Law (15, ll.603-13) but also the power of miracles to prove the truth of the sermon (16, ll.103-18).

In the sixth step of ascent, the higher Anima again summons the prophet's "vis imaginativa" and sublimates it. In turn, the sublimated "vis imaginativa" again creates speakers in a higher inner dream:[104]

> Non est autem longe ut, ab his actionibus comparatis ad intellectum sanctum potestate earum et virtute, emanet aliquid in imaginativam, quod imaginativa representet etiam secundum exempla visa vel audita verba, eo modo quae prediximus (It is not far from these activities, related to holy understanding in their strength and power, to the point that something flows into the imaginative power which the imaginative power, in turn, represents as exempla seen or words heard in the manner we described before).

"Eo modo quae prediximus" (in the manner we described before) refers back to the vivid image-making functions of the "vis imaginativa" in lower inner dreams. Ymaginatif's prophetic inner dreams reoccur, when they are stimulated by the "holy intellect" of Anima. By "sanctus intellectus," the natural prophet sees by a higher mirror. Vision through the higher mirror stimulates another inner vision and a higher syllogistic.[105] Ymaginatif's sensory powers are themselves elevated by the higher power of "sanctus intellectus," called the "Mirour" of

---

[104] *Liber de anima*, IV-V, Bk.5, ch.6; p.151, l.86-p.152,l.90.
[105] *Liber de anima*, IV-V, Bk.5, ch.6; p.153, l.14 (the prophet receives all divine questions from the divine Agent Intellect in syllogistic order).

Anima in Passus 15, l.162. Ymaginatif merely represents the "exempla visa et audita verba" (the examples seen and the words heard) as he did in the first inner dream, "in the manner as we said before" ("eo modo quo praediximus"), except that Ymaginatif is transformed into Piers Plowman because "something emanates" from Anima "into the imaginative power." Piers Plowman, the higher face of the higher Anima, shows a Tree of Trinite in the inner dream; but, instead of telling like Ymaginatif before him, he acts. He takes one of the props from the Tree of Trinite, occasions the Incarnation (16, ll.88–9), and proves the the truth of his act by performing the miracles of Jesus (16, ll.103–18).

The two faces and mirrors of Anima lead Will from the perfection of sensory prophecy by Ymaginatif, through the perfection of the patience and poverty, through the vision of "Actiua vita," to the vision of Anima. As there is a lower outer and inner vision by Anima's lower face, Thou3t and Ymaginatif (11, ll.7–406), so there is a higher outer and inner vision by Anima's higher face, Anima himself and Piers Plowman (16, ll.19–167). From 16, ll.19–167, Anima commands the sublimated Ymaginatif, i.e., Piers Plowman, to represent images appropriate to Will's holy intellect, in order that Will see the "persone" of Charite and learn a higher Clergie from within himself (15, ll.196b, 198). Thus Will "þoru3 wil oone" sees Charity by means of the higher face of Anima "Piers þe Plowman, *Petrus id est christus*" (15, l.210b, 212), in the second inner dream. As lower Anima had one face (sensory reason) broken into two in the lower inner dream (Thou3t from 11, ll.7–319, and Ymaginatif from 11, ll.320–410), so higher Anima's higher face, non-sensory reason, breaks into two here (Anima's showing of the "Tree of Pacience" in 16, ll.4–17, and Piers Plowman's showing of the "Tree of Trinite" in 16, ll.22–52).

In the highest act of the "intellectus sanctus," called the "virtus sancta" or holy power,[106] the natural prophet envisions angels and God Himself working in his soul (equivalent to Conscience's reception of a "tresore" of knowing within his five wits in Passus 19, ll.215–8) and receives the power to earn his livelihood in a craft (Grace's "*Diuisiones graciarum sunt*" or "gratiae gratis datae" or "craftes" from 19, l.228–57). Here, Will's ability to perfect Haukyn's power is granted: he knows how to judge good and evil in concrete cases, and he knows how to practise a "craft" to perform miracles, i.e., to provide food for his Anima and the Anima's of other men. But here the gift to Will's Conscience is to be tested by concrete cases of good and evil and by concrete cases of winning a livelihood (19,l.335b–20, l.386), i.e., by resolving who is "cristene" and who wins a livelihood with "right" (19, ll.348–50).

---

106 *Liber de anima, IV–V,* Bk.5, ch.6; p.153, ll.15–7.

An Introduction to the Higher Psychology of "Augustinisme Avicennisant"

The seven steps of ascent through a naturally prophetic "vis imaginativa secundum Avicennam" would well explain the psychological structure of the B-text from Passus 12 to Passus 19, if the B-text is structured not along the lines of the "three lives" of Dowel, Dobet and Dobest but along the lines of the perfection of Avicenna's "virtus activa" and "virtus contemplativa" in Will.[107] The "Augustinisme" in "Augustinisme Avicennisant" may suggest that the *Vita* represents the "three lives" of Dowel, Dobet and Dobest, structured according to Augustine's "tria genera visionum." But the "Avicennisme" in "Augustinisme Avicennisant," evident in Will's ascent from Ymaginatif through Haukyn to Anima and Piers Plowman, suggests that the seven steps of Avicenna's prophetic psychology govern Will's ascent to a "tresore," given at 19, ll.215-7, and tested from 19,l.335-20,l.386. In light of Avicenna's higher psychology, Will's vision through Haukyn would not be a second, separate vision, both unrelated to Will's first vision through Thou3t and Ymaginatif and unrelated to Will's third vision through Anima.[108] Will's vision, first through Ymaginatif, then through Haukyn, then through Anima and then through Piers Plowman, would represent, rather, the "opening stages of the life of Christian perfection,"[109] because *PP* is an "epistemological poem, a poem about the problem of knowing truly."[110]

Mary Carruthers' expression, the " 'logic' of the mirror," captures the lower and higher psychology of "Augustinisme Avicennisant."[111] Will's "seeing the world as a series of *specula*. . . is exactly in accord with the way in which God reveals himself to man in time through the . . . pattern of history," she says, intuiting the higher psychology:

---

[107] Derek Pearsall's note to C.X., ll.78–98 (pp.182-3) briefly discusses the relationship of the three lives to the structure of the *Vita* and the problems with the three lives in such a structure. If we make Will's vision by Avicennan "virtus activa" or Haukyn central to Will's ascent, the centrality of Haukyn clarifies the problem we have had with the so-called "mixed life" or life of Will's action and contemplation. Will's knowledge is that of the "mixed life" from Passus 13 to Passus 16, ll.1-2.

[108] Skeat, *The Vision of William Concerning Piers the Plowman in Three Parallel Texts*, 2, xxv–vi.

[109] T.P. Dunning, "Action and Contemplation in *Piers Plowman*," *Piers Plowman: Critical Approaches*, ed. S.S. Hussey (London: Methuen, 1969), pp.220-1, in light of the remarks on pp.216-9.

[110] Mary Carruthers, *The Search for St. Truth: A Study of Meaning in Piers Plowman* (Evanston, Ill.: Northwestern Univ. Press, 1973), p.10.

[111] *Search for St. Truth*, p.128; the continuing quotation is taken from pp.127-9.

Charity which is a 'fre liberal wille' manifests itself in the mirror of charitable works. Yet what is important is not the charitable work but the right will which it reveals. This is why, Anima explains, Will can never see the person of Charity without the help of Piers Plowman:

> 'Clerkes haue no knowyng,' quod he, 'but by werkes and bi wordes.
> Ac Piers the Plowman parceyueth more depper
> What is the wille and wherfore that many wyȝte suffreth,
> *Et vidit deus cogtaciones eorum.'*   (XV.156-7)

On earth men see *"in enigmate"*; in heaven men see face to face. The vision of Christ, true knowledge of the Savior, comes only through the mirror of charity in the deeds of his servants. . . When Will, after thanking Anima for his lessons "for Haukynnes loue the actyf man," complains that he is still "in were what charite is to mene," Anima gives him the vision he seeks of the "persone" of Charity, a vision guided by Piers Plowman. And it is surely no accident that this vision comes in the form of the most elaborately prepared and executed figure which the poem contains – the Tree of Charity.

" 'Logic' of the mirror" summarizes the steps of "Augustinisme Avicennisant:" Will's lower and higher mirrors, Haukyn's midway position between the lower and higher mirrors, the higher mirror of the "persone" of Charity, the perfection of free will, the image of the tree, the vision of "what charite is to mene" through Piers Plowman.

On the one hand, Will follows the syllogistic of the Avicennan mirrors to ascend; on the other hand, Will purifies himself of concupiscence as he ascends to knowledge of himself as "fre liberal wille" (15, 1.150). Showing Will how to prevent the three effects of concupiscence from collapsing such an act of free will, Piers Plowman sets two props and then a third at the roots of the universal Tree of Trinite, of which Free Will is a part (16, ll.48-50):

> 'Ac whan þe fend and þe flessh forþ wiþ þe world
> Manacen bihynde me, my fruyt for to fecche,
> Thanne *liberum arbitrium* laccheþ þe [þridde] planke.'

The elaborate image explains how Free Will performs an act of free will. That is, when Piers Plowman props the three roots of free will, Free Will does not commit the sin against the Holy Spirit (16, 1.47), for Free Will freely chooses to love all other men. Free Will practises " '*Dilige deum & proximum*' " as the Samaritan practises it (17, ll.134-7, 349-54).

Immediately after Will's exclamation to Anima (16, ll.1-2), Will perfects the "active" vision, begins the "contemplative" vision from which the "virtus sancta" will come (19, ll.215-8), and learns "what charite is to mene," by three means: by Anima's explanation of "*liberum arbitrium*" (16, 1.16-7), by Piers Plowman's explanation of an act of " '*liberum arbitrium*' " (16, ll.46-52), and by the Samaritan's resolution to problems created by the one faith of Abraham and the seemingly contradictory practices of *Spes'* *"Dilige deum & proximum"* (16, ll.26-49, 134-7). Having ascended from vision in the sensory Anima to vision in the non-sensory Anima and having ascended from the practice of patient poverty without charity to the practice of patient poverty with charity, Free Will's exclamation at 16, ll.1-2, surpasses Haukyn's response to Conscience's call for contrition (14, ll.1-4):

'I haue but oon hool hater. . . I am þe lasse to blame
Thou3 it be soiled and selde clene: I slepe þerInne o ny3tes;
And also I haue an houswif, hewen and children –
Vxorem duxi & ideo non possum venire –
(I have taken a wife and, therefore, cannot come [to the heavenly banquet])
That wollen bymolen it many tyme maugree my chekes.'

Haukyn's is the response of universal and active Christendom, summoned to the Heavenly banquet by God the Father (*Mt.*22:2-14), a response halfway between Scripture's reference to the clothing required for the banquet (baptism, in 11, ll.112-4) and Anima's reference to the food served at the banquet (15, ll.462-85). In the in-between at Passus 14, Haukyn practises patient poverty without charity, and Will has yet to learn from Anima how charity grows from patient poverty.

As soon as Haukyn asks Pacience, " 'Where wonyeþ Charite?' " (14, l.98a), Will and Conscience note the splotches on Haukyn's coat (13, ll.271, 273; 313-4). The rationale for the splotches (13, ll.288-9a),

Wiþ Inwit and wiþ outwit ymagynen and studie
As best for his body,

represents both that Haukyn has used his Inwit (9, l.18) and the "outwit" of Kynde (11, l.321b) to study and to think through the process of Ymaginatif's showing, but that Haukyn has not learned the basic lesson of Ymaginatif's Clergie: the importance of Charity (12, l.31b). Haukyn's baptism into patient poverty has produced no charity by which "crist" invests him for the banquet. This rationale shows how Will's vision through Ymaginatif is to be perfected by vision through Haukyn's practice of the active life (making judgments of good and evil, and bearing patient poverty in charity). For Will's "virtus activa" perfects the reason and love in Ymaginatif, only after Will dispels the concupiscence he sees in Haukyn and acquires charity by Anima's higher "shewyng" (16, ll.1-2).

Will's question of Anima, " 'What is charite?' " (15, l.149), differs from Haukyn's question to Pacience, " 'Where wonyeþ Charite?' " only because Will has achieved kynde knowyng (15, l.2) and because the "bisshop's" long harangue about the opposition of concupiscence and charity (15, ll.79–148) has prompted Will to ask the question. Will's "virtus activa" surpasses Haukyn's "virtus activa," for the fact that Will ascends to the fifth step of the perfection of prophecy by Avicenna's "vis imaginativa," i.e., to the "virtus contemplativa" and to vision by "holy intellect" (15, l.162):

> 'Ac I seiȝ hym neuere sooþly but as myself in a Mirour.'

Now Anima can "abstract" charity from Will's practice of Avicennan patient poverty in Passus 13 and 14, in order that Will envision how charity would give him Haukyn's power over matter (16, ll.1–2), in order to confirm his preaching (15, ll.605–13). Now Anima's higher face, Piers Plowman, does show Will how to exercise Haukyn's power in 16, ll.104–18.

That is, Piers Plowman perfects what Will perceived to be Haukyn's power of witchcraft in 13, l.337, so that Will became curious about the powers in Anima's various names (15, ll.46–7),

> 'Ye , sire!', I seide, 'by so no man were greued
> Alle þe sciences vnder sonne and alle þe sotile craftes
> I wolde I knewe and kouþe kyndely in myn herte.'

First glimpsing his higher Anima "as it sorcerie were" (15, l.12a), Will thought that Anima's Latin verb for the description of himself in 15, l.39a, " 'sortitur' " ("to separate" or "to cast lots"), signified not the "separation of Anima's powers" but the sorcery of "casting lots." Understanding "sortitur" to refer to magical powers in Anima, Will "conjured hym" (15, l.14), and requested a kynde knowyng of the subtle crafts (15, ll.47–8). As before in Passus 10–12, Will intended to use his subtle knowledge to be curious, even after achievement of kynde knowyng (15, l.2). That is, in imitation of the mendicant Franciscan, Roger Bacon, or the mendicant Dominican, Albertus Magnus, Will intended to practise patient poverty only to learn the occult arts of Avicenna's "virtus activa" and to use them for the amelioration of human life on earth. This is to say that, like Haukyn, Will continued to practise the konnynge he learned from Kynde's Reson by 13, l.15, assuming that he served the common good of Kynde in the life of a "mendynaunt" who intends to preserve the earthly integrity of Kynde's two Bodies (13, l.3). By preserving the human species within Kynde's two Bodies, Will hoped to use Haukyn's power to effect a Paradise on earth and so to keep his earthly "cors" immortal. But vision through Anima is to dispel Will's concupiscence for knowledge of the occult Avicennan powers over matter.

Anima intends that Will use his subtle knowledge to preach charity to all men and to convert men by the miracles produced by charity

(15, ll.605–13, 587–95); Anima does not intend Will to pursue the occult
sciences for the sake of themselves. Anima silences Will's curiosity with
the same *"Non plus sapere quam oportet sapere"* that Dame Studie used on
him (15, l.69), for Will is still possessed of the same flaw he had in the
first vision of the *Vita*: a "licames coueitise/ Ayein cristes counseil and
alle clerkes techyng" (15, ll.67–8). Like Dame Studie (10, ll.72–3), Anima
thinks that Will would preach the experimental sciences, based upon
obscure theological principles invented by friars (15, ll.70–2):

> 'Freres and fele opere maistres þat to [þe] lewed [folk] prechen,
> Ye moeuen materes vnmesurable to tellen of þe Trinite
> That [lome] þe lewed peple of hir bileue doute.'

Anima's rebuke of Will's curiosity cuts off the natural perfection of
prophecy by the "vis imaginativa secundum Avicennam" and com-
pletes prophecy by "Augustinisme Avicennisant."

At 15, l.162, Will replaces Avicennan mirrors with Pauline mirrors
(*I Cor*.13:9–10 and 12),

> Ex parte enim cognoscimus, et ex parte prophetamus; cum autem venerit
> quod perfectum est, evacuabitur quod ex parte est. . . Videmus nunc per
> speculum in aenigmate, tunc facie ad faciem; nunc cognosco ex parte, tunc
> autem cognoscam sicut et cognitus sum. Nunc autem manent fides, spes,
> caritas, tria haec; maior autem horum est caritas (In part, we know and in
> part we prophesy; when that which is perfect comes, that which is partial
> will disappear. . . We see now through a mirror in obscurity, then face to
> face. Now I know partially. The I shall know as I am now known. Now
> remain faith, hope and charity. The greatest of these is charity),

and Augustinizes Avicenna's "holy intellect" in Will who responds:

> 'I seiȝ hym neuere sooþly but as myself in a Mirour:
> [*Hic*] *in enigmate, tunc facie ad faciem'*
> (Here in a glass darkly, then face to face).

Now, Will's "light" of charity would come from the "Augustinisme" in
Gundissalinus' compendium *De anima*, which baptizes Avicenna's
mirror of "holy intellect" into the Pauline "speculum in aenigmate:"[112]

---

[112] Gundissalinus, *Compendium de anima* (Muckle, *Mediaeval Studies*, 99, ll.22–7), which
Christianizes Avicenna's two faces of the soul, "quicquid est per se scit," and "sanctus
intellectus" (Muckle, *Mediaeval Studies*, 95, ll.25–31, 95,l.32–96,l.15 and 99, ll.12–5).
Christians converted Avicenna's prophecy by "holy intellect" into a theology of the
beatific vision. The *Speculum Naturale* glosses "*Videmus nun per speculum in aenigmate*" in
these Augustinian terms (Bk.26, ch.85 [Douai-Graz, 1, 1893D]):

> Quia ergo in Deo species sunt & rationes rerum, nusquam inuenitur dictum a
> sanctis, quod Deus sit rerum speculum, sed magis quod ipsae res creatae
> sunt speculum Dei, prout dicitur in prima ad Corinthios 13. *Videmus nunc per
> speculum in aenigmate* (Because, then, in God are said to be the species and
> reasons for things, never is it found that the saints say that God [Himself] is

Hic oculus animae qui est intelligentia in contemplationem creatoris intendit. . . ipsa intelligentia tanta claritate divini luminis perfunditur ut in ipsa intelligentia sic irradiata lux. . . tamquam forma in speculo resultare videatur. Ipsa enim intelligentia creaturae rationalis quasi speculum est aeterni luminis de qua Apostolus 'Videmus nunc per speculum' (This eye of the soul, intelligence, intends toward contemplation of the Creator. This intelligence is suffused with such a brilliance of Divine Light that the irradiated Light is seen to leap in the intelligence, as though an image were leaping in a mirror. For the intelligence of the rational creature is, as it were, a mirror of eternal Light of Which the Apostle speaks: "We see now through a mirror").

Will's sight ("oculus") through Anima ("animae") christianizes Avicenna's "intelligentia." Seeing ("videmus") himself through Anima as a "Mirour" ("speculum") of Christ or charity, Will then intends ("intendit") toward the light of Christ or charity ("divini luminis"). Light from Avicenna's Divine Intelligence, now a Pauline Intelligence, radiates through Will's Anima. Will's partial line, "*[Hic] in enigmate,*" signifies the full psychology of *I Cor.*13:12: "Videmus nunc per speculum in enigmate" (We see now through a mirror in obscurity).

Until Passus 15, Will has had partial self-knowledge and partial prophecy of the means to his salvation, partial because only a vision of practical patient poverty without the illumination of charity. With the higher Reson of Anima (15, l.11) and the motive power of Charite, he now sees dimly ("in enigmate") the rest of the process of his perfection of vision through himself as if "in a Mirour." Anima's rebuke converts the subtlety of the knowledge that Will learns from his Avicennan "spiritus" in Passsus 9 to the subtlety of knowledge that Will learns from his Christian "Spiritus" in 15, l.36b. For Will has understood Anima's expression, " 'spirit specheless' " or " '*Spiritus*' " in the function " 'whan I flee from þe flessh and forsake þe careyne' " (15, ll.35-6), in an Avicennan sense: when an Avicennan Anima dies, Anima becomes a "separate substance" ("substantia separata"), "specheles" but living in the "perfection" of the ten spheres apart from the body. The "virtus activa" of an Avicennan prophet would derive

the mirror of things. Rather [it is said] that created things themselves are the mirror of God, as stated in *I Cor.* 13, *We see now through a mirror darkly*).
The Augustinians here use "speculum" to distinguish the beatific vision (God Himself as mirror to which the mind as mirror is conjoined in beatific vision) from the highest form of prophetic knowledge (the human mind as *created* mirror of all things).
Having so avoided the pantheistic "unity of intellect" in the highest form of Avicennan prophecy, Vincent proceeds to "Augustinize" Avicenna's "holy intellect" both as mirror for the beatific vision and mirror for the highest prophetic knowledge (Bk.26, ch.86 [Douai-Graz, 1, 1894C), quoting Thomas Aquinas (*De veritate*, quest.12, art.5, objections 5-7, and the respondeo). In the later *Summa theologiae*, "Secunda Secundae," quest.173, art.1, Thomas repeats the idea but modifies the "Avicennisme" in the words.

marvellous powers from the spirits in the ten spheres and from an Avicennan God, if his spirit were conjoined to planetary spirits. But a "cristene" Anima belongs to Pauline concept, Pauline language, Paul's Christ and Paul's incarnate charity. "Cristene" Anima's belong in the unity of the Holy Spirit, because they are "cristene" by the grace of the Holy Spirit.

Therefore, "spirit of Charity" received from Anima is not the "spiritus" of conjurers, philosophers or those who speak with the wisdom of the secular world. From 15, ll.50–69, Anima illumines Ymaginatif's reference to " '*Sapiencia huius mundi stulticia est apud deum*' " (12, l.138); Anima applies the *Glossa Ordinaria* on *I Cor*.2:11 to Will's Avicennan "spirit," to baptize Will into the "cristene" sense of "Spirit:"[113]

> *Non* utique accepimus *spiritum huius mundi*, id est spiritum pythonicum, qui solet conjecturis quae mundi sunt divinare. Vel non accepimus spiritum hujus mundi, id est spiritum elationis, quo doceamur sapientiam mundi, *sed* accepimus *spiritum qui ex Deo* est. Spiritus ergo Dei, spiritus charitatis est (*Not at all* have we received *the spirit of this world*, that is the spirit for divining, which is usually used to conjure things of the world. Nor have we received the spirit of this world, that is the spirit of pride which teaches us the wisdom of the world. *But* we have received *the spirit which is from God*. Therefore, the Spirit of God is the spirit of charity).

"Spirit" no longer means that "the spirit of man in Holy Scripture stands for the soul or the rational powers of the soul:"[114]

> Spiritus autem hominis in Scripturis accipitur ipsa anima, vel ipsius animae potentia rationalis (In the Scriptures, "spirit of man" is understood to be Anima itself or the rational power of Anima).

The Avicennan "holy intellect" cannot help Will to interpret his visions of the world to come.

Up to 15, l.162, of the *Vita*, Will has been impelled by an Avicennan Ymaginatif, Avicennan perfections of the concupiscible and irascible appetites (patience and poverty), an Avicennan "virtus actiua" (Haukyn), and especially by a subtle kynde knowyng ("solertia" or Will's ability to connect the terms of his syllogistic kynde knowyng by supplying the connecting "middle term" in a flash). Anima dismisses the rationality of this "spirit," and emphasizes knowledge " 'þoruȝ wil oone' " as the means to know the " 'persone' " of Charity or Christ (15, ll.210a, 196b). As a result of vision through the higher "Mirour," Will's higher reason and will intend to preach the common good,

---

[113] Actually, Peter Lombard's commentary on *I Cor*.2:11 (*PL*, 191, 1551C).
[114] *Glossa Ordinaria* or Peter Lombard on *I Cor*.2:14–6 (*PL*, 191, 1552A).

Charity or Christ, to all of "cristes creatures," all faithful souls or Anima's, whether they be Christian, Saracen, Jew or Greek (15, l.605). Anima ends Passus 15 and begins the higher inner vision, by calling upon Will to preach the unity of Christian belief "in the Spirit." For "*in Spiritum sanctum*" is to be found the "remission of sins, the resurrection of the body and life everlasting" (15, ll.611–3). Will's "Augustinisme Avicennisant" becomes a vision of charity, albeit a vision in an unusual sense of "cristene," i.e., a "Spirit" possessed by Jews, Christian, Greeks and Saracens in common.

When Will unites his Avicennan "spirit" to the Pauline Spirit Who is Charity ("spiritus" to "Spiritus" in 15, ll.36 and 39), then the "bisshop" Anima is inspired not by the spirit of divination but by the Spirit Who is Charity. Anima is not conjured but christened, filled with that Spirit Who divinized the human kynde of Christ, for Anima is "cristes creature" (15, l.16). Anima puts an end to the naturally subtle kynde knowyng Will derived from Aristotle and Avicenna, and converts the kynde knowyng to the subtle Clergie of Piers Plowman's " '*Dilige deum*' " (13, l.127a), so that Will preaches in the Spirit of Charity shown by Piers Plowman's act at the end of the showing of the Tree of Trinite (16, ll.87b–9):

> [happe] how it my3te,
> *Filius* by þe fader wille and frenesse of *spiritus sancti*
> To go robbe þat Rageman and reue þe fruyt fro hym.

Piers' act of driving off Satan from the Tree of Trinite occasions the Incarnation; by the Will of the Father and the Freedom of the Holy Spirit, Divine Free Will chooses to make " '*Filius*' " incarnate: to fill the human kynde of the Christ with the " 'Persone of Charity' " (15, l.196b). This Supreme Act of Free Will both enables Will to become "fre liberal wille" (15, l.150) or the Latin equivalent, "*liberum arbitrium*" (16, l.16), and to perfect Haukyn's miraculous power. This is also the Supreme Act of Piers Plowman's Clergie of "*Dilige deum*" (13, l.127): by the Charity Who is God, the Will of God the Father freely chooses that His Son become incarnate to redeem universal human kynde.

By the end of Will's vision in Passus 15, the two lower appetites of his sensory Anima are perfected by the practice of the "virtus activa;" the "virtus activa" is, in turn, perfected by the third Avicennan appetite, the "vis rationalis" (the rational appetite), so that Will sees through his "virtus contemplativa." According to Christian adaptation of Avicenna's "vis rationalis," i.e., "liberum arbitrium" or Free Will (16, l.16a, and "fre liberal wille" in 15, l.150b),[115] Will would be enabled

---

115 Avicenna uses Aristotle's image of a "tree" (*De anima*, Bk.2, ch.2; 413a, ll.25–30), we

by Anima to see himself as a Tree of appetites (an Avicennan psychology of the perfection of the prophetic will) in 16, ll.4–16. Mirrored by Anima as a "Tree of Pacience" in 16, l.8, Will would have the higher mirror to see the higher face of Anima in the second inner dream.[116] In the second inner dream, the higher "face of the soul" is Piers Plowman who shows Will the inner vision of himself as "Free Will," i.e., as a universal Tree of Trinite (16, ll.22–52). To repeat, the one grace of the Holy Spirit props up the three radicels of the Tree against the concupiscences of the world, the flesh and the devil ("world," "flessh" and "fend" in 16, ll.27, 31, 40, 48), in order to preserve the power of *"liberum arbitrium"* occasionally ("som tyme," in 16, l.46). By such a showing through Piers Plowman, the "Persone" of Charity enables Free Will to love all men, to perform miracles of feeding and healing, and to preach Anima's sermon (15, ll.605–13) by living Anima's sermon. The three acts of loving, performing miracles to confirm the preaching, and the preaching-by-practice all elucidate Piers Plowman's Clergie, *"Dilige deum"* (13, l.127a).

In Passus 19, ll.215–8, Will takes the seventh step toward the perfection of prophecy by the "vis imaginativa," when he receives an Augustinized "virtus sancta" (holy power). In Avicenna's language, Will receives

> unus modus prophetiae qui omnibus virtutibus prophetiae altior est. Unde congrue vocatur virtus sancta, quia est altior gradus inter omnes virtutes humanas (the one mode of prophecy which is higher than all the other power of prophecy. Whence it is fittingly called the holy power, because it is the highest among all human powers).[117]

In Augustinian terms (19, ll.215–8), Will's Conscience receives the

---

recall, in order to describe the relationship of the anima to the will. Anima is the "root" ("radix") from which the "tree" ("arbor") of the will grows (*Liber de anima, IV–V*, p.122, ll.69–72):

> [Anima] est substantia et radix (The soul is a substance and a root).

From the root, the tree of Will would grow two branches, the concupiscible and irascible appetites (*Liber de anima, IV–V*, p.56,l.6–p.57,l.9),

> Huius autem virtutis voluntatis rami sunt virtus irascibilis et virtus concupiscibilis: illa autem quae vult delectabile et quod putatur utile ad conquirendum, est concupiscibilis; quae vero vult vincere et id quod putatur nocivum repellere, est irascibilis (The branches of this power of will are the irascible power and the concupiscible power. The [power] which wills the delightful and what is thought to be useful for achievement is called the concupisicible. The [power] which wills to conquer and to repel what is thought to be harmful is the irascible),

from whose *corporeal* harmony emanates a "substance most like a separate substance. . ., as the celestial substances" ("substantiam quae est simillima substantiae separatae. . ., sicut substantiae caelestes" [*Ibid.*, Bk.5, ch.7; p.172, ll.6–7]).

116 *Liber de anima, IV–V*, Bk.5, ch.6; p.151,l.87–p.152,l.90.
117 *Liber de anima, IV–V*, Bk.5, ch.6; p.153, ll.15–7.

'' 'tresore' '' which Will sought from holi chirche (1, ll.138–9), i.e., the
'' 'kynde knowyng' '' by a '' 'craft in my cors:' ''

> 'For I wole dele today and [dyuyde] grace
> To alle kynne creatures þat [k]an hi[se] fyue wittes,
> Tresour to lyue by to hir lyues ende,
> And wepne to fighte wiþ þat wole neuere faille.'

Unlike the *Visio* where the dreamer's Conscience is encumbered for
coueitise of Mede (2, 1.51), Free Will's *Conscience* cannot be so
encumbered (19, ll.219–26):

> 'For Antecrist and hise al þe world shul greue
> And acombre þee, Conscience, but if crist þee helpe.
> And false prophetes fele, flatereris and gloseris,
> Shullen come and be curatours ouer kynges and Erles;
> And Pride shal be Pope, Prynce of holy chirche,
> Coueitise and vnkyndenesse Cardinals hym to lede.
> Forþi', quod grace, 'er I go I wol gyue yow tresore
> And wepne to fighte wiþ whan Antecrist yow assailleþ.'

In 19, ll.204–12, in the act of being conjoined to Conscience, Free Will's
"tresore" is called "synderesis" or "sunteresis" (Gk., meaning
"joining together"). At 19, l.220, in the act of unity with Conscience,
Free Will's same "tresore" is called "suneidesis" (Gk., meaning
"conscience").[118] In 19, ll.332b–3, in the acts of Grace's and Piers
Plowman's preaching,[119] the same "tresore" is called a "spark" of
"preaching" ("scintilla praedicationis"). The "tresore" so unites Free
Will's "wittes" with Conscience's judgment that Will's three appetites,
(concupiscible, irascible and rational) desire and know what the moral
good is. Will's Conscience, therefore, discerns moral good innately and
infallibly in the exercise of the "craftes" enumerated from 19, ll.228–49.

In the first division of Grace (19, ll.215–26), called the "tresour" for
the "fyue wittes," Conscience receives the power to discern good spirits
in the Law from malign spirits in the Law, so as to avoid Pride's first
attack on Conscience: '' 'That Conscience shal not knowe who is

---

[118] The term "suneidesis" or "sinderesis" is derived from Jerome's commentary on
Ezechiel 1:7–18 (*PL*, 25, 19–27) which, together with Gregory's *Homilies on Ezechiel*, forms
the gloss in the *Glossa Ordinaria*. Derived from Avicenna's "vermis" (i.e., the vermiform
part of the brain, described in *Liber De anima*, I–II–III, p.89, l.46), "synderesis" is
Augustinized in *Worcester MS F 57* (Callus, "Powers of the Soul," p.157, ll.6), in Jean de la
Rochelle's *Summa de anima*, ch.40 (p.298, p.300) and the *Tractatus* (p.98, note j), and in
Alexander of Hales' Commentary on *II Sententiae*, dist.40 (Bibliotheca Franciscana
Scholastica Medii Aevi, XIII, 380–5).

[119] The penitential canon "Pennata" (can.9, dist.2, quest.3, causa 33, "Secunda Pars,"
Decretum Gratiani [Friedberg, 1, 1193]), quoting Gregory the Great's *Homilies on Ezechiel*,
Bk.1, homily 3 (*PL*, 76, 812D–3A). The sparks fall into the "ground" ("terram") of good
men and become seeds to do the good works of the four cardinal virtues (*Ibid.*, 807–9).

cristene or heþene' " (19, l.348). For the Spirit Who has inspired such "cristene" helps Conscience to discern the true "cristene," and His "tresore" unites the wits of all such "cristene" Consciences into a Church whose pope is Piers Plowman. By this "tresore" in the "fyue wittes," each "cristene," according to his "couenant" and his "knewelich[e] to paie" (Christian, Saracen, Jew and those under Natural Law, e.g., Trajan) may receive pardon from the Pope, Piers Plowman, for acts of Dowel (19, ll.186–7).

In the second division of Grace (19, ll.228–49), called a "craft" (19, l.234), Conscience receives the various skills needed to earn a living, so as to avoid Pride's second attack on Conscience (19, ll.349–50):

> 'Ne no manere marchaunt þat wiþ moneye deleþ
> Wheiþer he wynne wiþ right, wiþ wrong or wiþ vsure.'

Conscience's "right" judgment of Will's use of the "craft" would enable Free Will to perform miracles among the society of "cristene" united by One Spirit under the Pope, Piers Plowman. For Piers Plowman's pardon would absolve these "cristene" of their sins and Piers Plowman's food would sustain these "cristene" (19, ll.383–90), provided that, in 19, l.394, the Conscience of each of them observes the New Law of the " 'Paternoster: *Et dimitte nobis debita nostra*' " (And forgive us our debts), and each Conscience practises the part of the New Law omitted by Conscience: "sicut et nos dimittimus debitoribus nostris" (as we forgive our debtors).

By Passus 19, ll.215–8, the *Holy Spirit* in Free Will's *body* so devotes his Conscience to such a kynde knowyng that Will cannot turn back from it, according to to the image in 19, l.335a, "Now Piers is to the plow." The image is taken from the old Law of penance, i.e., the canon "Pennata," and from the Scripture, i.e., the *Glossa Ordinaria* on *Ezech*.1:12:[120]

> Qui aratri stivam tenet, non debet respicere post tergum (*Luc*.ix, 62) (He who holds the plough handle ought not to look back over his back [*Lk*.6:62]).

Will achieves Piers Plowman's power of preaching-by-practice, by ascending the seven steps of Avicenna's psychology of the perfection of prophecy by the "vis imaginativa."

---

[120] *PL*, 25, 25B.

Certification by Inner and Outer Dreams and by "Makynges"

By 20, 1.33, awakened Free Will lacks not only formal Clergie but also Ymaginatif's powers. To understand why Will finds truth only in sleep and vision, and why Will completes his "makynges" only in sleep (by 19, ll.1 and 481), we look at the same text of the *Liber de anima, IV–V,* a third time:

> Contingit autem aliquibus hominibus quod haec virtus imaginativa sit creata in illis fortissima et praevalens. . . Isti habent in vigilia quod alii in somnis, sicut postea dicemus: haec enim est dispositio dormientis dum apprehendit visiones, ut certificentur ei. . . Saepe enim inter utrumque istorum [idest vigiliae et somni] contingit eos in ultimo absentari a sensibilibus et accidit eis quasi dormitatio;. . . multotiens apparet similitudo et videtur eis. . . quod sit locutio imaginis veluti verba audita quae tenent et legunt. Et haec est propria prophetia virtutis imaginativae (In some men the imaginative power has been made very powerful and predominant. . . Such men have in waking what others have in sleep, as we shall discuss a little later: the mental state of a sleeper who, while seeing visions, is certified of the visions. . . Sometimes between states [of waking and sleeping] they are taken out of their senses to experience a quasi-sleep;. . . many times the appearing image is seen by them as an image which speaks, as it were, in spoken words which they hold and read. And this is the essence of prophecy by the imaginative power).

For the reason that Will's Ymaginatif is weak in his waking but strong in his sleep, Will finds truth ("certificentur") only in sleep and composes "makynges" ("verba audita. . . quae legunt") only in sleep.

Answers to two more specific questions, how Will uses Ymaginatif to interpret his dreams and why Will writes "makynges," depend upon the antecedent of the pronoun "haec" in the sentence, "Haec est propria prophetia virtutis imaginativae." "Haec" has several antecedents. If "haec" refers to images which speak in inner dreams, the "vis imaginativa" prophesies by hypostatizing images into speakers. If "haec" refers to "quasi-dormitatio," the "vis imaginativa" prophesies by images which speak in inner visions. If "haec" refers to the prophet's certification of future events by means of dreams, the "vis imaginativa" prophesies by certifying to the prophet that his dream will come true. "Haec" thus refers both to the several states (sleep, waking, in between sleep and waking) and to the mental acts by which the prophet certifies the truth in his dreams:

1. a continuing outer dream
2. interprets an inner dream

3. whose images are so vivid
4. that they speak in the inner dream
5. and make a "book" for the prophet to hold,
6. so that, when he awakes from the continuing outer dream,
7. he remembers the interpretation given in the continuing outer dream.

Will certifies the truth in his first vision by the same process.[121] That is, Ymaginatif creates vivid images in Will's inner dream (11, ll.7–406) and interprets the images in the continuing outer dream (11,l.414–12, 1.297) while Will writes "makynges" (12, l.16); then Will awakes (13, l.1) and remembers both the vividness of the images in the inner dream and their interpretation in the outer dream (13, ll.4–19):

> And of þis metyng many tyme muche thou3t I hadde,
> First how Fortune me failed at my mooste nede;
> And how þat Elde menaced me, my3te we euere mete;
> And how þat freres folwede folk þat was riche
> And [peple] þat was pouere at litel pris þei sette,
> And no corps in his kirkyerd n[e] in his kirk was buryed,
> But quik he biqueþe [hem] au3t [or sholde helpe] quyte hir dettes;
> And how þis Coueitise overcom clerkes and preestes;
> And how þat lewed men ben lad, but oure lord hem helpe,
> Thoru3 vnkonnynge curatours to incurable peynes;
> And how þat Ymaginatif in dremels me tolde
> Of kynde and of his konnynge. . .
> And siþen how ymaginatif seide 'vix saluabitur [iustus]',
> And whan he hadde seid so, how sodeynliche he passed.

First, Will summarizes the acts of his hypostatized concerns, the speakers of the inner dream: how Fortune failed (11, l.12), how Elde threatened (11, ll.35, 60), how the friars promised easy absolution and burial (11, ll.55, 76), how the friars deceived the unkonnynge (11, ll.71–78), how Kynde taught images of konnynge (11, ll.320–404). Then, he summarizes Ymaginatif's resolution to the problem of salvation "*in extremis*," raised by Scripture (10, l.352). In the continuing outer dream, Ymaginatif said " '*Saluabitur vix Iustus in die Iudicii.*' " The statement prophesies Will's salvation by "truth" (12, ll.283, 287, 290–3) and by amendment (12, l.289). Upon his waking from the first vision, Will remembers how the interaction of the hypostatized speakers and Ymaginatif certified this truth.

---

[121] We are agreed that Ymaginatif interprets Will's dream. See Joseph Wittig, "Elements," 243–245, 263, 279–280; and Britton J. Harwood, "Imaginative in *Piers Plowman*," *Medium Aevum*, 44(1975), 251–253, among other good discussions. Harwood points out that Ymaginatif's interpretation of the inner dream fails, in some respects, to teach Will fully of the power in his body to know kyndely (p.251), and that Ymaginatif's rational powers need grace (p.254).

Avicenna's explanation of the process of certification and of the "book" ("verba. . . quae legunt"), promised "a little later" ("sicut postea dicemus"), is this:[122]

> Iam autem dicitur rex Hercules vidisse somnium quod nimis terruerat eum et non inveniebat apud interpretes qui solveret illud; qui cum postea obdormivit, interpretatum est ei suum somnium in somnis: in quo continebantur quaedam quae futura erant in mundo et praecipue in eius civitate et regno; deinde cum scripsissent ea quae predicta fuerant, impleta sunt omnia sicut interpretatum illi fuerat in somnis (The king Hercules is said to have seen a very frightening dream, and found no one among his diviners to interpret his dream. When he later went to sleep, his dream was explained to him in his sleep. The [later] dream contained things to come in the world, especially in his city and kingdom. Then, when they had written down what had been predicted, everything was fulfilled as it had been interpreted to him in his sleep).

The prophet certifies his dreams in two ways. First, a later dream certifies the truth in a former dream:[123]

> Videt homo interpretationem sui somnii in somnio suo (Man sees the interpretation of his dream in his dream).

That is, not only does the continuing outer dream (11,1.407–12,1.297) interpret Will's inner dream (11, ll.7–406), but also later visions in the *Vita* interpret some of Will's concerns raised both in the first vision of the *Vita* and even in the *Visio*:[124]

> Pluribus autem contingit percipere et allegorizare somnium suum in somniis, illis scilicet quorum anima sollicitata fuit circa id quod vidit cum dormiunt, remanet illis sollicitudo in ea sicut erat (It happens to many that they perceive and interpret their dreams in dreams. For to those whose soul was concerned about that which they saw when they sleep, the concern still remains in the soul as it did before).

"Percipere et allegorizare" translate Avicenna's term "ᶜabbara" ("to interpret").[125] "Allegorizare" means that Will interprets former dreams by latter dreams. Applied to the end of the *Visio*, "allegorizare" means that the first vision in the *Vita* interprets concerns at the end of the *Visio*. Applied to the end of the first vision of the *Vita*, the term means that Will's concern about the kynde knowyng of Dowel is to be interpreted by the next vision of the banquet of Conscience and Clergie. At the end

---

[122] *Liber de anima, IV–V,* p.26, ll.51–56.
[123] *Liber de anima, IV–V,* p.25, l.31.
[124] *Liber de anima, IV–V,* p.25,l.46–p.26,l.48. The power of the complete, written text of the visions is attributed not only to the prophet's "vis imaginativa" but to the strength and nobility of his imagination and memory (*Liber de anima, IV–V,* p.26, ll.59–60).
[125] *Liber de anima, IV–V,* p.25, note 2.

of the second vision (14, 1.335), the term means that Will has achieved
kynde knowyng by practice of patient poverty under "*Actiua vita*"
(15, 1.2). In the middle of the third vision and before the second inner
dream (16, ll.1–2), the term means that Anima's "faire shewyng" of
charity allows Will to interpret the meaning of the vision not only from
15, ll.11–613, but from 13,1.221–14,1.334. After the second inner dream
(16, 1.167), the term means that Will knows "what charite is to mene"
(16, 1.3). At the end of the third vision (17, 1.356), the term means that
Feiþ's liturgical illumination, from 18, ll.21–35, allows Will to interpret
how Piers Plowman's fruit is to be redeemed historically and how
Anima's sermon in 15, ll.605–13, is to be preached to all Anima's who
practise Piers Plowman's Clergie, "*Dilige deum.*" For Will sees what
"*Dilige deum*" means from 18, ll.110–431, and says specifically
(18, ll.110–2),

> What for feere of þis ferly and of þe false Iewes
> I drow me in þat derknesse to *descendit ad inferna*
> And þere I sauȝ sooþly, *secundum scripturas,*

and hears "*Rex glorie*" say (18, 1.376):

> 'For we be breþeren of blood, [ac] noȝt in bapteme alle.'

If the blood of "*Rex glorie*" redeems every man, then all are brothers by
Redemption but not by baptism. "*Dilige deum*" means that God's Son
has loved God by redeeming man ("*Dilige deum & proximum*").
Preaching "*Dilige deum*" to all men means preaching the vision in
Passus 18. From the first to the fourth vision, later dreams interpret
former dreams.

At the beginning and end of the fifth vision, however, "allegorizare"
means that the "I" writes down the events of the fourth vision in 19, l.1,
and the events of the fifth vision at 19, l.481. In the sixth and final vision,
"allegorizare" means that Free Will's awakening to Nede tests the
wisdom in all his previous visions (20, l.33). For, in the second process
of certification, prophetic dreams are recorded in a text, so that later
events, outside the text, interpret the dream. The event of Nede, outside
the completed "makynges," interprets the visions from 8, l.68, to
19, l.481. Thus, the B-text represents two ways by which Will certifies
his dreams. In the first, Will's continuing dreams and wakings interpret
the concerns of previous dreams; in the second, the "makynges" record
the concerns which have and have not been interpreted.

The second process of certification not only begins at 12, l.16 (in the
continuing outer dream) and is internally completed by the "I" at
19, ll.1 and 481, but is externally completed by the *PP*-poet himself at
20, l.386. At 12, l.16, when Will begins the "makynges" or a mental

text, the "makynges" show that Will has interpreted some of his concerns about Dowel, unresolved at the end of the *Visio*, in 7, ll.185–6. For, by 13, l.20, Will knows that Dowel "at þe laste" saves more surely than the pardon of Piers Plowman (7, ll.152–3) or the indulgences he was going to receive from the friars, from burial in his parish churchyard and from his scheming with Scripture (11, ll.53–67, 117–39). Will "makes" (12, l.22), then, in order that the "makynges" keep a record of both interpreted and uninterpreted concerns about his knowledge of the Dowel "at þe laste," i.e., at Doomsday (12, l.26).

Then, the second process of certification develops into the completed "makynges." For Will's mental acts, after the "makynges" (12, l.16), certify the truth of the first vision; but Will's mental acts are not complete, until Will as Free Will comes to a full realization implied by the "do" (in Dowel, Dobet, Dobest) and by the "I" of 19, ll.1 and 481, when he, identified with "I," writes down both the sermon to be preached and the reception of the "tresour" in his "fyue wittes" (19, l.217). For he he has been looking for this "tresore" in order to "do," since Passus 1, ll.138–9; and, finally, all the faculties, acts and objects of knowledge which lead to this "tresore" are unified by the pronoun "I." At this point, Will is one with all his acts, faculties and objects of knowledge and knows what to intend; and, at this point, when, in 20, ll.1–50, Will wakes to Nede, events external to the "makynges" completed by 19, ll.1–481, interpret the visions from Passus 8, l.68, to Passus 19, l.481. Nede, the event external to the complete "makynges," opposes the "tresore" Will has received and described in the completed "makynges." So, from 20, ll.51–386a, a final dream represents Will's fundamental concern: Free Will's actual waking and actual "doing" in in conditions of necessity, opposed to Free Will's envisioned "tresore" and completed record of "makynges."

Finally, at 20, l.386b, i.e., at the last half-line of the B-text where Will *actually* awakes and the B-text *actually* ends, the second process of certification *begins* for the fourteenth-century reader. Events, *historically* external to Will's final awakening and to the final line of the B-text, interpret the B-text of the *Vita* for the reader. This is to say that the truth in the B-text is certified by the reader of the B-text, when the mental events described within the B-text correspond to the fourteenth-century reader's experience of religious events outside the B-text. The B-text *actually* prophesies for the reader, when the reader follows Will's mental acts to their logical conclusion: Nede does oppose the unity of Free Will's Conscience. For fourteenth-century readers, well aware of the practices of mendicant confessors, use Conscience's predicament to answer this question posed to them by the B-text: whether their gifts, given to a mendicant confessor in return for pardon, are more profitable to them "at þe laste" than their acts of Dowel, i.e., their use of Mede to make amends (which would alleviate their mendicant confessors' needs for food, clothing, shelter).

All this certification originates in Will's interaction with his animal Anima, Kynde and Ymaginatif, we recall:[126]

> Cito aderit comparatio quae est necessaria inter absentiam et animam et inter virtutem imaginativam, et videbitur subito visum (The comparison [of images], necessary between the soul and the world of invisibles and [between these two] and the imaginative power, will be seen quickly).

Ymaginatif joins Will's intelligence of Dowel to Kynde's Intelligence ("absentia" or "caelestia" in Latin, but "ghayb" or "malakut" in Arabic[127]), so that Will's "konnynge" or "ingenium" achieves insight into the elements of kynde knowyng in a flash, we recall. To facilitate the insight, Will's *animal* Anima creates the inner and outer dreams, we recall:[128]

> Animae autem necessariae sunt virtutes interiores ad recipiendum origines absentium (The soul needs the interior faculties of knowledge to receive the beginnings of the world of invisibles).

In his sleep and dreams, Will imagines his "intent seen permanently," we recall:[129]

> Animae autem necessariae sunt virtutes interiores ad recipiendum origines absentium duobus modis: uno, ut imaginetur in illis intentio visa stabiliter (The soul needs the interior faculties of knowledge to receive the beginnings of the world of invisible in two ways: in one way, so that the soul's intent may be imagined permanently in the world of invisibles).

Therefore, only in sleep do Will's faculties of knowledge serve Will's Anima and not impede his vision:[130]

> alio, ut sint iuvantes et deservientes ei ad libitum eius, non impedientes eam nec trahentes eam post se (in another way, so that the faculties of knowledge help the soul and serve it at will, and do not impede the soul and drag it off after themselves).

---

126 *Ibid.*, p.28, ll.76–8.
127 *Liber de anima, IV–V*, p.27, ll.64, 66–70 and notes; p.29, l.2 and note.
  As we have seen in the discussion of Avicenna's "unity of intellect," Will's images would be a "material intelligence" fused with with the Divine or "Active Intelligence." Avicenna explains in the *Kitab al-Najat* (Rahman, *Avicenna's Psychology*, p.34,l.30–p.35,l.13): "some of these actions attributed to the 'Divine Intelligence'. . . overflow into the imagination which symbolizes them in sense imagery and words."
128 *Liber de anima, IV–V*, p.27, ll.65–6.
129 *Liber de anima, IV–V*, p.27, ll.65–7.
130 *Liber de anima, IV–V*, p.27, ll.67–8.

Since, therefore, Ymaginatif compares Will's permanent intent to his present progress toward that intent (we recall [131]),

> Est igitur necesse comparationem esse inter absentiam et inter animam et inter virtutem interiorem imaginativam (Therefore, there must be a comparison among the world of invisibles and the soul and the interior imaginative power),

then Will is enabled to know the full consequences of his intent toward the degrees of the kynde knowyng of Dowel only in dreams. If only dreams and vision allow Will to perceive the development of his intent as a "permanent sight," Will's certification of his progress toward that intent depends very much upon Ymaginatif's divining powers.

This psychology in the *Vita* develops the dreamer's lack of "songewarie" in the *Visio*. After the dreamer dares not interpret his vision in the "Prologue" (ll.209–10), his first attempt (1, ll.1–2) fails for lack of a "craft" in his "cors." After his vision of Mede (Passus 2–4) and of amendment for the misuse of Mede (Passus 5–7), he awakes at 7, l.145, to find that he cannot rely on "songewarie" to interpret the unresolved problem of Dowel, introduced by Piers Plowman's appearance (7, ll.154–6). Although, in the *Visio*, the dreamer knows that Mede's true use is for purposes of amendment (2, l.119b) and that Piers Plowman has shown to ways to make amends by either the high way of interior pilgrimage (5, ll.560–629) or the by-way of communal labor (6, ll.5ff.), nevertheless, his vision of the use of Mede and of amends for the misuse of Mede leads him to another concern, represented at the end of the *Visio*: whether the Dowel of actual amends is more helpful "at þe laste" than the Dowel of indulgence granted to Piers Plowman by Truth (7, l.186b). In 8, ll.2–4, in waking and beginning the *Vita*, he states the concern about Dowel, uninterpreted at the end of the *Visio* (7, l.186b):

> Al in a somer seson for to seke dowel,
> And frayned ful ofte of folk þat I mette
> If any wiȝt wiste where dowel was at Inne.

At 8, l.70, Avicennan faculties of knowledge infuse the mental acts by which the dreamer becomes the "wil" who, in turn, uses his innate faculties of kynde knowyng to resolve objects of knowledge (Dowel), unresolved at the end of the *Visio*. Will develops an Arabic "songewarie," i.e., the prophetic psychology of the "vis imaginativa secundum Avicennam" applied to the continuing dreams of the *Vita*, to interpret an unresolved concern raised in the *Visio*. The hypostases, Will ("appetitus"), Thouȝt ("vis cogitativa"), Wit ("sensus communis"),

---

[131] *Liber de anima*, IV–V, p.27, ll.68–70.

perhaps Dame Studie ("meditatio"), Ymaginatif ("vis imaginativa"), Kynde ("Virtus Animalis"), begin to resolve whether pardon or Dowel is best for the soul "at þe laste." Will's first vision in the *Vita* resolves some of the concern (the "konnynge" to amend is more important than indulgences or pardons), but leads to another concern (kynde knowyng perfected by the amendment of patient poverty in the practice of "*Actiua vita*"). After the visions and "makynges" are complete (19, ll.1 and 481) and "Crist" gives Piers Plowman the power to pardon "cristene" whose Consciences are illuminated to practise their craft in unity (19, ll.183, 215–335a), then in Passus 20, a final waking (ll.1–51) and vision (ll.52–386a) pit all the truth and "makynges" envisioned in sleep (from 8, l.68, to 19, l.480) against the truth done in wakefulness (i.e., Free Will's Conscience's actual choice to Dowel after the last line of the B-text).

The *Vita* of the B-text interprets the *Visio* of the B-text, by applying Avicenna's psychology of the certification of dreams to the resolution of a theological problem raised at the end of the *Visio*: salvation by Dowel or salvation by pardon. Concatenations of visions and "makynges" (12, l.26, written down in 19, ll.1 and 481) both develop the problem and the psychology. The fourteenth-century reader interprets the whole of the B-text, in light of religious practice external to the B-text.

Conclusions and Suggestions

When we apply Avicennan psychology and "Augustinisme Avicennisant" to the meaning and function of Ymaginatif, we reach some definite conclusions and some plausible conclusions about the structure of the *Vita* in the B-text. First, we know precisely what is meant by "spokesman of Reason" when Jones' expression is applied to Ymaginatif's functions in the B-text. In a general sense, the "vis imaginativa secundum Avicennam" refers to instinctual reasoning in the human imagination, predicting a joy and sorrow to come from the perfection of instinctual reasoning in Will. In the first vision of the *Vita*, Ymaginatif hypostatizes the power of the "vis estimativa" in Will (to intuit the good or bad intents in his Wit) and the "vis imaginativa" in Will (both to deliberate the good and evil in his images and to motivate him toward the good in the images). In a precise sense, Ymaginatif hypostatizes the animal, sensory reasoning in Will's human imagination, when opposed to the "vis cogitativa" or human sensory and *sensual* reasoning in his imagination. Ymaginatif is simply the twin of Thouȝt.

Second, we know that, as the twin of Thou3t, Ymaginatif has been operative in the first vision of the *Vita* since Passus 8, 1.70. " 'Ydel was I neuere,' " in 12, l.1b, means that Ymaginatif has been present since 8, 1.70. A baptized "vis imaginativa secundum Avicennam" opposes the reasoning of a "vis cogitativa," even though both stem from the same sensory reason. In 12, 1.2, " 'Thou3 I sitte by myself in siknesse and in helþe,' " precisely describes Ymaginatif's power to reason. When Will is "frenetike of wittes" (10, l.6b), Ymaginatif sits by himself; " 'in helþe,' " Ymaginatif also sits by himself because he is not part of human Anima's powers. In Will's health, Ymaginatif is commanded by the Reson of Kynde in all animals, i.e., by a "Virtus Animalis" Celestial but yet Animal. When Thou3t's reason becomes contradictory because of Will's sensual "likyng" (11, 1.45), Ymaginatif's Reson addresses the natural good in Will's kynde and teaches Will the sensory elements of kynde knowyng. Thou3t is besieged by Will's human sensuality. Ymaginatif is not.

Third, we know that Ymaginatif is the spokesman for animal Reson in naturally prophetic dreams. Especially powerful when Will's powers of kynde knowyng are turned inwards and operate together, Will's animal Anima causes an inner dream which, in turn, produces self-knowledge as instantaneous as Ymaginatif's appearance and disappearance. Will looks into Anima's lower mirror of "middelerþe," where Ymaginatif hypostatizes concerns of Will's outer dream into speakers in an inner dream. Will hears and sees the speakers, as if holding onto a book. After Ymaginatif interprets the inner dream in the continuing outer dream from 11, 1.411, to 12, 1.297, Will, awakening at 13, l.1, certifies Ymaginatif's interpretation of the inner dream (13, ll.14–9).

Fourth, we know that sensory knowledge in Will's imagination is elevated to Avicenna's "supernatural," i.e., to Adam's natural Paradise (" 'Adam, whiles he was heere' "), as Ymaginatif declares in 11, 1.417a, in the "F-group" of mss. Avicenna's Divine Anima and his Angel transform into the *PP*-poet's "Kynde" and "Ymaginatif." Ymaginatif is Kynde's "angel," as it were, the angel who brings Will's natural reason to Paradise. Ymaginatif is the spokesman for innocent reasoning and, therefore, the naturally "cristene" Clergie, evidenced by the development of "Augustinisme Avicennisant" in thirteenth-century England, possibly in the environs of Worcester. In the continuing outer dream in Passus 12, Ymaginatif converts the data of Will's sense experience (learned from Thou3t, Wit, Dame Studye, Clergie, Scripture, his consequent concupiscences, and the Reson in Kynde) into a natural-supernatural Clergie. Will's knowledge of "kynde and of his konnynge" becomes the naturally known substrate for the revelation that " '*vix saluabitur [iustus]*,' " proved by the salvation of one empowered by only natural reason (Trajan). Now aware of his need for amendment, Will converts his sensuality into a sensory kynde knowyng by the practice of patient poverty in Passus 13. That practice, because it is a natural practice of all Kynde, becomes the substrate for Will's " 'vix saluabitur [iustus].' " Patient poverty will teach Will to know how to be saved; for, from the patient poverty of Passus 13 and 14, comes the kynde knowyng in 15, 1.2, and the showing of salvific charity for the rest of the Passus. Patient poverty is both the "joy" and "sorrow" predicted by the "spokesman of Reason:" "Pacience and pouerte" is the place where Charity grows (12, 1.61).

Fifth, we know that Ymaginatif teaches Will to recognize an innate syllogistic. Immediately after Will awakens from the inner dream, he defines Dowel: " 'To se muche and suffre moore, certes, is Dowel' " (11, 1.412). The logic comes naturally to Will, i.e., without external books or discipline, so naturally that Will calls it a "konnynge" (13, 1.15). The flash of insight is predicted by Dame Studie in 10, 1.119, and shown by Ymaginatif, in the slow motion of 11, ll.320–406, where Will sees images of natural "Reson" and "Suffraunce." The first vision of the *Vita* represents, then, a mental dialectic in Will. By 11, 1.412, Will combines the objects of his thought, as if the objects were extreme terms of a syllogism (e.g., the extreme term "dowel" and the extreme terms provided by every hypostatized faculty of knowledge's definition of Dowel). Ymaginatif and Kynde's Reson teach Will to recognize an innate logic.

Sixth, we know that Will begins "makynges," in order to explain how he acquired the syllogistic (12, 1.16). Will learns how to "make" from Ymaginatif. The "makynges" in 12, 1.16, become complete at 19, ll.1 and 481. When paralleled by the written words of the B-text, the "makynges" are a second means for the certification of Will's dreams; and the B-text itself is the means for fourteenth-century readers to certify the "truth" of Will's dreams.

Other conclusions seem plausible. First, upon Ymaginatif, Will builds the natural foundations for the perfection of himself as an Avicennan prophet and thaumaturge. Inspired to accept poverty and patience in Passus 13 and 14 as preconditions to the kynde knowyng of Dowel in 15, 1.2, Will ascends to the charity which perfects the power of Haukyn in a second inner vision, where Piers Plowman's charity permits him to work miracles. Although sitting by himself, Ymaginatif underlies Will's perfection of prophecy by ascent through Haukyn, to Anima, to the inner dream of Piers Plowman, and to the reception of the "tresour" in Passus 19. Second, Ymaginatif's developed powers help Will both to preach the Law and to confirm the preaching by performance of miracles. Third, Will awakes to Nede, after he has perfected prophecy by Ymaginatif, so that the final vision is a test of his ability to will freely to Dowel in conditions of necessity. If this heterodox interpretation of Ymaginatif is convincing, then the structure of the B-text of the *Vita* becomes somewhat more accessible to readers of the B-text.

Some assertions await more demonstration: e.g., the type of poetic operative in the B-text (a very literal, logical and non-apocalyptic poetic), the dense coherence of the theological questions raised and answered in the first vision of the *Vita* (the first vision has a coherence as artistically crafted as the best Cantos in the *Divina Commedia*), and an account of the Franciscan "Augustinisme Avicennisant" in Piers Plowman's Clergie, *"Dilige deum"* (the "cristene" in Piers Plowman's Church include Jews, Saracens, and Greeks, as well as those who live by the Natural Law, e.g., Trajan and Aristotle).

Primary Sources Quoted

Aegidius Romanus, see Giles of Rome.

Alexander of Hales, *Magistri Alexandri de Hales Glossa in Quatuor Libros Sententiarum Petri Lombardi: In Librum Primum, In Librum Secundum*, Bibliotheca Franciscana Scholastica Medii Aevi, XII–XIII, ed. PP. Collegii S. Bonaventurae (Florence: Quaracchi, 1951–2).

——, *Magistri Alexandri de Hales Glossa in Quatuor Libros Sententiarum Petri Lombardi: In Librum Tertium, In Librum Quartum*, Bibliotheca Franciscana Scholastica Medii Aevi, XIV–XV, ed. PP. Collegii S. Bonaventurae (Florence: Quaracchi, 1954, 1957).

——, *Quaestiones Disputatae "Antequam Esset Frater"*, Bibliotheca Franciscana Scholastica Medii Aevi, XIX–XXI, ed. PP. Collegii S. Bonaventurae (Forence: Quaracchi, 1960).

——, *Doctor Irrefragabilis Alexandri de Hales Summa theologica* (Quaracchi: Florence, 1924–48), 4 vols.

Alonso, M. Alonso, *Temas Filosoficos Medievales (Ibn Dawud Y Gundisalvo)* (Madrid: Universidad Pontificia Comillas, 1959).

d'Alverny, M. T., "Avicenna Latinus," *Archives d'Histoire Doctrinale et Littéraire du Moyen Age*, 28(1961), 281–316; 29(1962), 217–233; 30(1963), 221–72; 31(1964), 271–286; 32(1965), 257–302; 33(1966), 305–327; 34(1967), 315–343; 35(1968), 301–335; 36(1969), 243–280; 37(1970), 327–361; 39(1972), 321–341.

——, "Bibliotheca Capituli Q.81: Codex Wigornensis: Avicenna Latinus," *Archives d'Histoire Doctrinale et Littéraire de Moyen Age*, 32(1965), 297–302.

Aristotle, *On the Soul (De anima)*, transl. J.A. Smith, *Basic Works of Aristotle*, ed. Richard McKeon (New York: Random House, 1941).

——, *Posterior Analytics*, transl. G.R.G. Mure, *Basic Works of Aristotle*, ed. Richard McKeon (New York: Random House, 1941).

Augustine of Hippo, *De Trinitate (PL*, 42, 819–1098).

pseudo-Augustine of Hippo, *De spiritu et anima liber unus (PL*, 40, 779–831).

Averroes, *Averrois Cordvbensis Commentarium Magnum in Aristotelis De Anima Libros*, Corpus Commentariorum Averroes in Aristotelem, VI, pt.1, ed. F. Stuart Crawford (Cambridge, Mass.: The Medieval Academy of America, 1953).

——, *Averrois Cordvbensis Commentarium Medium in Aristotelis Poetriam*, ed. William F. Boggess (unpublished doctoral dissertation, Univ. of North Carolina at Chapel Hill, 1965; repr. University Microfilms at Ann Arbor, Michigan, §65–14, 314, in 1987).

——, "Averrois Cordubensis Compendium Libri Aristotelis De Sompno et Vigilia," *Averrois Cordubensis Compendia Librorum Aristotelis Qvi Parva Naturalia Vocantur*, Corpus Commentariorum Averrois in Aristotelem, VII, ed. Emily L.

Shields and Harry Blumberg (Cambridge, Mass.: The Medieval Academy of America, 1949).

Avicenna, *Avicenna Arabum Medicorum Principis Canon Medicinae* (Venice: Apud Iuntas, 1595).

———, *Avicenna (Ibn Sina,* †1037): Opera Philosophica: Venice, 1508 (facs. ed., Louvain: Edition de la bibliothèque S.J., 1961).

———, *Avicenna Latinus: Liber de anima seu sextus de naturalibus, I–II–III*, ed. S. van Riet and G. Verbeke (Leiden: E.J. Brill, 1972).

———, *Avicenna Latinus: Liber de anima seu sextus de naturalibus, IV–V*, ed. S. van Riet and G. Verbeke (Leiden: E.J. Brill, 1968).

———, *Avicenna Latinus: Liber de philosophia prima sive scientia divina, I–IV*, ed. S. van Riet and G. Verbeke (Leiden: E.J. Brill, 1977).

———, *Avicenna Latinus: Liber de philosophia prima sive scientia divina, V–X*, ed. S. van Riet and G. Verbeke (Leiden: E.J. Brill, 1980).

———, *Avicenna Latinus: Liber de scientia divina sive scientia divina, I–X: Lexiques*, ed. S. van Riet and G. Verbeke (Leiden: E.J. Brill, 1983).

———, *Logica, Avicenne perhypatetici philosophi: ac medicorum facile primi opera in lucem redacta: ac nuper quantum ars niti potuit per canonicos emendata*, ed. D. Cecilius Fabrianensis (Venice, 1508; rpt. Minerva, 1961). fols. 2–12.

Badawi, A., *Histoire de la Philosophie en Islam* (Paris: J. Vrin 1972), 2 vols.

Bartholomaeus Anglicus, *De proprietatibus rerum* (Frankfurt: Apud Wolfgangum Richterum, 1601, repr., Minerva, 1964).

———, *On the Properties of Things: Trevisa's Translation of De Proprietatibus Rerum*, ed. M.C. Seynour (Oxford: Clarendon Press, 1975), 2 vols.

Biblia Sacra cum Glossa Ordinaria Walafridi Strabonis aliorumque et interlineari Anselmi Laudunensis (Strassburg, Adolf Rusch for Anton Koberger, 1480), 4 vols.

Blumberg, Harry, see Averroes.

Boggess, William F., see Averroes.

Boniface VIII, "Unam sanctam," *Extravagantes Communes,* or *Extravagantes Decretales quae a Diversis Romanis Pontificibus post Sextum Emanaverunt*, Corpus Iuris Canonici, Editio Lipsiensis Secunda post Aemilii Ludouici Richteri, II, 1245-6, ed. Emil Friedberg (Leipzig: B. Tauchnitz, 1879; repr. Graz, 1955).

Callus, Daniel A., "The Powers of the Soul: An Early Unpublished Text," *Recherches de théologie ancienne et médiévale*, 19(1952), 131–70.

———, "The Treatise of John Blund on the Soul," *Autour d'Aristote: Recueil d'Etudes de Philosophie Ancienne et Médiévale Offert à Monseigneur A. Mansion*, Bibliothèque Philosophique de Louvain, XVI, ed.? (Louvain: Publications Universitaires de Louvain, 1955), pp.471–95.

Canivez, J.M., "Alcher," *Dictionnaire de Spiritualité Ascétique et Mystique*, I, 294–5, ed. M. Viller, F. Cavallera, J. Guibert (Paris: Gabriel Beauchesne, 1937–).

Courtenay, William, *Schools and Scholars in Fourteenth-Century England* (Princeton, New Jersey: Princeton Univ. Press, 1987).

Decker, Bruno, *Die Entwicklung der Lehre von der prophetischen Offenbarung von Wilhelm von Auxerre bis zum Thomas von Aquin*, Breslauer Studien zur Historische Theologie, VII (Breslau: Müller and Seiffert, 1940).

Doucet, V., "Prolegomena," *Magistri Alexandri de Hales Glossa in Quatuor Libros Sententiarum*, Bibliotheca Franciscana Scholastica Medii Aevi, XII, 5*–130*, ed. PP. Collegii S. Bonaventurae (Florence: Quaracchi, 1951).

———, "Prolegomena," *Quaestiones Disputatae' Antequam Esset Frater'*, Bibliotheca

Franciscana Scholastica Medii Aevi, XIX–XXI, 5*–41*, ed. PP. Collegii S. Bonaventurae (Florence: Quaracchi, 1960).

Floyer, J.K., and Hamilton, S.G., *Catalogue of Manuscripts Preserved in the Chapter Library of Worcester Cathedral* (Oxford: James Parker & Co., 1906).

Fournier, P., ''Alcher,'' *Dictionnaire d'Histoire et de Géographie Ecclésiastiques*, II, 14–5, ed. A. Baudrillart, P. Richard, U. Rouziès, A. Vogt (Paris: Letouzey et Ané, 1912–).

Friedberg, Emil, see Gratian.

Gardet, Louis, *La Connaissance Mystique chez Ibn Sina et Ses Présupposés Philosphiques* (Cairo: Institut Francais d'Archéologie Orientale du Caire, 1952).

——, *La Pensée Religeuse d'Avicenne* (Paris: J. Vrin, 1951).

——, ''Quelques aspects de la pensée avicenienne dans ses rapports avec l'orthodoxie musulmane,'' *Revue Thomiste*, 45(1939), 537–75.

Giles of Rome, *Giles of Rome: Errores Philosophorum*, ed. Joseph Koch and transl. John O. Riedl (Marquette, Wisconsin: Marquette Univ. Press, 1944).

Gilson, Etienne, ''Les Sources Gréco-Arabes de l'Augustinisme Avicennisant,'' *Archives d'histoire doctrinale et littéraire du moyen age*, 4(1929), 5–127.

——, *History of Christian Philosophy in the Middle Ages* (New York: Random House, 1955).

——, ''Pourquoi Saint Thomas A Critiqué Saint Augustine,'' *Archives d'Histoire Doctrinale et Littéraire du Moyen Age*, 1 (1926–1927), 5–127.

Glorieux, P., ''Pour Revaloriser Migne: Tables Rectificatives,'' *Mélanges de Science Religeuse*, 9(1952), Suppl.

Goichon, Amélie-M., *Lexique de la langue philosophique d'Ibn Sina (Avicenne)* (Paris: Descleé de Brouwer, 1938).

Gratian, *Decretum Gratiani*, Corpus Iuris Canonici, Editio Lipsiensis Secunda post Aemilii Ludouici Richteri, I, ed. Emil Friedberg (Leipzig: B. Tauchnitz, 1879; repr. Graz, 1955).

Gregory I, *Homiliae in Ezechielem*, PL, 76, 785–1072.

Gundissalinus, *Compendium de anima*, ed. by J. T. Muckle as ''The Treatise De Anima of Dominicus Gundissalinus'' (*Mediaeval Studies*, 2[1940], 23–103).

Hermannus Alemannus, see Averroes.

Jean de la Rochelle (Joannes de Rupella), *Summa de anima*, ed. by Teofilo Domenichelli as *La Summa de Anima di Frate Giovanni della Rochelle* (Prato: Tipografia Giachetti, 1882).

——, *Tractatus de divisione multiplici potentiarum animae*, ed. Pierre Michaud-Quantin (Paris: J. Vrin, 1964).

Jerome (Hieronymus), *Commentarii in Ezechielem* (PL, 25, 15–490).

John Blount, *Tractatus de anima*, ed. D.A. Callus and R.W. Hunt (Oxford: Univ. Press, 1970).

Ker, N.R., *Medieval Libraries of Great Britain: A List of Surviving Books*, 2 ed. (London: Offices of the Royal Historical Society, 1964).

Liber de causis primis et secundis et de fluxu qui consequitur eas, ed. R. de Vaux, *Notes et textes sur l'Avicennisme Latin aux confins des XIIᵉ–XIIIᵉ siècles*, Bibliothèque Thomiste, XX, 88–140 (Paris: J.Vrin, 1934).

Lohr, Charles, ''Medieval Latin Aristotle Commentaries,'' *Traditio*, 23(1967), 313–413; 24(1968), 149–245; 26(1970), 135–216; 27(1971), 251–351; 28(1972), 281–396; 29(1973), 93–197.

Lottin, Odon, "A propos de Jean de la Rochelle," *Problèmes d'Histoire Littéraire de 1160 à 1300*, Psychologie et morale aux XIIe et XIIIe siècles, VI, 181-223 (Gembloux: J. Duculot, 1960).

——, "L'influence littéraire du chancelier Philippe," *Problèmes d'Histoire Littéraire de 1160 à 1300*, Psychologie et morale aux XIIe et XIIIe siècles, VI, 149-69 (Gembloux: J. Duculot, 1960).

——, "Les mouvements premiers de l'appétit sensitif de Pierre Lombard à Saint Thomas d'Aquin," *Problèmes de morale*, Psychologie et morale aux XIIe et XIIIe siècles, II, pt.1, 493-589 (Gembloux: J. Duculot, 1948).

Mandonnet, Pierre, *Siger de Brabant et l'Averroïsme Latin au XIIIme siècle*, 2 ed. (Louvain: Institut Supérieur de Philosophie de l'Université, 1911).

——, "Tractatus de erroribus philosophorum Aristotelis, Averrois, Avicennae, Algazelis, Alkindi et Rabbi Moysis," *Siger de Brabant*, 2 ed., pt.2 (Louvain: Institut Supérieur de Philosophie de l'Université, 1911).

Marsilius of Padua, *Marsilius of Padua: The Defender of Peace*, transl. Alan Gewirth (New York: Columbia Univ. Press, 1956), 2 vols.

——, *The Defensor Pacis of Marsilius of Padua*, ed. C.W. Previte-Orton, (Cambridge: Cambridge Univ. Press, 1928).

Muckle, J.T., see Gundissalinus.

Norpoth, L., *Der pseudo-augustinische Traktat: de spiritu et anima* (Cologne: Institüt für Geschichte der Medezin, 1971).

Peter Lombard, *Magistri Petri Lombardi Parisiensis Episcopi Sententiae in IV Libris Distinctae*, 3 ed., Spicilegium Bonaventurianum, IV-V (Rome: Quaracchi, 1971-1981).

——, *Collectanea in omnes D. Pauli Apostoli Epistolas* (PL, 191-2).

Portaliè, E., "Augustinisme: Développement historique de l'," *Dictionnaire de Théologie Catholique*, I, pt.2, 2502-61, ed. A. Vacant, E. Mangenot, E. Amann (Paris: Letouzey et Ané, 1908-50).

Raciti, Gaetano, "L'Autore del '*De spiritu et anima*,' " *Rivista di Filosofia Neo-Scolastica*, 53(1961), 385-401.

Rahman, Fazlur, *Avicenna's Psychology* (London: Geoffrey Cumberledge, 1952).

——, "Ibn Sina," *A History of Muslim Philosophy*, ed. M.M. Sharif (Wiesbaden: Otto Harrassowitz, 1963), I, 480-506.

——, *Prophecy in Islam: Philosophy and Orthodoxy* (London: George Allen & Unwin, 1958).

Reines, A.J., *Maimonides and Abrabanel on Prophecy* (Cincinnati: Hebrew Union College Press, 1970).

Richard of St. Victor, *Benjamin minor* (PL, 196, 1-64).

——, "A Tretyse of the Stodey of Wisdom þat Men Clepen Beniamyn," *Deonise Hid Diuinite*, ed. Phyllis Hodgson, *EETS*, o.s.231 (London: Geoffrey Cumberledge, 1955), 12-46.

Robert Bradwardine, *De causa Dei contra Pelagianum* (London: Apud Ioannem Billium, 1618, rpt. Minerva, 1964).

Rohmer, J., "Sur le doctrine franciscaine des deux faces de l'ame," *Archives d'Histoire Doctrinale et Littéraire du Moyen Age*, 2(1927), 73-7.

Seymour, M.C., see Bartholomaeus Anglicus.

Thomas Aquinas, *Quaestiones Disputatae: De Anima*, Quaestiones Disputatae et Quaestiones Duodecim Quodlibetales, II, 366-467 (London: Burns & Oates, 1897).

——, *Quaestiones Disputatae: De Veritate*, Quaestiones Disputatae et Quaestiones Duodecim Quodlibetales, III, 1-351 (London: Burns & Oates, 1897).

————, *Summa theologiae* (Madrid: Biblioteca de Autores Cristianos, 1955), 5 vols.

de Vaux, Roland, ''Avicenne et les décrets de 1210 et de 1215,'' *Notes et textes sur l'Avicennisme Latin aux confins des XIIe et XIIIe siècles*, Bibliothèque Thomiste, XX, 45–52, (Paris: J.Vrin, 1934).

————, ''Le Première Entreé d'Averroes chez les Latins,'' *Revue des Sciences Philosophiques et Théologiques*, 22(1933), 193–245.

Vincent of Beauvais, *Speculum Naturale* (Douai: Ex Officina Typographica Baltazaris Belleri, 1624; repr. Graz, 1964).

pseudo-Vincent of Beauvais, *Speculum Doctrinale* (Douai: Ex Officine Typographica Baltazaris Belleri, 1624; repr. Graz, 1964).

William of Auvergne (Guilelmus Arvernus), *De anima*, Opera Omnia, II, 65–228 (Paris: Andreas Pralard, 1674, rpt. Minerva, 1963).

Wolfson, H.A., ''The Internal Senses in Latin, Arabic, and Hebrew Philosophic Texts,'' *Harvard Theological Review*, 28(1935), 69–133.

de Wulf, Maurice, *Le Traité De unitate formae de Giles de Lessines* (Louvain: Institut Supérieur de Philosophie de l'Université, 1901).

Index of Lines

(according to Kane-Donaldson edition of the B-text)

1,138–9   (kynde knowyng by a craft in the cors): 1, 44, 83, 118, 120, 136, 142

1,142–3   ("kynde knowyng. . . to louen þi lord"): 121

1,85–207   ("tresore"): 120, 136

1,140   (dulle wittes): 1, 120

2,4   (craft to knowe the false): 1

2,51   (encumbrance of Conscience): 7, 136

2,119   (Theologie's definition of Mede): 51–2, 57

7,3–4   ("pardoun *a pena & a culpa*"): 123(note 101)

7,152–3   (the worth of Piers Plowman's pardon): 142

7,154   ("songewarie"): 144

7,185–6   (the worth of "dowel" at Doomsday): 144

Passus 8–19   (structure of the *Vita*): 122–8, 140–1, 144–5

8,28–56   (the friar's "forbisne"): 52, 59

8,49   ("flesshes wille"): 59, 61

8,57–8   (kynde knowyng to conceive): 57–8, 119

8,68–13,1   (first vision of the *Vita*): 2, 5–6, 34, 35(note 41), 39–40, 58–61, 67

8,68–13,1   (structure of the first vision): 4, 17–18, 58–61, 66–7, 114–15, 117–18, 138–9

8,70   (Thouȝt): 5, 14–15, 34, 39, 40–8, 59–60, 84–6

8,112   (savor or wisdom): 81, 85

8,113   ("coueite"): 3–4, 75, 86

8,125   (Thouȝt's "purpos"): 7, 9, 14, 19, 37–8, 84

8,129   (the name "wil"): 5, 19, 24

8,130   (whether Will is man or no man): 6, 14, 19

8,131   (Will's intent): 5–6, 8, 39, 43–4, 52

9,2   (the "Castel" for Anima): 60

9,19   (Inwit's five fair sons): 42

9,31   (man's likeness to Kynde): 23–4, 41, 52–3, 84–5

9,32–46   (Creation by Speech): 55

9,38, 53   ("myȝt" of Kynde): 79–81, 83–5, 109, 114, 117

9,57–8   (the animal soul emanating from the heart to the head): 41

10,1   (Dame Studie): 35(note 41), 38, 45, 71, 81
10,6   (''fooles þat frenetike ben of wittes''): 3, 72
10,9   (''hogges''): 45
10,14   (''lond and lordshipe on erþe''): 3
10,104–36   (theological ''purpos'' answered by Ymaginatif): 7–11, 13
10,119   (Dame Studie's prophecy of Ymaginatif's answer): 7, 14–15,
                  37, 44, 71, 85
10,120   (''Non plus sapere quam oportet''): see Passus 15, line 69
10,140–4   (Dame Studie silences Wit): 3, 8
10,238–335   (Clergie): 3, 8, 18, 22, 36(note 41), 45
10,336   (Dowel of ''*dominus* and *knyʒthode*''): 45
10,344–8   (baptism into patient poverty): 45
10,361   (''loue þi lord god leuest. . .''): 121(note 95)
10,377–11,4   (Will's rebellion against Scripture): 3, 38, 45, 68

11,3   (''Multi multa sciunt et seipsos nesciunt''): 3, 45
11,6–406   (lower inner vision): 2–4, 17–18, 20, 39, 58–64, 112–17, 138–41
11,7   (Anima causes the first or lower inner dream): 17, 20, 62, 114–
                  17
11,7a   (''I was rauysshed''): 62, 80, 115–16
11,7b   (Fortune): 3, 22, 53–54, 116
11,7–319   (the first half of the inner dream): 3, 38, 62, 90, 95, 116
11,9   (''Mirour of middelerþe''): 3, 62, 90, 116–17
11,9   (''middelerþe''): 22, 79, 113
11,13–5   (Sisters Concupiscence): 3–4, 54, 75–6, 116
11,34   (Rechelesnesse's reckless thought and speech): 24, 46–7, 54
11,37–8   (''Man proposes and God disposes''): 32; see Passus 20, line
                  33
11,44–5   (''wit'' ruined by Will's ''likyng''): 3, 10, 60, 95
11,53–67   (salvation by membership in a ''Fraternitee''): 52
11,112   (''Multi to a mangerie''): 129
11,319   (confusion of Thouʒt): 46, 116
11,320, 410   (Ymaginatif as ''oon''): 4, 10–11, 18–19, 37, 40–8, 52, 58, 60,
                  63–4, 80, 115
11,320–3   (Ymaginatif's prophetic powers): 5–6, 49, 61–4
11,320–406   (Ymaginatif's showing of images of Reson): 4, 38, 90
11,320–406   (second half of the inner dream): 22–3, 84
11,320–12,297 (Ymaginatif's showing and telling): 8, 45, 63, 92, 119
11,321   (the name ''kynde''): 41, 116
11,321–68   (images of Kynde's Reson): 2, 46, 52, 82, 84, 129
11,322   (Kynde calls Will by his kynde ''name''): 5, 19, 60
11,323   (Kynde's Wit): 38, 43, 46–7, 61
11,324   (''me [þo] þouʒte''): 80
11,334   (''And how men token Mede and Mercy refused''): 10, 49–53
11,335   (Kynde's Reson): 10, 18, 30, 38, 46–7, 49, 52–4, 56, 61, 82, 87–
                  8, 114
11,335   (''sewen''): 49, 52, 61
11,336   (''in etynge, in drynkynge and in engendrynge of kynde''): 24,
                  49, 61
11,347   (''I hadde wonder''): 39, 48–54
11,360   (''Muche merueilled me''): 10, 34, 39, 48–54
11,364   (''Manye selkouþes I seiʒ''): 48–54

11,369–72   (Will's anger at human reason's failings): 10, 52
11,373–5   (Will's reenactment of Adam's sin): 8–9, 55, 83, 86, 114
11,375   ("sewest"): 23, 53,
11,376–7   (Reckless speech opposed to patient speech): 24, 46–8, 54–6, 64
11,379   (Kynde's sufferance or patience): 9, 46–7, 54
11,382   (God's sufferance for "som mannes goode"): 10, 24, 47, 54
11,383   ("Be subject to *every creature* for the sake of God"): 56–7
11,386   (the power of patience and patient speech): 48–58
11,387   (["þow] rule þi tonge bettre"): 54–5
11,397   (man's likeness to Kynde in "shap" and "shaft"): 24–55
11,401–2   (the "matere" of Will's body as a cause of concupiscence): 8,
             73, 75–6, 84–5
11,405   (Will's shame): 8–9, 34, 39, 65–6, 117
11,406   ("awaked"): 63, 117
11,412   ("To se muche and suffre moore, certes, is Dowel"): 10, 64
11,413–6   (Will's loss of innocent Clergie): 9, 22, 64, 84–5
11,414–12,297 (Ymaginatif's telling of Kynde's Clergie): 4, 114–15
11,417,   in the "F-group" of mss ("heere"): 9, 83, 114–15
11,419   ("wisedom and þe wit of god"): 84
11,432–4   (Ymaginatif's prophecy of Nede): 11

12,1   ("ymaginatif"): 4, 34, 39, 58
12,2   (Ymaginatif's solitude in sickness and in health): 20
12,4   ("[mynne] on þyn ende"): 64
12,7   ("lest myȝt þe faill[e]"): 95
12,16   (Will's "makynges"): 20–21 and note 19, 62, 83(note 16), 119–
             21, 138–45
12,26   ("dowel. . . at þe laste"): 119
12,63   (Ymaginatif's reference to the Holy Spirit): 21–2
12,66   ("Quod scimus loquimur, quod vidimus testamur"): 23
12,71   ("cristes loue"): 82
12,95   (Clergie and kynde wit as "Mirours"): 90
12,138   ("Sapiencia huius mundi stulticia est apud deum"): 133
12,155–9   (the truth and falsehood in Will's rebellion against Scripture):
             45
12,162   (swimmming as a metaphor for penance): 45
12,223–4   (Will's study of the wits of animals): 9
12,297   (Ymaginatif's sudden disappearance): 34 and note 40, 39, 66–8,
             115

13,1   (awakening from first vision): 2, 11, 63, 67, 92, 114
13,3   ("walke in manere of a mendynaunt"): 109(note 75)
13,13   ("vnkonnynge"): 71
13,14, 19   ("Ymaginatif in dremels me tolde"): 4
13,15   (konnynge): 2, 9, 27, 34 and note 40, 39, 42–3, 68–72
13,5–15   (summary of first vision): 2, 63
13,19   ("vix saluabitur [iustus]"): 117
13,4,21   ("þouȝt"): 63
13,21–14,335 (second vision of the *Vita*): 6, 26–7, 48, 57, 69, 71, 91, 119, 130,
             140
13,127   (Piers Plowman's Clergie, "Dilige deum"): 30, 121 and note
             95, 134

13,224   ("Actif" or Haukyn): 26, 88–91, 94, 123–4, 128–30
13,240–59   (Haukyn's power to perform miracles): 122–3 and notes 100–101
13,288–9a   (splotches on Haukyn's cloak): 129
13,337   (Haukyn's consultation of witches): 130 and note 100
14,3   ("Vxorem duxi"): 129

15,2   (achievement of kynde knowyng): 6, 27, 69, 90
15,11–17,356   (third vision of the *Vita*): 128–35
15,11   ("reson"): 90, 92, 99(note 41), 132
15,12–3   (the higher, non-sensory Anima): 90
15,16   ("cristes creature"): 90, 124
15,23–39   (Anima's catalogue of powers): 83, 90, 95
15,24, 40   (the name "animus"): 41
15,25   (human Thouȝt in the "R-group" of mss): 5, 18, 43, 95
15,40   (Anima the "bisshop"): 88–90, 95, 119, 121, 134
15,46–7   (Will's higher curiosity): 130–31
15,69   ("Non plus sapere quam oportet"): 131
15,149   ("What is charite?"): 129
15,150   ("fre liberal wille"): 6, 27–8, 128, 134
15,161–2   (the higher mirror): 28, 125–6, 130
15,162   ("[Hic] in enigmate"): 131–3
15,196   ("persone" of Charite): 126, 133
15,210   ("þoruȝ wil oone"): 126, 133
15,584   ("Dilige deum & proximum"): 121
15,603–15   (Anima's sermon): 30, 134
15,605   (the Creed held in common by Christians, Saracens and Jews): 125, 134
15,605–13   (the sermon to be preached to Christians, Saracens and Jews): 119–20, 130, 141

16,1–2   (Will's perfection of Haukyn's power): 6, 26, 90, 124, 128, 141
16,4,9   (so-called "Tree of Charity"): 28
16,4–17   (the image "tree"): 28–9 and note 31, 134(note 115)
16,8   ("Pacience hatte þe pure tree"): 29, 90, 126
16,16   ("liberum arbitrium" [free will]): 6, 27–8, 91, 134
16,19–167   (second inner dream): 6, 29–30, 91, 125–6
16,30,36, 50   (props of the Tree of Trinite): 25(note 25), 29(note 32) 101(note 72)
16,47   (sin against the Holy Spirit): 128
16,48–50   (world, flesh, devil: three effects of Adam's sin, i.e., concupiscence): 128
16,63   (Tree of Trinite): 29, 126
16,88–9   (act of Divine Free Will): 29, 126, 134
16,90   (act of Divine Speech): 29–30, 119
16,93   ("plenitudo temporis"): 30
16,103–16   (Piers Plowman's power to perform miracles): 27 and note 28, 31, 126
16,168–17,356   (continuing outer vision): 6, 27, 30

17,26–49   (conflict between faith of Abraham and Spes' hope in the Law): 129

Index of Lines

Passus 18–20 (last two visions of the *Vita*): 31–3

18,5–35   (summary of the third vision of the *Vita*): 141

19,1 and 481   (completion of the "makynges" in 12, 16): 141–2
19,215–8   (grace to perfect the wits): 6, 121–2, 126–7, 135–7
19,217   ("tresour" for the wits): 31, 136, 142
19,219–20   (encumbrance of Conscience): 6, 136–7
19,228–49   (conferral of the crafts): 31, 135–7
19,335b   (Pride's attack): 6, 32, 126
19,348–50   (Pride's attack upon "cristene" Conscience): 32, 126
19,394   ("Et dimitte hobis debita nostra"): 32, 137

20,1–51   (Will is awakened to Nede): 6, 141–2, 145
20,10   (nede has no law): 6
20,12–3   (need for food, clothing, shelter): 6
20,14   ("sleighte"): 6
20,33   ("Man proposes and God disposes"): 32
20,33   (Nede's attack upon a wise Ymaginatif): 11, 32
20,209   ("catel. . . to cloþe me and to feede"): 33